THE CALL
OF THE
RED-WINGED
BLACKBIRD

THE CALL
OF THE
RED-WINGED
BLACKBIRD

essays on the common
and extraordinary

TIM BOWLING

WOLSAK
& WYNN

Published by Wolsak and Wynn Publishers
280 James Street North
Hamilton, ON L8R2L3
www.wolsakandwynn.ca

Editor: Noelle Allen | Copy editor: Ashley Hisson
Cover and interior design: Jen Rawlinson
Cover image: Red winged Starling, or Marsh Blackbird from Birds of America (1827) by John James Audubon, etched by William Home Lizars.
Author photograph: Jacqueline Baker
Typeset in Adobe Caslon Pro, Tw Cen MT and Centaur
Printed by Rapido Books, Montreal, Canada
Printed on certified 100% post-consumer Rolland Enviro Paper

10 9 8 7 6 5 4 3 2 1

The publisher gratefully acknowledges the support of the Ontario Arts Council, the Canada Council for the Arts and the Government of Canada.

Library and Archives Canada Cataloguing in Publication

Title: The call of the red-winged blackbird : essays on the common and extra-ordinary / Tim Bowling.
Names: Bowling, Tim, 1964- author.
Identifiers: Canadiana 20210258659 | ISBN 9781989496428 (softcover)
Classification: LCC PS8553.O9044 C35 2022 | DDC C814/.54—dc23

In loving memory of Dorothy Jean Bowling (née Stevens)
1926–2021

The greatest sorrow arrived
as the greatest source of comfort departed

CONTENTS

PREFACE

ALL MY LIFE, I HAVE RESPONDED MOST STRONGLY TO THE SENSIBILITY behind a piece of writing rather than to its content or style. F. Scott Fitzgerald said, "We don't fall in love with a story; we fall in love with a voice." For me, the personal essay, even more than the poem, celebrates this distinctive individual voice while at the same time opening one door after another into the shared mysteries of the world. Where the novelist and poet adopt guises to heighten their effects, the essayist more often seeks the kind of direct connection with the reader normally associated with letter writing. That I happen to be an inveterate letter writer, still handwriting and posting missives to several long-time correspondents, is therefore not surprising, for the purpose in both forms is to bring the blood of life to the surface without the protective trappings of other genres. When Pablo Neruda writes that he is tired of being a man, he writes as himself but also, more dramatically, as all men. There is always an oracular quality in a great poem. The essayist works on a more modest and immediate scale, even when tackling the most freighted universal subjects. It is that scale these essays hope to find.

With the exception of the title essay, all of the pieces here were completed before the pandemic, which is of note only in relation to "The Hermit's

Smoke," a lengthy narrative meditation on solitude. Readers might naturally wonder, in light of the past two years of masks and social distancing, whether my views on the subject have changed. They have not. In fact, in many ways, my desire to withdraw from society and busyness has only intensified, dangerously so, and I must constantly fight against the hermit instinct, at least for the sake of my family if not for myself. As recent history should teach us, the deification of the self over the greater good serves only those powerful interests who seek a material benefit from eroding our natural capacity for community and compassion. Yet it is also undeniably a potent part of human nature to stand alone at times, outside of societal influence, as a means of grappling with those eternal questions that the day-to-day world of getting and spending doesn't want us to confront.

In this book, then, you will encounter a nonconformist but empathetic voice, in love with nature and literature, on the side of working people and animals, and wholly skeptical of romantic mythologies passed off as truths, whether by priests, politicians or other artists. It is, in the end, the voice of an almost sixty-year-old man who, in the heartache of losing his mother this past spring, keeps in touch with the loving world she made for him, and with his own wondering child self, by continually listening for the call of the red-winged blackbird.

PART ONE

ON THE RAILS

ON OCTOBER 4, 1895, JOSEPH FRANK KEATON ENTERED THE WORLD IN a clangorous railroad town called Piqua, Kansas. Sixty-nine autumns later Buster Keaton, now a legendary silent screen comedian, crossed Canada on a mechanized railway handcart for the making of *The Railrodder*, a 1965 National Film Board production promoting the scenic splendour of our country. Less than a year later, the Great Stone Face, as he was nicknamed due to his stoic onscreen expression, was dead.

Rarely is a life so neatly and perfectly framed. That Buster Keaton – whose most celebrated film, *The General* (1926), involves the theft of a Confederate locomotive during the American Civil War – should enter and exit the world to the clatter of trains is a poignant and artistic structure worthy of the man's own directorial genius. Ironic, too, given that Keaton's name – along with those of Charlie Chaplin, Harold Lloyd, Douglas Fairbanks, Mary Pickford and so many others – is synonymous with silence, that golden and increasingly rare commodity.

But it is the silencing of that silent culture that intrigues me, the vanishing of one rich world and the emergence of another that might be less rich, less human, less moving, for this is perhaps what we are experiencing

5

now in our "age of ubiquitous computing," as Adam Greenfield describes it, an age where the line between the real and virtual worlds becomes increasingly blurred.

I know something about this vanishing myself, having spent the first thirty years of my life actively involved in a vital industry that has all but disappeared (commercial salmon fishing) and the last seventeen years labouring along as a writer in a culture with ever-diminishing patience for the apparently complex devices of metaphor, symbolism and extensive character development; a culture intent on exchanging physical interactions for digitized ones. In fact, it's my growing sense of frustration with contemporary life's pace, attention span and attitude toward reality that has drawn me into Keaton's dramatic spiral circa the late 1920s, when sound changed the movies forever, when he lost artistic control over his projects and when he began a thirty-year slide into alcoholism and obsolescence that almost made his story a classic tragedy instead of a classic comedy.

But it is wonder and joy, as much as frustration, that focuses my weary middle-aged gaze on Keaton when, in the final scene of *The Railrodder*, he arrives at the shores of Boundary Bay, in White Rock, British Columbia; climbs off the railway handcar; and, hands behind his back, gazes at the Pacific. Much of the past 115 years since Keaton's birth have condensed into the figure of that lonely old man at the edge of the sea, and his own mortality. So much of our modern sense of what constitutes entertainment, art and meaning washes up against those legendary flat shoes and lifts the brim of that iconic porkpie hat. But what really haunts me is the revelation that a few miles down the highway, in Ladner, British Columbia, that same October in 1964, I lay in my crib, eight months old, pre-language, pre-walking, but already forgetting the mysterious art of the first silences and the first rhythms that we are all destined to forget.

It is, in the grand scheme of "brushes with fame," a small matter. And yet small matters are the origin of creativity. Would Keaton, for example, even have made *The General* if he'd not been born in a railroad town? Would I be fascinated with Keaton and silence if I had not, at the age of five, watched with avid delight several of his short films projected onto the side of a neighbour's house one summer evening as the familiar musk of salmon washed over the town and the larger-than-life black-and-white figures on the clapboard moved with all the rippling, disorienting speed of the sockeye seeking to escape my father's net?

A small matter. Like silent film, railroads and poetry.

And already I can see Keaton turning away from the ocean, and the close-up reveals the iconic, unsmiling expression on his face, which is not stone or unchanging, but alive with stoic incredulity at the fate of humans in the hands of the Fates.

Buster Keaton experienced the death of two vibrant cultures: vaudeville and the silent cinema. In the first case, he was an incredibly gifted young man in his early twenties who realized that movies were set to replace vaudeville as the dominant form of popular entertainment. In 1917, he took a large pay cut to leave the stage and team up with Roscoe "Fatty" Arbuckle to begin making two-reel comedies in which bags of flour hit people square in the face and the logic of the perfect gag ruled the day. In the second case, a mere decade later, after he had made all of the films on which his reputation is based, the advent of "the talkies" demoted Keaton to a contract player in the Hollywood studio system and effectively wiped out all opportunities for his genius to flourish. By 1933, still famous but now hopelessly drunk and miserable, he was not prepared for change, perhaps because years of celebrity and an unhappy marriage had eroded his confidence.

For the next twenty years, until a widely read James Agee article celebrating the silent screen comedians appeared in *Life* magazine, Buster Keaton disappeared from the public consciousness. When he re-emerged, his stoic face much-wrinkled, worn with the decades of heavy drinking and smoking, he took whatever work was offered to him, appearing in hundreds of television shows and a string of movies such as *Beach Blanket Bingo* and *How to Stuff a Wild Bikini*. Imagine Laurence Olivier making a bit appearance in an Adam Sandler movie and you'll have a sense of the sadness involved.

But Keaton, who never considered himself an artist, and who distrusted all intellectual efforts to deem him one, was delighted to have the work;

he was old, and he had been neglected a long time. To take bit parts and exchange unfunny dialogue with teenagers in bikinis was perfectly fine by him; he was not a pretentious man in any way, and often resented high praise for his silent films, dismissing it as all that "genius bullshit." But still, his work through the '50s and early '60s was sad. He was one of America's greatest film directors, yet for nearly three decades he directed nothing.

Then Canada came calling. To be precise, a young director working for the National Film Board named Gerald Potterton came calling. He wanted Keaton to cross Canada by mechanized railway handcart and he wanted him to play himself, as in the glory days, with silence and the artistry of expression and physical movement, with gags. And Keaton wouldn't be acting with teenagers in bikinis this time. This was Canada in 1964, still a land known for dramatic and even imposing natural grandeur, not a wannabe sophisticated urban playground seemingly anxious to leave its rural past and hokey history behind. This was a Canada built by the railroad. Under the hum of the steel on the rails you could hear Don Messer's violin, you could hear Tommy Douglas fighting for Medicare, you could hear people talk about national dreams without sneering or chuckling, but you could also hear the machinery destroying the very land Potterton and the NFB were setting out to celebrate.

At first, Keaton resisted Canada's call. Then, in July 1964, when Potterton visited him in New York and asked if he'd be interested in appearing in the Canada travelogue film, Keaton, according to biographer Marion Meade, experienced a rapid change of heart. "Keaton looked at the kid director and rolled his eyes. 'Sounds crazy,' he said. Suddenly a racket down on Central Park South sent him clomping to the window. He pulled it up and stuck his head out. 'Quiet!' he bawled at Manhattan. Then he closed the window and turned back to Potterton. 'I'll do it. When do we start?' He never could resist trains."

The Railrodder began shooting in Halifax on September 5. The weather was already cool, and everyone involved in the film shuddered to think what the conditions would be like once they hit the Rockies. But Keaton was in his element. A documentary on the filming of *The Railrodder*, made at the same time and narrated by the legendary NFB filmmaker Donald Brittain, revealed Keaton as a moody, shy, sometimes petulant man, but one whose personality exploded into life whenever he discussed the delicious mechanics of a gag. His voice might have been gravelly from the decades of chain-smoking, his iconic face flaccid with the ravages of time and alcohol, but the creative spark that took him to the heights of movie stardom in the 1920s remained.

So did the physical courage and stamina. From the beginning of his screen life, Keaton always performed his own stunts, including the breathtaking scene in *Steamboat Bill, Jr.*, from 1928, when a whole housefront collapses on him and he escapes because he's standing exactly where the frame of an open second-storey window falls. An inch to either side and he never would have been around to visit Canada at all in the autumn of 1964.

But there he is, emerging fully clothed from the cold Atlantic (his character, in London, had read the newspaper headline "See Canada Now," jumped off a bridge and swum over); there he is, finding the abandoned railway handcar on the tracks, climbing aboard and rapidly heading west; and there he is again, on a two hundred-foot-high trestle bridge with a giant fold-out map wrapped around him, covering his face, as the handcar zips ever onward. That last gag caused some turmoil between the star and his young director. Potterton thought the stunt was far too dangerous and ordered a safer scene. Keaton demurred but shot the scene Potterton's way, and the documentary records his frustration afterwards. "I generally know what I'm doing," he says. "That's not dangerous. It's child's play, for the love of Mike." The next day, Potterton reshot the scene the way Keaton wanted it. The map on the trestle bridge is one of the comic highlights of *The Railrodder*, along with the scene of Keaton having a formal tea complete with fine china (all miraculously stored in a box on the handcar). In essence, Keaton co-directed and co-wrote the film; Potterton himself admitted as much. "Let's face it," said the man who would go on to be one of the main animators of the Beatles' *Yellow Submarine*, "he was Buster Keaton, and who the hell was I to tell him what to do?"

Across Canada the crew travelled, over the Prairies and through the Rockies, along the banks of the Fraser, finally arriving at White Rock. The five-week journey had been a comfortable one, accomplished in style on a private railroad car with sleeping compartments and a lounge in which Keaton and his wife, obsessive bridge players, could take rubbers and chain-smoke to their hearts' content. The travellers even had their own chef and steward. Keaton thoroughly enjoyed the trip. At one point in the documentary – which itself was a black-and-white tribute to a vanished Canada with everyone shrouded in cigarette smoke – the citizens of Rivers, Manitoba, gave Keaton the key to their city. A painfully shy man who loathed public appearances, especially when he was the centre of attention, Keaton was nonetheless moved nearly to tears by the gesture. A kilted band had piped him and his wife into the ceremony ("O Canada" of the kilts and Manitoba mayors handing out keys!), and even this quaint homage humbled the great comedian. The emotion on his famously stoic face is deeply moving to witness now. He had lived large for a long time, and his life, like *The Railrodder*, was approaching its terminus. The blend of the comic and tragic, the blend that defines our lives, is writ clearly on the private Keaton's face as he blinks at the citizens of Rivers, and writ with even greater clarity on the screen Keaton's back as he stands on the shores of Boundary Bay and gazes westward.

I want to read so much into that old man's stance. We're now in the midst of another great technological transition. The world is being rapidly digitized. Hundreds of millions of people worldwide spend endless hours playing virtual reality computer games. Google tracks everyone's private lives for commercial, and no doubt political, purposes. E-books are replacing material books, and the reading culture of the past several centuries is, like vaudeville and wild salmon and the Amazon rainforest, doomed to extinction, gone the way of nationhood and manners and other quaint rejects from a time when public figures at least paid lip service to values other than money-making and money-counting. And here, now, I want to read my own five-decade journey from childhood's enthusiasm to middle age's cynicism in Buster Keaton's lonely figure on a shore only a few miles from my hometown.

I want to see him turn, tears on his face, and tell me that it's all futile but that I have to make the best of a bad situation. "Get a Facebook page, kid," he growls. "For the love of Mike, buy one of them iPhones with apps, or at least a laptop computer. You're doomed if you don't." I want to hear him admit that change is painful and that it defines us.

But I can't. To do so would be to dishonour the wonderful comedian who never for a moment accepted that his life had ever been tragic. As biographer Meade puts it, "He dealt with the pain of looking back by ignoring it." Indeed, he always felt sorry for his fellow stars of the silent screen, those elderly, moaning nostalgics who never heard a Beatles song. When television first appeared, Keaton liked to tease Charlie Chaplin about his elitist disdain for the new medium. Stoic and bravely engaged with the Fates to the end, Buster Keaton wanted only one thing: to make people laugh. *The Railrodder* is a charming coda to a life spent in pursuit of that goal. That it is also a heartbreaking song to the inevitability of change and its consequent losses is entirely my problem. For *The Railrodder* does not end with Buster Keaton staring at the Pacific. It ends with a fully clothed Asian man emerging from the bay, a man dressed in a Keaton-like outfit who, on reaching the tracks, finds the railway handcart reversed and begins his own silent journey eastward across Canada.

And Keaton? When he discovers that his ride is gone, the Great Stone Face simply begins walking the tracks back in the direction he had come. Such an unrelenting adjustment to fate is the reason we continue to love and celebrate the man's films. For this reason, I cannot dishonour him. I can only do the opposite. Unwired and unrepentant, I sit in my biological frame and write in longhand the stories and poems that I hope will transcend the limitations of my private self, trust to the old connections between the single imagination and the collective heart, look down the rails at my own and my country's past, and, like Keaton, walk, stone-faced and off-camera, into the future.

INITIATION

I FIRST SKATED IN 1969 ON A FROZEN SLOUGH AT THE MOUTH OF THE Fraser River, so far west of our nation's capital that you could taste the brine of the Pacific on your tongue and hear Tokyo accents on the breeze. The ice had that 1950s' black-and-white grainy television look — the shadows under my blades were killer whales poised to break through and gnash an ice floe–napping seal to shreds. Oh, learning to skate wasn't just a sweet and happy experience; it possessed some of the terror of a religious experience undergone by a Christian who genuinely believes in the Old Testament God.

First of all, there was the isolation. The slough intersected a small silt island reached by driving out of town for ten minutes along a winding, unlit dike road, crossing a wooden suspension bridge, driving another five minutes past dark-rutted potato fields and barns like the hulking shoulders of head-less giants, until finally reaching the entrance to a bird sanctuary donated decades before by a rum-running millionaire to the federal government way off in the east. Here, the slough was long, narrow and alarmingly secluded.

The second part of the terror involved authority. My brother — twenty-three years old to my five — wasn't particularly threatening, but he smelled like beer (which he drank copiously from stubby brown bottles), Old Spice (which he wore liberally, and which emanated off a wicker ball dangling from his Mustang's rear-view mirror) and animals (which he hunted and trapped, when he wasn't salmon fishing and driving a tractor on the potato fields for a living – my hand, in fact, rested on a tanned muskrat hide on the console between the car's front bucket seats). Somehow, in a way I couldn't possibly understand, my brother's world was adult and intimidating rather than inviting; he was a peculiar Canadian cross between Hugh Hefner and Relic from *The Beachcombers*, right from his open-necked silk shirts and heavy jewellery to his scale-flecked toque and flapping rubber gumboots. Nonetheless, he was, like most young men of his era, conservative; he had one foot firmly in the gentlemen's only side of the local tavern, the other only tentatively in the free-love house parties of the swinging sixties.

Third, was the terror of winter. We didn't get as much of it as the rest of Canada, and so when it came, it came with the fully regal fury of the white witch to Narnia. This night, however, it had come without snow. The landscape glittered white with frost and moonlight from a porthole-sized full moon (the reason we could skate after dark), but the ice on the slough itself shone no brighter than isinglass.

I sat on a crispy bank and gazed as far as I could into the night. Overhanging oak branches all along the near bank, only a skiff of stars low over the far bank. Something flitted through the moonlight like a flipped hockey card. And again. Something black, the size of a gloved fist. My brother, taking no notice of the hunting creature, began to lace my skates. They were like the irons from a Victorian scullery. When he tightened the laces, I almost gasped.

"They have to be good and tight, bud," he said. "Just like your own feet."

Because I was a contemplative child, fated to become that loneliest of citizens – an intellectual – I wondered how exactly my feet were tight. They certainly didn't feel tight. Not like the skates. It felt as if my legs ended in stumps of pumping blood. I stood, tentatively. Off in the night, near the entrance to the slough, a pair of headlights swung across the bushes, then glided ghostlily toward us. Another pair followed. My brother's body prickled like a hunting dog's. Without looking at me, he said – and it might have been Canada itself speaking – "Here's your stick."

Now, at last, came the final and most important component of this Old Testament experience. Out of his white, swirling breath, my brother had spoken. And what he had said began my lifelong love-and-hate affair with the game that most of the Canadian media and our politicians – if not quite Canadians themselves – consider a major part of our national character. For the first time, I stood in skates on ice, holding a sawed-off Sherwood that was, even so, as heavy as me, its blade like a paddle's, its shaft thick enough to be a safe climbing branch. My brother might just as well have handed me a shotgun. I immediately felt a charge of power, followed by a curious mixture of apprehension and confidence. We were a secular family of Anglo-Saxon heritage who'd been in Canada since the middle of the nineteenth century: this was the only coming-of-age ritual I was ever going to have, and I was having it before I even went to school; others, even today, have it not long after they learn to walk. But no gathering of community, of friends, family, neighbours necessarily attends the ceremony. In my case, that would come, and soon. On this night, however, I was Joseph alone with one brother, and I wasn't quite sure I could trust him.

He reached into the pockets of his peacoat, pulled his hands back out and threw something on the ice. He repeated the motion three times until six pucks were scattered like buckshot for rhinoceros on the frozen slough.

"Use your stick for balance," he said, his eyes still on the headlights – which had stopped. Then blinked off. Now music floated over the stillness, probably from a car radio. "I'm just going to have a quick skate up the bank. You'll be okay?"

It was the first test of the hockey/Canada code. Could I be alone with my fear? Was there enough joy in this new faith to overcome whatever natural panic floated through my veins? This wasn't my father sending me over the boards to take out the other team's goon, but the challenge made me swallow hard. I knew I couldn't refuse it.

My brother vanished in a quick burst of grace and power. His first few strides over the black ice sounded like the workings of a scythe – then the dark swallowed him. The small roar of human welcome that followed came as a kind of dry splash. Trembling, I got to my feet. Immediately – though I did not move again – I felt my balance forsake me. If I should move either foot, I thought, I might vanish too, but not with an eagle's fierce glide; my fate would be the eaglet's, downward to death. And yet, the blood flow that bound my brother to me also gave me courage. I took a small step. Another. From the tangled woods across the slough, the non-human eyes took my efforts in, blinked and waited. I looked down, the blade of my stick resting on cold, black space; the solid, heavy shaft keeping me grounded. One deep breath and a moist helmet of cloud formed around me. Now. Go now.

The crunch under my blades, first one, then the other, felt and sounded like the crushing of beetles. Second by second, I expected the slough to open and a great icy hand to yank me down. What protection did I have? From the loneliness of five years, from the indifferent wilderness, from that oddly disturbing burst of human voices somewhere in the dark? What protection from my own lack of skill?

I had the stick. And it is no exaggeration to say that the stick compensated for my weakness and fear. I leaned on it as I lurched ahead, that intermittent crowd roar turning my attention to the loose constellation of pucks. If I could just reach one.

It happened as much violence happens – before it was possible to prevent it. The stick clattered away. Pain flared along my hip and in my elbow. Earth and sky tilted. And then the great inrushing silence of my insignificance joined the metaphysical to the physical. The eyes blinked from the trees as if nothing had happened. The wind did not howl. My numb hands touched the ice rough as loose gravel. I might have laid there forever staring at the dim stars had the world not returned to me like a rapid scissoring of the hair close to my skull. Scritch, scritch, scritch.

"Are you okay, bud? That was quite a spill."

My brother's mildly amused face and voice hovered close. I caught the familiar powerful mix of tobacco and beer, and the smell did comfort me:

hockey, the outdoors, cigarettes and alcohol. Were these not the Canadian masculine ideal?

I nodded, and did exactly what hockey players – especially Canadian hockey players – are still widely celebrated for. That is, I toughed it out, I gritted my teeth against the pain and went looking for the number of the guy who'd . . . except there wasn't any obvious enemy. In a real dark night of the soul, perhaps, the enemy never has a face or a number. And perhaps it is this primitive simplicity of the hockey code that explains its grip on the Canadian psyche? Perhaps the "eye for an eye," or, much more aptly, the "tooth for a tooth" logic, and the Darwinian dog-eat-dog philosophy *are* the Canadian value system? But if so, how to beat what lacks a jersey and a number? Tim Horton, drunk and weary at the end of his career, driving off the highway, or Jean Béliveau, graceful and celebrated all his life long, gritting his teeth against the Reaper. Derek Boogaard downing painkillers against the concussive goon whose jabs never weaken, or Guy Lafleur, in court, wondering what a father can ever really do to help his son.

The questions, the doubt, would not begin for decades, of course. At five, climbing up from the grainy surface of a frozen slough, I merely smelled the tobacco and beer, and I *trusted*. After all, my stick was there, and the pucks. I stood in the centre of the Saturday night TV screen, with the wilds of the world's second largest country pushing in from all sides. If the wolves had begun to howl, what of it? Even outside, there had to be a horn to end the period.

Wobbly, I stood, waiting while my brother returned my stick to me. He performed a tight turn on his edges, his grin a river in the wilderness. I watched his breath through my breath, amazed all over again that someone who skated so well should choose not to.

A CAR HORN BLARED. DOORS SLAMMED IN RAPID SUCCESSION. I LOOKED behind me. One pickup truck had even crept a little onto the ice, then sat like a stalled Zamboni. Within minutes, dark figures flitted along the

bank. Men's voices. And . . . women's laughter. Our last name suddenly shouted like an invitation, or a challenge. My brother, still grinning,
whirled away. More shouts. Laughter. A pair of headlights flicked on, then
another, and another; the slough was like an airfield in a WW II movie.
The lights almost reached my skates, where I stood, leaning on my stick,
my heart throbbing like a bruise.

"Come on, Bowling! Strap 'em on!"

Minutes later, the figures along the bank became figures on the slough,
cutting swiftly through the faint beams, shouting, laughing, speeding in
my direction. One by one, the still pucks vanished. Then echoed the hard
slap of sticks. Swearing. A puck whizzed past my blades. Jovial swearing.

My brother re-emerged, no longer grinning, and swooped me close,
holding me against his chest, bent over, our two faces close, his legs providing the power and the guidance, mine barely touching the ice.

"Just wait here a bit, okay. Maybe I can get you a bag of chips."

I sat on the hard bank. Behind me, thirty yards away, three young,
long-haired women stood by the hood of a car, smoking, so close together
they must have been whispering. On the ice, the skaters – there might
have been five of them; it was hard to be sure, as they changed positions so
rapidly – placed two beer bottles in the headlight glow to make a net. My
brother came down from the women, carrying what looked like two huge
suitcases. He sat on the bank beside me, mussed my toque and began to
strap on his pads. They were dark and heavy as saddles left out in the rain,
each one the size of a dog's grave. The leather straps dangled like the straps
of an electric chair. Slowly, with that peculiar, existential isolation that
marks all goalies, he did them up. It was 1969. He was twenty-three. My
brother did not even stuff a balled-up towel down the front of his pants for
protection, as he often did for games when he forgot his cup. He skated out
onto the slough without a mask, like Johnny Bower or Terry Sawchuk. Or
at least without a mask that I could recognize. My heart beat faster.

The moonlight and the headlights together cast a dreamy quality over
the scene, but something distinctly un-dreamlike had settled on the slough

now. The hard slapshots, the hollow echo of the puck when my brother made a save – like an axe blow on wood. The figures sped up. The shouts increased. Suddenly a goalpost exploded.

Everything paused, but only briefly. A skater tilted his head back to empty a bottle, then used it to make another goalpost. Behind me, more vehicles arrived, their headlights adding a slight brightness to the cold moon glow. Engines idling. Blast of rock music suddenly cut off. A young man in a duck hunting cap with orange earflaps whooped and ran onto the slough with a stick but no skates. Ten feet from the bank, he slipped and hit the ice hard. Two skaters whirled close to him, poked him with their sticks and laughed. He swung his own stick at their legs but missed. Then he leaned on his stick, like an ancient Roman on his sword, except to live and not to die. Seconds later, he was skidding around after the puck, which the others easily kept from him. His cap fell off, and for a while it became the puck. Even I could tell that his drunkenness was different somehow, a matter of sport and mockery.

On the bank, by the cars, the women kept right on smoking and whis-pering. Whenever I looked back at them, they didn't seem to be watching the skaters at all. There was a ghostliness to them, for they stood out of the glow of most of the headlights, their long hair and smoke rings captured mostly by the moon. I couldn't hear their voices, but I understood their gestures as a kind of speech.

My brother did not forget me. After a while, he skated over, very heav-ily, his long hair wet at the tips, his cheeks red, his eyes vivid.

"How are you doing, bud?" he almost gasped. "Enjoying the game?"

At my assent, he merely smiled, then tucked the large lobster claw of his trapper underneath the opposite arm and reached into the pocket of his coat. "No chips. But I forgot I had these for you." He gave me two slim packs, each about the size of my open hand. "Maybe you'll get a Bobby Orr." He winked. "I'm just going to play for a few more minutes. Do you want to skate some more after, or are you getting cold?"

In truth, I was already cold, sitting on the hard bank, torn between the desire to be warm and the desire to actually send a puck sliding along the slough. The latter desire won out. I told my brother I wanted to skate.

He tapped my shoulder with his lobster claw. "Sure, bud. Just let me stop a few more, then you can take some shots on me yourself. How's that sound?"

It sounded fine, but my toes were numb, I shivered, and the slapshots and the shouts and the rock songs rising and falling on the breeze seemed to go on forever. I put my mittened hands, each one gripping a pack of hockey cards, into my coat pockets. And waited. After a while, a skater swooped along and shouted at the young women to bring a case of beer from his trunk. With it tucked under his arm, he returned to the game. I went on waiting.

The cold intensified. The time between shivers grew shorter. The dark all around the headlights thickened and grew blacker, despite the moon, which, though full, was small and grubby as a much-used goalie mask. I no longer wanted to slide a puck along the ice. I wanted to go somewhere warm and open up my packs of hockey cards.

At last, one shouted word changed everything, the one four-letter word most commonly associated with hockey and Canada, the fierce competitiveness of both institutions, declaimed in the rink and the boardroom and the caucus meeting.

Then out of the darkness the skater approached me. Second by second, he loomed larger and clearer, gliding through the headlights, becoming solid as if carved out of the ice and the night. Slightly bent at the waist, his right hand cupping his jaw, he came on. Two other skaters trailed behind him to either side, falling back like wingers.

He shouted the word again. Then muttered it savagely several times, his face vivid as the moon and moving toward me as the moon moves outside a speeding car. And his cupped hand trying to hold the spilling blood, either from his mouth or nose I couldn't tell. His hand like a muskrat's bloodied paw being gnawed from a trap. With his skates still on, he clambered up onto the bank, a few feet to my side. I caught a whiff of beer, a brief, bewildered glare of pain, the same look cast by tens of thousands skating off the ice on their own power to stitches and scars and worse.

The music stopped. And the slapshots. A strange silence descended, one I had never been inside of before, but which I now know too well, the silence of "too late." Not the trivial silence after an overtime goal by the visiting team, but deeper, more complex; the silence of three o'clock in the morning, fifty years already played, the scoreboard clock frozen; the human silence that the wilderness feeds on without particular appetite or even interest.

"Let's go, bud. It's late. I'd better get you home. We'll come back another time."

His trapper was under his arm, and he held a stubby beer bottle in his hand. He sat on the bank beside me and delicately placed the bottle down. Then he took off his pads, one strap at a time, wearily, just as, for years, he'd pull in salmon nets by hand, because it was what the land gave him to do. The fishing, the farming, the hunting, as well as the hockey and the drinking that went with it: all somehow came from the land. And it was a complicated, confusing gift, a Greek gift.

I never received it. At least not in the same way. In fact, the rain that fell a few days later and turned the slough back to water, rained all the rest of the winters of my childhood. I wouldn't skate outside again for over two decades, when, almost thirty, I moved to Edmonton in the middle of a fiercely cold February and discovered a little-used outdoor rink in my neighbourhood. But why had I even packed a pair of skates? Instinct, perhaps, or hope. My hands reached into my pockets for those hockey cards, again and again for years, but not to find a piece of cardboard depicting a famous athlete. No, the reach was much more important than that, and much harder to explain: it was the reach of innocence for belief and community and home, the reach we hope our children make, though I have long since taken off that mask and given away that coat. I'm fifty-five years old. The comforting lies don't always comfort. And hockey, beyond all else, is this country's most comforting lie.

THE COMMON
CURRENCY OF LIFE

ONCE, I RECEIVED AN 1893 AMERICAN INDIAN HEAD PENNY IN CHANGE from an Edmonton Starbucks.

Look ye! D'ye see this Spanish ounce of gold? – holding up a broad bright coin to the sun – D'ye see it? Mr. Starbuck, hand me yon top-maul.

I didn't notice until I returned home, several hours later, and idly glanced at the change pulled from my pockets – an old habit, the natural inheritance of a low-income, working-class upbringing provided by parents raised during the Great Depression, parents to whom the idea of a four-hundred-penny latte would be as foreign as the idea of reading *Moby Dick*. Sometimes – as when I find one of the 1967 centennial coins designed by the painter Alex Colville, or one of the 1973 Mountie quarters that my mother collects and keeps in long Black Velvet Whisky cylinders – I'm in luck. As if I had suddenly discovered a penny on the sidewalk.

Find a penny
Pick it up

And all the day
You'll have good luck.

But this 1893 coin was a great deal more than ordinary run-of-the-mill good fortune; this was eerie and unsettling. The little brown penny on my palm – the United States of America on one side, Liberty in headdress on the other and no mention of God or trust – had been in circulation for almost 120 years! I gazed at the coin a while, marvelling at its survival, marvelling at all that had happened since the year it had left the mint. Flight. Wars. Space travel. Splitting the atom. The Internet. Billions of childhoods and marriages and deaths. I froze, much as I had frozen the day the hundred-year-old columnist from my hometown newspaper telephoned to congratulate me on an award I had recently won. What do you say to a person born the year the *Titanic* sank? That man, as a boy in short pants, could have had a nice treat in a sweet shop with my Indian Head penny, this penny already two decades old in his childhood. In wonder, and almost dizziness, I gazed at the coin – smaller than the modern Canadian version, and smooth as a beach stone – and then I did exactly what my culture and my times had prepared me to do.

I jumped online and did a quick Google search to see if my surprising Starbucks experience (I had been to no other stores that day) had dramatically increased my wealth. No such luck. Except in uncirculated condition, shiny, unrubbed, never dropped into the palm of a shouting newsie for the latest *Times*, an 1893 Indian Head penny fetches about ten (Star) bucks. And even coins from Ancient Rome and Greece can be bought for mere dollars – age, as in many collectable things, is no guarantee of material value. Pristine condition combined with scarcity is generally the combination that leads to early retirement. For example, if a smiling barista had handed me a 1936 Canadian dot penny, of which the Royal Canadian Mint in Winnipeg struck only a few on account of the Prince of Wales's unfortunate involvement with a Yankee divorcee, I'd be a great deal closer to Freedom 55. Indeed, in the 160 years since Canada started minting its own money, the 1936 dot penny remains one of our most valuable coins.

One sold to a private collector in 2013 for $253,000. The most valuable, however – a 99.9 percent solid gold dollar from 2007 – sold at auction for over four million. As for the most valuable coin in the world, that honour goes to the 1794 Flowing Hair American silver dollar, which sold in 2013 for just over ten million.

My Indian Head penny, then, is at once common and extraordinary. It might be no monetary star (to coin a phrase), but how often in the daily drudgery of commerce – a commerce rapidly becoming exclusively plastic and electronic – does your great-great-grandfather reach out and touch your hand? Besides, as the creator of the original Starbuck points out, "And some certain significance lurks in all things, else all things are little worth, and the round world itself but an empty cipher."

Well, I have witnessed three births and sat by one deathbed to the end – life eventually moves us on from all miracles. So I put the 1893 penny in my special drawer, with my children's baby teeth, my Bobby Orr–autographed Vancouver Canucks program from 1979 and the first cheque I ever received for a piece of writing. Then I forgot all about it, and put my nose to the grindstone, my shoulder to the wheel, à la Allen Ginsberg:

America two dollars and twentyseven cents January 17, 1956

. . . .

America I'm putting my queer shoulder to the wheel.

Until 2012, that is, when the Canadian government decided to make us all penniless. After a hundred and sixty years, the Royal Canadian Mint ceased production of the little (mostly) copper coin, and – remarkably – within a year, the penny virtually disappeared, at least from ordinary circulation. As losses go, it wasn't particularly tragic. Most people shrugged, some jokesters lightly mourned the imminent extinction of favourite sayings and phrases, such as "A penny for your thoughts," "penny ante" and "That must have cost a pretty penny," and businesses rounded purchases up or down, except on debit and credit card transactions, which can more easily record single cent numbers. Many people even applauded the abolition of the penny, regarding such a miniscule amount of coinage as an irrelevant nuisance. After all, not even the most money-conscious among us will religiously go through their pennies, searching for one from 1936 with a tiny dot under the date. Most won't even collect the centennial coins designed by the staunchly conservative Alex Colville, whose paintings, by the way, sell for millions. As for the 1973 Mountie quarter, I've never known anyone except my mother to collect those, and I don't even know why she does, except out of some curious nationalistic instinct that itself seems as, well, un-current as the penny. Besides, it doesn't take a John Maynard Keynes or an Adam Smith to see that the days of actual touchable cash are numbered – too inefficient and inconvenient in this era of rapid digital transactions.

And yet, a penny saved is still a penny earned. When the major banks raise service charges by a few cents, that doesn't seem like much of an increase. But the banks make millions with such seemingly innocuous moves, and they use those millions to make billions, and they use all that wealth to exert a vast influence on the world in which we live. I simply can't forget the penny.

After all, I grew up in a time when men fought one another over pennies. All through the 1960s and '70s, on the west coast, salmon fishermen and canneries battled over the price paid per pound for each of the five species of Pacific salmon. My father, uncles, brothers and cousins voted on whether to accept the canneries' offer of $1.21 per pound for sockeye and 47¢ for pinks, or else to go on strike. Often they voted to strike. Over a penny. There was no rounding up or down for families who needed to eke out all the income they could from the hard labour they performed.

And so did Ishmael seek more than the three hundredth lay on his maiden whaling journey on the *Pequod* (which, incidentally, Starbucks' founders also considered for the shop's name). Who doesn't want a higher crew share? My own often depended on those negotiated miniscule amounts – and still does, though I fish mostly in inky waters now.

And if Starbucks raises the price of a latte by a few pennies, who really notices? And if Starbucks – the largest coffee chain in the world, named for the fiscally conscious first mate of the *Pequod*, who said of Ahab's obsession with Moby Dick, "How many barrels will thy vengeance yield thee even if thou gettest it, Captain Ahab? It will not fetch thee much in our Nantucket market" – if that Starbucks threatens and intimidates its employees who try to unionize, if that Starbucks promotes a benevolent capitalism wholly dependent on the whims of the wealthy, who will raise a harpoon against that implacable twenty-first-century white whale?

No, the penny is not so easily dismissed.

Also in my special drawer are a handful of Newfoundland pennies that my father carried as lucky charms all the way through the Second World War. Pennies of the independent nation of Newfoundland, a nation which, per capita, lost more men than any other during World War I, a conflict that most historians now agree was extended for years largely in the name of profit. Money – even in the form of pennies or Ahab's Spanish doubloon nailed to the mast as a prize for the sailor who first spied Moby Dick – is always power, and power is often bloody. It was Sitting Bull, after all, who said, "What white man can say I ever stole his land or a penny of his money? Yet they say that I am a thief." A coin can be many things: "a white whale's talisman," a young telegrapher's survival on a minesweeper in the north Atlantic or a rare gift in the bottom of a knitted sock on a Christmas morning in the slums of Toronto in 1932. But a coin is always a coin of the realm, and pennies once were placed on the eyelids of the dead. And what are the dead if they are not unaware?

So I will not only keep my 1893 Indian Head penny, but I will also take it out of hiding every now and again, to hear the voice of over a hundred years whispering, but also to relearn the lessons of basic human rights. There are the powerful and the disenfranchised. Always. I hold the penny up to hear its last words, Ishmael's last words, my gift from the Canadian government and the Starbucks chain: "And I only am escaped alone to tell thee."

ON HANDWRITING
AND NATIONHOOD

FIFTY YEARS HAVE PASSED SINCE I LEARNED CURSIVE WRITING, A FINE motor skill fast going the way of blacksmithing and lamplighting. That seven-year-olds in the Canadian school system are no longer taught to connect one letter to another in a graceful swoop without breaking off (like peeling an orange in one long peel) is unfortunate but not surprising – the powers that be in government and education routinely put economics ahead of individual agency and cultural richness. Indeed, it would be naive in the extreme to expect those powers to do otherwise. The world of business is the world of communications technology: penmanship, therefore, is, as many online commenters confidently point out, "a colossal waste of time." It matters not that most neurological studies connect the use of mobile phones to a widespread decrease in focus (the average North American's attention span has dropped by five seconds in the past decade) and the use of handwriting to the opposite. What does it profit a society to think clearly, especially about its past?

The question is ominous, and would surely still be so if I typed it on a keyboard instead of, as I'm doing, writing it longhand in the script first taught to me by Miss Gallagher who, during that school year of 1971, would marry and become Mrs. Noble, a fact I remember clearly perhaps only because I sat in my desk trying to run the g in *good* smoothly into the two *o*'s and then into the *d*, the circles in the four letters maddeningly refusing to remain uniform as I pressed the pencil down on the lines of one of those tan-covered exercise books that I painstakingly filled day after day and which my ninety-three-year-old mother, who herself won an award for penmanship at Alexander Muir elementary school in the west end of Toronto in 1931, still keeps in the bottom drawer of her bedside chest. But if I had typed the question, and then typed the word *good*, would the efficiency of the keyboard have allowed me to linger over those *o*'s so long and lovingly that – presto! – I suddenly recalled that Miss Gallagher sometimes wore round clear granny glasses on the bridge of her tiny nose and would look up and out over them at us as we looked over her blonde bunned head at the cursive examples of the whole alphabet pinned up on square cards, one for each letter in both capital and lower case, all around the room?

My answer is no, but I cannot demonstrate scientifically the way handwriting deepens and enriches memory, nor can I explain how the use of script requires a physical coordination and intimacy that is markedly different from the use of a keyboard. If I tried to prove, for example, that my antiquated habit of writing poems, stories and personal letters by hand has made me comfortable with long, complex sentences – comfortable enough to love them in an age that seeks greater and greater condensation of communication, to the point of using abbreviations (lol) and emojis (sad face here) – I would undoubtedly be dismissed as a Luddite, a dinosaur, an enemy of the obvious truth that a language must adapt in order to survive. And besides, there's little hard scientific evidence, at least so far, to suggest a link between typing/texting and decreased levels of literacy.

So all I can say, with accuracy, is that I *feel* the difference between writing by hand and typing. The past comes alive for me in more surprising and detailed ways when I use cursive, as if each swooping stroke is like the waving of a tiny magic wand that reawakens that small boy at his desk and encourages him to look again at the world in which he first came to written expression.

My elementary school lay almost exactly at the midpoint between the Fraser River to the north and the CN railroad lines to the south, which means that I learned to write words and then sentences between two long sentences, the one alive with the salmon's flowing and leaping silver syllables and the other heavy with mournful phrases of deep-black coal and the detritus of history. The river and the salmon were my family's world, but the railroad with its ghostly cadences captured more of my attention as I sat at my desk trying to make a *z* not look like a *y* or a *g*.

Outside, at recess, in the easy black script of the slanting autumn rains, I always looked to the south, which was apt for a Canadian, then and even more so now, hemmed in by the syntactic structures of a larger empire, yet one employing a language that had grown out of a dying empire whose queens and kings gazed dolefully back at me from the money I sometimes carried in my pants pockets to buy candy. America, after all, was television, movies, comic books, sport – cultural influences that saturated my early consciousness to such an extent that, even now, if not for the more power-ful impact of the land and water on which my family worked, I might not know where the American in me ended and where the Canadian began. Certainly, without that land and water, my formal education would have made me an Ontarian, because the Canadian history, politics and enter-tainment of my developing years were almost exclusively the product of a province thousands of miles away – what Canadian culture I learned, in other words, taught me that Ontario was Canada and that my home was . . . what? At best, a place of stunning physical beauty; at worst, an afterthought, the "west beyond the west," the electoral region where, due to a three-hour difference in time zones, our votes rarely mattered during a federal election.

But that seven-year-old boy, just entering written language, also looked westward, to the Pacific Ocean a few short miles away, that rich broth of motion and mysterious life somehow escaping all nationalistic influence, a mercurial surface and profound depth where human communication seemed tiny and vulnerable and all but meaningless. The sea, I knew, was where those rivery and coal-blackened sentences stopped, where the Stars and Stripes and the Maple Leaf and the Union Jack dissolved into the same crab-eaten fabric. How could I be Canadian, American or English, standing on a slippery deck of words over a reality that cared nothing for the discipline of any language? I couldn't be, and I can't be. The idea's as absurd as the Apollo 11 astronauts *feeling* American rather than human as they looked back at the Earth from the moon. Yet when I read the famous last sentence from *The Great Gatsby*, am I not at least participating, through those letters that form those words and the words that form those rhythms, in a kind of American rhapsody? When I read the famous opening sentence about the best and the worst of times in *A Tale of Two Cities* is my spirit moved solely by the music or does the sentiment's aural relationship to its expression also stir my distant and dormant English blood? And does the fact that no single Canadian sentence even comes to mind, let alone one that speaks directly out of my own distinct region of the country, make the letters I formed as a child nothing less than the bars of a cage that keep me forever on the margins of myself?

The matter is at once complicated and simple. The poet Adrienne Rich, explaining her relationship to English from a feminist perspective, claims that she must use "the enemy's language" to combat oppression. And while my position is certainly not as dramatic or tragic as that of a woman resisting the patriarchy or an Indigenous person resisting industrial capitalism, I am nevertheless forced to draw on linguistic resources that do not come from the same place as my love for the land and water that has always been the most potent inspiration for my writing. As a result, my literary expressions speak out of a particular geographical location whose distance from power renders it voiceless to that power. How, then, should I feel about the memories of the past evoked in me by the handwriting of what is fundamentally a foreign language when it comes from England, and a borrowed foreign language when it comes from America or Ontario? Is there any sense in which my lived experience along the British-named Fraser River in British Columbia can ever find its natural lived voice?

After all, I had little exposure to the Indigenous languages of the coast, and no opportunity to learn them at a time when the people for whom those words and rhythms were a birthright were actively prevented from doing so. Although my family fished, mended nets, attended union meetings and sometimes relaxed alongside members of the Stó:lō First Nations, we had limited access to their cultural practices and, frankly, no serious interest in them. In any case, the Stó:lō define themselves as "the people of the river," and that is not a claim, despite my upbringing, that I can make in all conscience. So I must return to the question: Is there any sense in which my lived experience along the British-named Fraser River in British Columbia can ever find its natural lived voice?

In a word, no. Yet the little boy at the desk, given a set of beautiful but imperfect tools, has become a man who cannot deny or impugn the joy he finds in the carpentry of these second-hand letters. That I formed them for the first time without knowledge of their power and its meaning, and that I form them still, as somewhere Miss Gallagher looks on approvingly through her granny glasses, is at once a sadness and an opportunity. Regardless of background, a writer, no matter their subject, ought to write *against* power and not in complicity with it. We close one exercise book and open another. The salmon move, the trains move, the past moves through the present into the future and the past. Outside, the slanting autumn rains merging into the deep ocean still write the true story.

SHOULD I REALLY READ
THE REMAINS OF THE DAY
IN WHAT REMAINS
OF MY DAYS?

ROBERTSON DAVIES, THE CANADIAN NOVELIST AND ESSAYIST, WROTE OF great books that they need to be read once in youth, again in maturity and once again in old age. As we change, he argued, the books change. Of course, Davies lived and died on that other planet – the pre-digitized Earth – and so his relationship to reading great books was a little different than ours. His leisureliness and dedication remind me of D.H. Lawrence's view that a novelist should write a first draft and then . . . throw it away and write a second draft from scratch. Here was a writer doomed to an early death by tuberculosis, yet he had the time for wholesale revision, just as Davies, apparently, had time to reread *The Brothers Karamazov* and *The*

Life and Opinions of Tristram Shandy, Gentleman and who knows how many other classics at least three times.

We live in an age of a more accelerated pace. And while I have certainly written first drafts of novels and then thrown them away, I haven't gone on to write the second drafts at all, which isn't exactly what Lawrence had in mind. Still, close enough. As for rereading, I can't even get around to a first reading of many great books, including *The Brothers Karamazov*, the King James Bible, *The Remembrance of Times Past* and *Don Quixote*. But, of course, I could produce an essay – or even a whole book, and there are hundreds of these – in which I regale you with revelations about how, at twenty, I thought *On the Road*, *The Sun Also Rises* and *The Catcher in the Rye* were wonderful and about how, at fifty-four, I find them much less captivating. But what would be the point? That great books change so much as we age that they sometimes end up being ordinary books? No. I suspect that *On the Road*, *The Sun Also Rises* and *The Catcher in the Rye* will go on being great books, at least to twenty-year-old men.

I'm interested in something else, something that few writers appear to have discussed: the not-classic book from childhood that has long stayed in the memory but that no one else even remembers. Let me explain.

Back on that other Earth, the Earth before Google Earth, I occasionally asked people of my generation, including specialists in children's literature, if they had ever heard of Homer Pickle. The answer was usually a bemused look followed by a no, or, in the case of the specialists, "You mean Homer Price."

I didn't mean Homer Price. I knew all about Homer Price, the boy detective of a whole series of widely read books. I meant *Homer Pickle, the Greatest*. And before you start thinking that I've made this book up, who would possibly imagine a title like *Homer Pickle, the Greatest*? Not D.H. Lawrence, not Robertson Davies and not me either. I didn't invent the book, nor could I remember much about it except the title and the main character, an all-around boy super-athlete of great personal integrity who always did the honourable thing and never let the cheaters get the better of him. In fact, Homer Pickle stood out in my memory with great clarity as a more selfless, noble figure than either Jesus or Peter Parker. A few times (desultorily – remember, this was pre-Internet, and a slower pace was allowed) I tried to find the book in public libraries, but public libraries generally de-accession non-famous juvenile books from the 1970s. So Homer Pickle remained a lost character in a lost narrative from a lost time.

Then the Internet arrived. With it came, eventually, book search sites such as the Advanced Book Exchange (AbeBooks). Finally, one day, not too long ago, I decided to type in *Homer Pickle, the Greatest*. Lo and behold, several copies immediately appeared (confirming the book's publication date as 1971), so I ordered one in dust jacket for the grand sum of fifteen dollars US plus shipping. On its arrival last week, I began my long-overdue reread.

The results were at once surprising, sobering and amusing. First of all, the cover image was far more American than I had remembered, with the block capital letters of *Homer Pickle* entirely in stars and stripes. Of course, a Canadian child's cultural experience is often an American one (even more so today, with the erosion of national institutions and the ubiquity of the homogenizing Internet), and in the early 1970s I had no doubt looked right past the Yankee Doodleism, being more interested in the sporting images on the cover: a teenaged boy throwing a football, holding a bat at the plate, in a diving position and poised to sprint in track and field kit. And without question the dust jacket copy would have quickened my boyhood pulse:

> Into this age of anti-heroes – enters Homer Pickle, super-hero of the 70s . . . Whatever Homer attempts, he brings off: as a swimmer, he breaks the world free-style record; he leads his high-school football team to a national championship; he wins the Olympic gold medal for the grueling decathlon; as a switch-pitcher and awesome slugger, he personally wins the deciding game of the World Series.
>
> Homer Pickle is truly THE GREATEST!

And on the back cover: "Blessed with incredible natural ability, Homer Pickle also possesses the kind of character and integrity that everyone admires but seldom encounters. A modern Frank Merriwell, he is an inspiring hero for the 'now generation.'"

"This age of anti-heroes"? "The now generation"? Frank who? By the time I finished the story – which basically involves Homer triumphing in a variety of sports while looking after his kid brother, who seems constantly tempted by a life of drugs and criminal activity – I realized that I'd been drenched (re-drenched) in reactionary conservatism. Homer Pickle is more straight and narrow than a ruler – he even achieves excellent grades and has a remarkably chaste relationship with a childhood sweetheart named, oddly enough, Zelda. (Was the author Alfred D. Laurence perhaps a fan of the Jazz Age Fitzgeralds?) His brother, meanwhile, is a long-haired guitar player, bizarrely named Plutonious, prone to dark and sullen moods – obviously the author's idea of a now-generation anti-hero. I had completely forgotten about Plutonious, which suggests that that particular marketing angle had failed dismally, as of course it would. Who in 1971, post Woodstock and the Age of Aquarius and with the long-haired Beatles' breakup still fresh, would look to a juvenile sports book for a pop star fix? In fact, I had also forgotten the most significant backstory to the plot: the murder of Homer's shopkeeper father by a gang of "thugs." But not just any father. No, Homer's dad is the kind of patriarch prone to the following sort of guiding wisdom:

> Never forget, Homer. We live in this world only one time. If we're smart, we don't make the same mistakes twice. That's what I want you to remember. If you have to sweep the floor or trim heads of lettuce, or even if you have to fight a guy in the boxing ring or play first base with the Yankees, whatever you do, always do your best and give of yourself more than the other guy gives of himself. That's the secret of life, my boy. Never forget and someday you'll make it right up there to the top.

Why, Homer Pickle's father even gave him the name Homer as a nod to "a great author he'd read about in school one day." How could our hero possibly let his father *and* the great bard of Ancient Greece down?

Well, he couldn't. And therein lies the problem with the book. Kids – whether the now or the then generation – are sophisticated readers. When the dust jacket copy of a book announces "he personally wins the deciding game of the World Series," and the entire story is framed around that momentous plate appearance with, natch, two out and the bases loaded (it opens and closes the narrative, with the rest of the plot in flashback), even a short-haired well-behaved Canadian boy several years away from buying his first Led Zeppelin album is going to feel the lack of suspense. More than that, he's going to feel – and reject – the moralizing. Even today's more blasé teenagers, my own included, would likely roll their eyes at the book's dedication: "To all the boys and girls who will eventually realize that their parents and teachers are their best friends."

Uh, no. As much as I love and respect my parents, they were never exactly my friends, and the less said about many of my teachers the better. And yet, did I ever really fight off the reactionary conservatism that so much of any North American childhood is awash in? How old was I before I learned that morality and society have about as much in common as Homer and Plutonious (related, but not at all alike). I mean, for crying out loud, Homer's father even holds Ty Cobb – widely known for his violent temper, miserliness and racist attitudes that were shocking even by early twentieth-century standards – up as a role model because of his greatness on the ball diamond.

Naturally enough, that notion of athletic greatness was all I really remembered about the book. Humble Homer always came through in the clutch. There was never any chance he was going to lose, not even when accused of dealing heroin (oh those untrustworthy pals of Plutonious!). Because if he lost, America would lose the Cold War and will lose the war against terrorism. There's a straight line, in fact, between Homer Pickle and the recent celebrated Nike ad in which a variety of athletes – from the amateur to former NFL quarterback Colin Kaepernick – are encouraged to be not just the best but the greatest ever. Kaepernick, who refused to stand for the US national anthem as a means of protesting racial injustice (at least until the NFL blacklisted him) is, at least for the purposes of the advertising campaign, nothing less than a modern-day Homer Pickle, a beacon of integrity and athletic excellence. And if you believe that Nike or any other corporation is closer to Homer Pickle than to a gang of hooligans in its values, I have a nice little product from the publishing firm of Platt & Munk that you might enjoy.

How old was I – fifteen? sixteen? – before I learned about the Civil Rights Movement, resistance to the Vietnam War, the CIA's toppling of the democratically elected Chilean government just two years after Homer Pickle was published? How old was I before I understood that the expression "If you're not cheating, you're not trying hard enough," made famous by former Chicago Cub Mark Grace, is at least one definition of capitalism and nationalism, and that Bobby Clarke's successful elimination (by wicked slash) of the Soviet Union's star player in the 1972 Summit Series more accurately reflected my culture's values in the athletic arena?

In the mid '70s, of course, when I first read *Homer Pickle, the Greatest*, I thrilled only to the idea of being a superhero athlete admired by everyone. What aspiring young athlete wouldn't revel in Homer's shining example? Humble, blushing Homer always came through in the clutch, always thought of others first, always lived up to his promise.

Perhaps, in the end, Robertson Davies's point can also apply to books that are obviously not great. After all, any story can be a measure of our growth or lack thereof. What I can't answer – what no one can answer – is to what extent the messages in the books of our early selves shape our essential character. Though I have come to question many of the values my society promotes, I have never seriously rebelled against society, nor have I acted in my personal life with any less integrity than Homer Pickle. Were my behaviour and my moral compass in part shaped by this formulaic juvenile book and dozens of others that my memory hasn't held onto? Possibly.

But I suspect that I won't ever read *Homer Pickle, the Greatest* again, not unless some app developer decides to condense juvenile books from the 1970s into three-minute reads (for busy but nostalgic professionals). After all, in what remains of my days, do I really want to reread anything when I still haven't got around to *The Remains of the Day*, *War and Peace* and *Catch-22*, not to mention Burt L. Standish's 1903 juvenile bestseller *Frank Merriwell at Yale*? Robertson Davies, no doubt, would encourage me to reread, but what would the middle-aged Homer Pickle say? Somehow, I have the feeling he'd sound a bit like Jay Gatsby when he advises, "Steady on, old sport, you can't go wrong with a little tale called the *Odyssey*."

ON LITERARY SUCCESS
AND GROWING OLD

THE POET JOHN BERRYMAN ONCE DESCRIBED FAME AS "RECEIVING A LETTER from a younger man." The elderly W. Somerset Maugham, in what is perhaps the saddest summation of a life in writing that I've ever read, told a friend, "I'm through. The young men don't write essays about me."

I'm sitting in a café in downtown Edmonton, listening to a male poet thirty years my junior tell me about his life. He had a great summer of writing poems; he's trying to finish his English degree as fast as he can so he doesn't accrue any more personal debt; he's in love but the young woman is moving across the country to do her MFA and he's not sure if what they have can survive a long-distance relationship.

Whatever I say in response sounds hollow to me, just as most of what I say outside of my written art sounds hollow. I could say, instead, that I also had a great summer of writing poems; that I wish I'd done almost anything else with my love of literature than earn two English degrees; that romantic love, like everything else, is subject to unpredictable change, and that, in essence therefore, it's not romantic at all. But what do I say? This young man

– like me, from a small rural town in western Canada – is gentle, thought-ful, talented and a complete and utter stranger, just as my own children are strangers, just as I'm mostly a stranger to myself. So I don my father-mask (it is close to Halloween, after all) and clasp my father-hands and in my wise father-voice ask the young man if his girlfriend wants him to follow her.

His smile is full of rue. "I'm not sure. But as much as I'd like to go somewhere else and get some job and just write for a year, I don't think I'd look good to her doing that." Long pause. "Of course, if I don't do that, our relationship might not even last more than a few months. The problem is, I'm in love."

Ridiculously, but not without an awareness of the futility of my re-sponse, I mention the old chestnut of "better to have loved and lost than never to have loved at all." Too late, I realize that I'm forecasting the failure of his romance, but he smiles slightly, worldly enough at twenty-three to have already grasped the stakes.

We talk of other subjects – creative writing programs, his fondness for e.e. cummings, his own poems (five of which I have made comments on, mostly of a technical nature) – and the whole time I'm painfully aware of the absurdity of midlife, which is like nothing else but the absurdity of youth. "Professor," the students call me, though I'm not a professor and have little enough to profess. In fact, in my own consciousness, I'm still a young man and a student, trying to figure things out, but the world gives us roles to play, and being a middle-aged man often involves playing them when you'd rather just tear the playhouse down.

I tell him that poetry has been my best friend all my life and I mean it, because there's nothing else I've ever really believed in. The excitement of reading and writing poems – of creation – still makes the world bearable. No one can touch that faith. No one has touched it. Not reviewers, not editors, not English departments, not governments. If you can find a way to negotiate the world . . .

A way? His eyes widen and he leans forward. I suddenly realize that my position is enviable to this young man, this shadow-self of my youth.

Widely published, award-winning, a homeowner, a father: everything that's certain in me is uncertain in him. But I can't pretend a calmness that has never – and will never – exist.

Indeed, it is the great truth of growing older that age is remarkably akin to youth. Capitalism, which profits immensely by pitting the generations against one another, relentlessly sells us the idea (OK Boomer) that the young must push out the old to survive and that the old must resent (OK Slacker) the young seeking to establish themselves. Any way that the system can keep the workers divided is a way to further empower the elites. This toxicity even spills over into the arts, where a bias for youth and novelty is obviously disastrous for anyone who intends to keep maturing as an artist beyond the age of thirty. But where poetry, one of the most marginalized art forms, is concerned, the "work, work, work" of it (to use Don McKay's phrase) ought to bring people of all ages together. In fact, it does, as my coffee meeting with this twenty-three-year-old poet and my postal correspondence with an eighty-year-old poet attest.

Even so, to everything there is a season, and the concerns of a young person aren't exactly the concerns of a middle-aged or older person. As a result, I can't even tell my own children anything of use that they couldn't discover more powerfully on their own by reading the letters of John Keats – "the holiness of the Heart's affections." Trust in that holiness, even if Keats, the doomed young man, never had to subject his faith to the barnacle accretion of the years.

In the main, therefore, I refuse to pretend, as my culture encourages me to pretend, that youth is enviable or even interesting simply because it's young. I can't share Berryman's enthusiasm for his fan mail or Maugham's depression about his lack of reviews, even if I won't go to the extreme, à la Willa Cather, of titling a book *Not Under Forty* because I don't think anyone below that age can possibly understand what I'm trying to say. In fact, it depresses me – has depressed me – to see the work of my middle years in the careless and inexpert hands of not the young per se but of a materialist culture that has no respect for or interest in a deeply engaged and thoughtful record of any stage of life. The problem is this: If I'm true to my life in my work, how can a culture terrified of aging possibly understand? And if I'm false, how can I even bear to look a young poet in the eye and proffer any advice at all?

I realize, in the end, that my *human* purpose is to give this young man exactly what he wants and what he will inevitably find elsewhere: validation for his love, for the "holiness of [his] Heart's affections." And since it is a quest appropriate to any age, I am not a hypocrite for reminding myself, out loud, of the love I still feel for poetry.

In any case, I'm in some sense peripheral to him, as I must be, else I humiliate myself. To depend on attention from younger men is, at some level, to remain immature. I'm embarrassed for Berryman and Maugham – in midlife, I would like to correspond with my peers. Regardless of how old they are, I would like my peers to read and review my work.

But we live in a culture, for better or worse, where the "established" are duty bound to "launch" the young; where the parent, no matter how uncertain and stumbling, is duty bound to guide and support the child. It's all too romantically linear for me, even if I do want to subscribe still to the generative faith of the young Keats. Age, however, requires a different master, or at least a more exacting and impatient one. There simply isn't any time to waste; if the work is to matter to others, now it must be the truest work of all, and damn the consequences.

For the young artist across from me, encouraged by the culture that will almost inevitably turn away from his mature art, all of these lessons will be learned in time, and the hard way. There's really nothing I can say or do to help with that education, no digital seminar on successful writing I can recommend that isn't abysmally middle-class and fake. So I do what I always do in these situations: smile, listen, suggest a few good books and pay for the coffee. It isn't the *least* I can do; it is *all* I can do without being disloyal to my own long, lonely and confused apprenticeship.

THE PROOF OF LOVE

OF ALL THE TYPES OF LETTERS IN THE WORLD, THE LOVE LETTER IS AT once the most fascinating and the most boring: fascinating if you're the recipient, boring if you're not. Certainly, the story of Abelard and Heloise is compellingly tragic – the medieval French philosopher who arranges to tutor a much younger woman, conducts a torrid illicit relationship with her, is set upon and castrated by her guardian's kinsmen and then retreats into a celibate monkhood of remorse while his ex-lover writes to him that she can't and won't stop thinking about the pleasure of their physical exploits. But, in all honesty, would their love letters still be widely read today if not for the castration?

An interest in other people's love lives is always prurient, or at least dependent on factors other than the love itself. If John Keats, for example, had lived to a ripe old age instead of succumbing to consumption at twenty-five, would his impassioned letters to Fanny Brawne be even remotely interesting?

Many people would respond with an emphatic yes. Judging by the fascination the public has for the romantic lives of celebrities, I suspect that a compilation of the letters between, say, Meghan Markle and Prince Harry would rocket to the top of the bestseller lists (or rather, a compilation of their text messages, given that almost no one under the age of fifty posts a pen-and-ink letter anymore).

But how much variety can there really be in such correspondence? I love you, I want you, I need you, I can't think of anything else but you, when will we be together again, I think of your body constantly, my life is in your hands, etc., etc. Or an emoji of a heart filled with quivering Cupid's arrows or throbbing like a bullfrog's throat.

I don't mean to be dismissive of the genuine human need to communicate the most intense of emotions in epistolary form. Believe me, at the deepest possible level, I understand the lure of the love letter. Between the years 1993 and 1995, before the personal computer and the Internet and email had fully taken over our means of communication, I conducted a romantic postal correspondence with the woman who is now my wife. The details aren't anyone else's business, but for the sake of this essay, I'll point out that we had been encouraged to write to one another by a mutual friend, that I lived near Vancouver and that she lived in Edmonton, that we exchanged letters twice a month for a year before we met in person, and that after our meeting the letters intensified in frequency and – ahem – content until, eventually, we moved in together in Edmonton and the correspondence came to an abrupt end.

Why should any of this matter to anyone else? Clearly, it doesn't, but I'm going to assume that, at least for people my age and older, a similar situation and decision might arise as the one currently facing me and my wife.

In her book, *Signed, Sealed, Delivered*, Nina Sankovitch writes, "There are many examples of love letters, personal and revealing, that might have been better off destroyed, but who can bear to erase proof of love, when that might be the only talisman left to declare its existence?"

Who, indeed? The experience of reading other people's love letters becomes more and more diluted the further removed one is from the correspondents involved. John Keats and Fanny Brawne have been dead a long time, and we read his letters to her only because he's a famous poet, and they shine some light on the imagination that created the poems. More pertinently, we can choose not to read them because all love letters, if you're not the recipient, are so much cold mutton and, frankly, none of our business.

But when you have written love letters and received them and – here's the point – kept them, can you bear to destroy them? No? What if you have children who will one day have to sift through all of your worldly possessions? Would you choose to know how much your parents once desired each other's bodies, in graphic detail? How about the banal sentiments of longing – for these are always banal, except to the correspondents – would reading them truly be akin to holding a talisman?

Recently, my ninety-two-year-old mother had to go into a nursing home and her house was sold. When my sister was cleaning out the drawers of a bedroom dresser, she found the love letters that my father, who had died twenty years earlier, had sent to our mother while he was serving in the navy during World War II. My sister cannot bring herself to destroy these letters, nor does she feel entitled to read them. Our mother is still mentally sound but has obviously freed herself of material objects except for some cherished photos, so the physical letters no longer serve a talismanic purpose for her. To quote Vladimir Lenin, whose own love letters would be just as banal as anyone else's, what is to be done?

Perhaps we can return to the poets for an answer – more specifically, to the most famous poetry affaire de coeur of the twentieth century. Ted Hughes, a compulsive letter writer all his life and a dark, brooding Heathcliff-like lover who apparently, on their first meeting, bit Sylvia Plath's lips hard enough to draw blood, once responded to one of her letters by writing that it was "wonderful" and would be "a relic for our fifteenth child's fifteenth child."

Now, overlooking the fact that having fifteen children is decidedly less romantic for a woman than a man, Hughes obviously regarded letters – even the most intimate kind – as talismanic messages to the distant future rather than as ephemera of the moment to be destroyed. All fine and good, as long as the love endures, which, alas, it most definitely did not between modern poetry's most ill-fated pair. To be succinct about a relationship whose delineation is by now the very definition of shopworn,

Hughes's infidelity led, directly or indirectly depending on your biographer of choice, to Plath's suicide. But months before she placed her head inside that gas oven, she enacted a sequence of three ritual bonfires in which she destroyed many of Hughes's manuscripts and his love letters (but not all of them). Then, because she was every bit like Hughes in her approach to poetry and its role in life, she wrote a poem about her actions.

Entitled "Burning the Letters," it opens with a metaphor of the letters as "white fists" with a "death rattle," proceeds to describe the handwriting as "spry hooks that bend and cringe" and to employ various other images of violence, and concludes with dogs "tearing a fox," a "dead eye" and the idea that immortality is immortal.

So, clearly, no relics for the grandkids at this point. As for Hughes, he was soon urging his new paramour Assia Wevill, who'd eventually kill herself and their young daughter, to burn his letters so that "bloody eaves-droppers & filchers" couldn't "make hay" with them.

Well, more than a few hundred barns full of hay resulted when Hughes, several months before he died in 1998, published his final book, *Birthday Letters*, a sequence of epistolary poems addressed to his long-dead first wife. Comfortably able to present a one-sided correspondence, Hughes doubtless went to his grave satisfied that he'd had the last word. When, in 2007, *Letters of Ted Hughes* appeared, running to over seven hundred pages, the volume's almost universal acclaim surely must have pleased Hughes's ghost, if only because it revealed that so few of his correspondents destroyed what he had posted to them. The immortality of the immortal, I suppose.

Interestingly, when we go back to 1878 and the publication of Keats's letters to Fanny Brawne, the critical reception was decidedly more hostile. George Saintsbury, for example, wrote, "There are, it is to be hoped, few people who read such letters . . . without an unpleasant consciousness of eavesdropping." It seems that even the British, renowned for their reserve and desire for decorum and privacy, have now, considering the popularity of Ted Hughes's letters, moved fully into the Digital Age.

But Keats and Fanny had no children, whereas Hughes had a son and daughter with Plath. By most accounts a good father (if one discounts his affairs while they were toddlers), Hughes perhaps saw his letters, manuscripts, etc., as commercial goods whose sale would benefit his children one day. For his part, Keats asked that Fanny's letters be buried with him, and there, presumably, they remain, unread, unsold, not immortal.

Another famous literary couple, also childless, might shed a more useful light on the question of old love letters and what to do with them. Thomas Hardy and his wife Emma had a tempestuous marriage that began passionately and ended bitterly, so Hardy's poem "The Love-Letters" offers perhaps more of a general commentary on the strange relationship lovers can feel for their romantic missives. The speaker meets an acquaintance "quite by accident" who holds up "a square packet" of his old love letters. Turns out his love has "broken off" with him. He then tells the speaker,

> Quite right
> To send them back, and true foresight;
> I'd got too fond of her! To-night
> I burn them – stuff of mine!

The poem then concludes with the speaker's blunt summary: "He laughed in the sun – an ache in his laughter – / And went. I heard of his death soon after."

Incidentally, no love letters between Hardy and Emma have survived, because, more Plath than Plath, she burned them all in the garden and needed only one fire to do so. Presumably, Hardy was not with her at the time.

But my wife will be at my side when the conflagration of our early written romance occurs, which makes a considerable difference. Though we are both writers, we do not think ourselves "important" enough to sacrifice our children's peace of mind for the sake of posterity. The letters will soon be ash, and here's hoping we don't, like Hardy's acquaintance, follow soon after. And I'm sure a similar fate awaits my father's love letters. Unread by his four children, they will be burned when the woman he lived with for over fifty years dies, and all of the ashes of their life together will be scattered in the estuary of the Fraser River.

Will there be loss when these material artifacts disappear? Of course. What my wife and I had to say about Canada and literature in the late twentieth century has some minor cultural significance, as does what my father likely wrote about serving on a minesweeper in the North Atlantic during World War II. But loss isn't necessarily tragic. And our transition from the world of material relics to what comes after can itself constitute a gentle posting. As the Japanese poet Kiyu wrote in his death poem around 1820,

Evening:
I, too, the dew of those who bred me,
am twilit.

Of course, here in the Digital Age, few pen-and-ink love letters continue to be written and mailed, even as the human fascination for the love letter remains as keen as ever. How else to explain Hannah Brencher, a young woman who, in 2011, launched a website called The World Needs More Love Letters, whose raison d'être is the sending of love letters to strangers? (Two hundred fifty thousand and counting, like McDonald's Big Macs.) Or Samara O'Shea, a writer who launched a website in 2005, LetterLover.net, among whose services the writing of personalized love letters is the most highly sought? I suppose that writing love letters to complete strangers or hiring someone to write a love letter for you isn't going quite so far as Fats Waller when he sang about sitting right down and writing himself such a missive, but the difference between romantic love and self-love would take more than one essay to explore.

It's no longer the mid-1990s, and romances now can't even avoid a written component. In a review of *Where the Nights Are Twice as Long*, a compilation of love letters and poems by Canadian poets (not including me, thank God), the reviewer, recoiling at the "cringiness" of some of the content, metaphorically sighs. In the twenty-first century, she explains, few people are going to conduct a romance without doing some kind of writing – emails, texts, etc., are inevitable components of romance now in a way that pen-and-ink letters never were. Whether this means that my children, a half-century from now, will be deleting endless files from yet-to-be-imagined devices, or whether there can never again be any escape from the "bloody eavesdroppers & filchers," is less pertinent than the fact that the love letter will carry on, one way or another.

In the end, it all comes down to one of our world's most abused and vanishing resources: privacy. I happen to believe that romance should be the preserve of the lovers involved and no one else, which means I've already sullied my own valentines. Ah well, there's no sense in preserving them now. Where is that box of matches? It's a chilly night, so we might need an extra layer of clothing. Perhaps we should take turns: I'll burn one of hers, and then she'll burn one of mine. It will almost be like writing and sending them all over again, even though the recipients, like the age they inhabit, have long since moved on from the luxurious romance of the slow and ardent post.

THE FLOATING LIBRARY

MY FAMILY WAS POOR BUT WE DIDN'T LIVE IN POVERTY. MY FATHER MADE a subsistence living from the commercial salmon fishery at the mouth of the Fraser River, and my mother sometimes clerked in the five-and-dime store when the domestic budget required a boost. If poverty is living without hope of an improved situation, we didn't live in poverty, because each fishing season promised, if not riches, at least something better. The life cycle of the Pacific salmon works on a four-year, sometimes five-year cycle, which means that different runs of the fish return from the ocean to the rivers of their birth at different times. A fishing family, therefore, learns to budget according to natural rhythms – to the caprices of wind and tide and to the mysterious and ancient link between starlight, rain, ocean and the salmon's genetic code. Unfortunately, given the human interference in these rhythms (pollution, clear-cut logging, overfishing, government mismanagement, etc.), a fishing family's income – or at least my family's – always involved a considerable amount of unpredictability. If we counted on a large return of Stuart River sockeye, for example, that return might be surprisingly small. Or perhaps the federal department of fisheries, for some reason known only to the Ottawa-appointed minister in charge, would close the river. We never really knew what to expect, either year by year or tide by tide. It was a perilous way to make a living, and it's no exaggeration to say my family's economic challenges lie behind every word I've ever committed to print.

BUT ALL THAT LAY DECADES AHEAD. I'M GOING BACK TO THE FALL OF 1970, when the local pub still had separate men's and women's entrances and when our town's one Vietnam draft dodger – an erratic and Lincoln-bearded Oregonian by the name of Thomas Plum – still lived inside the stone tower of the old town clock. I had just started grade one two months earlier, an experience that involved learning to print and – something almost impossible for a child of the sloughs and fields – learning to sit silently at a desk for hours. At least I was quiet and introverted by nature, which made the days less painful than they must have been for many of my peers. In any case, I was becoming a cog in a machine whose workings I couldn't begin to recognize let alone understand, and my attendance at school only made me gloomy and restless.

So whenever the weekend arrived, I was relieved. If that weekend also included an outing with my father, I was delighted. For our bond contained almost none of the tension that is supposed to exist between father and son, an absence probably due to my late arrival on the scene. My father was forty when I was born, and my mother thirty-seven. They had been young parents twenty years before, to my two brothers, and then, in a span of five years, my sister arrived, followed by a stillborn brother and finally – because the doctors feared a repeat of the lost child – I was, like Macduff, from my mother's womb untimely ripped. Family lore has it that I was special from the start, the chosen one, but family lore, if you've ever been part of a family, is dubious. All I know is that, in some strange sense, I had a grandfatherly father, a grandmotherly mother and two fatherly brothers. Tolstoy's suggestion that all happy families are alike has never held much water for me. We were happy but not at all like any other family.

"Why shouldn't I take him along?" my father said that Saturday morning. "He likes books. And he loves being on the boat."

My mother turned her back on me and lowered her voice. "Because you spoil him." Then her voice was whispery, and I barely made out her words, though I sensed that the conversation was about finances. "Anyway, Grandma always thought that they were valuable."

My father nodded and began to pull on his Floater jacket. Any reference to his mother's opinion always decided matters. But I could sense that he wasn't really looking forward to whatever task he had been set. He began to whistle "Santa Lucia," his favourite means of distracting himself. Then he bent down and picked up a large cardboard box.

"Valuable or not, they're sure heavy. If they were sockeye, there's enough pounds here to sink a cork line."

"If they were sockeye," my mother said, opening the door for us, "we wouldn't need to sell them."

I KNEW THAT THEY WERE TALKING ABOUT BOOKS, BECAUSE I HAD LOOKED in the box earlier and had been disappointed by the contents. Comic books would have interested me, but not these grubby old volumes that had been on the one bookshelf in my late grandfather's plumbing shop. None of them had colourful dust jackets, and most of them contained gift inscriptions to various aunts and uncles and other more distant relations. There was a particularly heavy book about hunting dogs, heavy because of the two dozen colour plates inside. But who wanted to read about hunting dogs in a town as full of them as the night sky with stars? A few Zane Greys looked promising, or at least more promising than *Matched Pearls* or *The Adventure Girls at Happiness House*. As for *Measurement and Mechanics* and other manuals and texts of a mathematics or engineering bent, they might have been bricks for all I cared. But my investigation had been surreptitious and cut short, so perhaps some *Hardy Boys* rested at the bottom of all the grime and dust.

The rain-rich air soon took my mind off the box of books. As so often in my childhood seasons, the rain had just ended or was just about to start. The sky, mucilage grey, couldn't detract from the bubbling cauldron of smells and sounds that somehow seemed a veritable kaleidoscope of colours. The eavestroughs and drainpipes gurgled, the muddy ground and puddled streets hissed and steamed, the rotted mulch of maple leaves and the briny breeze off the river mixed with the just-departing or just-about-to-arrive rain, and I was walking in the black-and-white opening scenes of *The Wizard of Oz* as if they were also the dazzling Technicolor scenes.

Five minutes of such walking, beside my father's comfortable silence, and we had ascended the fifteen-foot-tall dike and descended the planked, nearly horizontal gangway to where my father's gillnetter was moored. Shallow-bottomed and narrow, its green and white paint flaked off by the weather to leave only strips, the *Nautilus* was twenty-four feet of almost genteel decay. Old car tires, green with slime, hung from creosoted ropes off its gunwales, the three softball-sized portholes on each side of the blackened wedding-cake-shaped cabin had clasps grown rusty with disuse, and even the two flags near the top of the twenty-foot-tall mast were seagull-grey and flapped disconsolately. But the net, with its cork line of multicoloured corks, was wrapped neatly on the large wooden drum in the stern, and that was all that mattered. If our boat looked more like some outsized old Remington typewriter caked in scales and grease, my father didn't mind so long as the engine caught and the net, still smelling strongly of mud and fish slime, rolled off the drum.

Five minutes later, once the reluctant engine had indeed caught and warmed up, and I had helped to untie the stern and bow ropes, we idled downriver, over a channel surface like chipped black lacquer; past, on the mainland shore, the carcasses of half-sunken rowboats, ash-grey wooden net sheds and the occasional two-storeyed houseboat festooned with hanging baskets of spider plants and sad ochre-tipped ferns; and the opposite shore showed its endless battalion of tan bulrushes to no enemy in particular. Nearby, behind one of the net sheds, a dog began to bark fiercely, as if to accept the challenge of the salt marsh, but within a few minutes we had turned north again and left the barking behind.

Now appeared the view that defined my childhood. It wasn't a view that I'd ever read about in books, nor does it appear much in our literature now: a muddy river flowing away into a blue mountain range with, somewhere, the skyscrapers of a major city nestled between. For all the years of my childhood, I would look up from the water – often the same colour as my father's Red Rose tea after the Carnation evaporated milk had been poured in – to the heron-wing-blue of Grouse Mountain rising three thousand feet above the hidden city of Vancouver. That one North Shore mountain, necklaced year-round with lights from the resort near the peak, was as close as the back of my eyelids when I closed my eyes, and yet, like all mountains, sang a low hymn of great distances. Between the sentinel deadheads stuck in the mud and silts along either side of the channel – almost completely submerged logs whose leaning toward the ocean gave them a floating Victorian ghost quality – and the coastal mountain range to which Grouse belonged nestled a sleepy, unfashionable Vancouver of sawmills and steep cherry-blossomed streets and still-working neon signs from the 1940s. It was a place of faded gentility then, a china teacup half-filled with rice wine and left out in the rain; even the legendary counterculture of the sixties had begun to fade away, replaced by a Greenpeace-led environmental movement still in its infancy. For me, as a child, Vancouver meant the high excitement of late summer's Pacific National Exhibition and the bizarre spectacle of indigenous killer whales performing tricks in captivity at the Stanley Park aquarium; it meant skyscrapers that didn't seem like skyscrapers at all, and certainly not the kind that Marlo Thomas or Mary Tyler Moore would go to work in; it meant rainy car rides to play soccer in grubby east end neighbourhoods and Christmas shopping downtown where, peering north between all the buildings, I would find again my familiar mountain, closer now and yet, unbelievably, even farther away; it meant the promise of urban glamour and the delivery of an uncelebrated sleepiness that somehow wasn't disappointing at the time; it meant a kind of working-class self-confidence before all the insecure aspirant crowing of world-class this and world-class that. Vancouver, in the mid 1970s, still wore black, red-tipped, scale-flecked gumboots and still smelled of salmon, that indefinable musky mixture of blood, brine and silt.

But we weren't going as far as the city. In fact, our little gillnetter chugged out of the familiar fishing grounds and – after travelling briefly to the west in the much larger main channel where foreign freighters black as slate Welsh hills loomed up in the drizzly air – approached the stone breakwater protecting Steveston, a fishing town once so prosperous with canneries that it was known as Salmonopolis. Before we skirted the breakwater and entered the harbour, however, my father cut the engine and ducked into the cabin. He re-emerged on the deck holding something I'd never seen before and didn't even know existed. Now, my father was such a quiet and shy sort of man that, in our close-knit local community of fishing and farming families, he had earned the nickname of "Ghost" for his propensity to be absent at town functions. Even the way he fished was curiously disengaged, as he would idle out onto the river only a few minutes before the scheduled opening times and would never leave his one drift on the river, regardless of how poor the fishing was. I knew, from a very young age, that he was famous for two things: shyness and patience. With regards to the former, he would even disappear from our house into his backyard shed to avoid visitors; with regards to the latter, he would calmly untangle sticks and fish from his net, without breaking any meshes, even on a raging tide sweeping his boat violently oceanward toward all varieties of disaster.

The morning was still and blackly dripping. I could hear the faint cry of seagulls and smell the brine wafting in off the Gulf of Georgia. My father smiled at me from under his woollen skullcap. He flicked the cigarette in his left hand into the river, a motion which only fixed my gaze more intently on what he now lifted in his right hand.

"It's been a while," he said. "I don't have the lip anymore."

Then he leaned his head back, put the trumpet to his mouth and blew a sequence of discordant notes that were nonetheless remarkably clear. When he stopped, and let his hand with the instrument drop, the notes seemed to come from all directions to surround our slowly drifting boat. It was as if we now stood in the middle of a raised flock of invisible seagulls. My father let the silence rebuild before he tried again. This time, the notes came louder though no more smoothly, but my father held them longer, his cheeks swelling the way I'd only ever seen them do blowing up balloons for my birthday parties.

"Getting there," he said, and winked at me. "Just like riding a bike." I could hear him breathing heavily as he added with a smile, "A bike with flat tires."

He blew into the trumpet for another few minutes, the brassy notes like a joyous splashing that didn't leave us wet. I had never heard a trumpet played before, and had rarely heard any instrument played live, other than at a few school concerts. It was an unnerving experience, mostly because my father seemed entirely alone and fighting against something that he couldn't defeat. Yet the rippling music, clumsy as it must have been, sounded entirely natural in that setting, a more audible extension of the river flow and the roiling lavalike scud above us.

I didn't know what music he played, but it had a lively staccato energy that I would eventually come to associate with my father's swing-band youth in and around Vancouver in those two or three years before he enlisted in the navy, served on a minesweeper in the Atlantic theatre and, while on leave in Toronto, met my mother. It isn't easy to imagine our parents' youth, at least not until our own is sufficiently behind us to incite both interest and empathy. That my father played "The Last Post" on the deck of his minesweeper several times probably explains why he lost the taste for playing any kind of horn after the war, but I never really asked him why he stopped. In fact, after this one impromptu concert, the subject of his trumpet-playing youth in a band called the Rhythm Kings rarely came up. When it did, I must not have been old enough or interested enough to mention this one odd solo in my eighth or ninth year.

"Not exactly Harry James," my father said as he turned to me, holding the dull silver instrument out like a salmon he'd just picked from his net. "Care to have a go?"

I took the trumpet from him, intrigued by its clunky elegance, the three mechanical valves in the middle somehow enhancing the morning-glory elegance of the bell flare as it opened to the sky. Both the weight and the size were indeed similar to a small sockeye's or jack spring's – only some blood and a blank gaze were missing. Cautiously, I put my lips to the mouthpiece and blew. No sound issued.

"It takes some getting used to." My father's distant expression suggested that he might have been looking back on many long hours of practise. "Have another go."

After a few more efforts, I managed to blow a sort of wheezing sound out of the flare, but that was all. Manipulating the valves, however, proved much more entertaining. I might have kept at it, hoping the movement of my fingers would encourage my breath into greater music, but my father eventually took the trumpet from me and slid it back into its battered black case.

"Well, Monk, I guess we ought to see a man about some books, eh?"

With the case under his arm, he stooped into the cabin and, a half-minute later, the engine started up and the bow pointed toward Steveston Harbour. We had drifted beyond the breakwater a few hundred fathoms, but it wasn't long before we were moored at the huge government wharf, our little mast like a twig amongst the hundreds of seiner and trawler masts.

The main street of old Steveston lay almost right alongside the wharf, and we were soon hurrying along it, borne on a curious tangy air of gasoline, rain and vinegar-drenched fish and chips. My father huffed a little as he carried the box of books against his chest, his arms underneath like the forks of a forklift, but the effort didn't stop him from whistling "Santa Lucia," a music even more unsettling to me than the surprising brassiness of the trumpet because it signalled my father's unease. By the time we stopped outside the used bookstore, its large window displaying wooden corks, Japanese glass buoys and linen gillnetting, along with a variety of titles relating to BC's maritime history, the rain had picked up enough to leave dark splotches on the tan cardboard of the box. I suspect that the weather, more than the weight of the books or the weight of the task, finally forced my father over the threshold.

Even after nearly fifty years, I can recall the musty smell of the cramped interior, the sound of low classical music on a transistor radio and the broad, sagging face of the Chinese bookseller as he peered scowling into our box that my father had placed carefully on the man's desk. Slowly, one by one, the musty volumes emerged, each one greeted with a grimace and a discouraging grunt. My father, who didn't have a salesman's bone in his body and who couldn't even arrange private sales of salmon the way most fishermen did, as a way to increase profit and to avoid taxes, stood silently by, a few raindrops pearled in the wool of his skullcap.

"I can't take these," the man suddenly said, rearing back. He literally threw the fifteen or so books back into the box and violently forced the flaps into place. "Take them out, take them out. They have bugs. I can't have bugs in here."

When my father, without protest and with a genuine look of dismay on his face, immediately picked up the box, the man calmed down. "I'm sorry," he said. "But even without the bugs, these are not books I could sell. They're in bad shape. And they're not the sort of books anybody wants."

My father nodded, thanked the man for his time and turned toward the door. I can only guess, after all these years, that the passive integrity of my father's character must have somehow touched the owner, for he seemed almost sheepish about his outburst. "It was a bad season on the water," he said, softly stroking his chin. "That makes it hard for everyone. Here, young fellow." He suddenly held out a bowl of mints and urged me to take one. But the sweetness in my mouth couldn't sweeten the day's scudding gloom when we eventually returned to the empty street and stood listening to the far-off gull cry and the infrequent whoosh of car tires on the wet pavement.

My father lifted his head and sniffed the air. "Mmmm, smells pretty good, eh, Monk? What do you say to some lunch?"

A block down the street, at Dave's, Steveston's legendary fish and chip restaurant, I sat alone, eating battered cod and fries and protecting our box of books, which, in some strange way, seemed more valuable than ever. My father, meanwhile, said that he had a little business to do at one of the canneries and would be back as soon as possible. I don't know how much time passed, but I didn't feel any anxiety about waiting, so I imagine it wasn't more than a half-hour before he returned. Despite the dark rain splotches on his dull orange Floater jacket, he seemed lighter, the burning cigarette held nonchalantly between his lips while he paid for my meal through skillfully manipulated puffs of smoke. It didn't even occur to me to wonder why he hadn't eaten anything.

Outside in the teeming rain, my father said, "We'll have to go fast. Don't want the box melting in my arms. But careful as you go on the wharf, now. It'll be slippery."

Several minutes later, we reached our boat. My father unlocked the cabin door and we descended the two little steps down to where the un-covered engine almost completely blocked the way to the narrow bunk at the bow. Here, the smell of gas and oil from the uncovered engine was thick enough to make you sick in minutes if the engine was running. Even now, the atmosphere was unpleasantly smothering, though it was a relief to escape from the rain. My father shoved the box of books all the way up to the front of the bunk, where it stayed for years. No one could sleep in the cabin because of the fumes, so there was no reason to move the books again, although in later years I would take one of the old bug-ridden volumes out, maybe a copy of Thomas Costain's *The Black Rose* or William MacLeod Raine's *Rutledge Trails the Ace of Spades*, and read a few pages or chapters until the tide turned and the river gave me something better to do.

The tide has turned thousands of times since that day, and there has never been anything better to do, not in terms of the heart, at least. I sup-pose my father gave some money to my mother, saying nothing about the trumpet. And I suppose too that my father trusted me not to say anything, or perhaps he asked me not to – my memory grows cloudy on this point.

But a surprising clarity comes to me now in my fifty-fifth year, my father dead these two decades, my mother recently in a nursing home and the family house sold, gone fully into the past where the family boat van-ished thirty years ago. I can see the interior of that gillnetter cabin, with its mackinaw jackets scattered around like parts of a crazy quilt, with old cans of motor oil and worn-out fan belts and wooden hanging needles of frayed string, and I can see the boat's small deck too, a kind of theatre in which a man and a boy, a ghost and a monk, play their unimportant and unworldly roles, hunched over a poisonous engine or standing scarecrow-still in summer moonlight, as the rain-chased metal of the Fraser's bell flare fills over and over with rapid silvery notes until the musician of grandeur at last runs out of breath and everything I ever loved stops. Sound the trumpets, summon the town, as the stage direction in Shakespeare says. But if the trumpets have all been sold for survival, and the town no longer goes out on the water, all that plays across these years is silence, the silence of the counting house when all the counting has been done and there's nothing left to tally but the years.

OF CHERRY TREES AND RED-WINGED BLACKBIRDS

I know noble accents
And lucid, inescapable rhythms;
But I know, too,
That the blackbird is involved
In what I know.
  – Wallace Stevens, "Thirteen Ways of Looking at a Blackbird"

You don't need a pandemic to experience a new normal:
You just have to get older.
  – the author

AT THE BEGINNING OF THE PANDEMIC, I RETURNED TO WATCHING THE television news for the first time in decades. But after a month, the bizarre combination of conservative bias, fearmongering and complacent middle-class sentimentality that passes itself off as mainstream journalism once again aroused in me such feelings of despair that I knew I had to stop watching and return to a place of sanity and affirmation. Which brought me, almost immediately and as if by some protective instinct, back to the cherry trees and red-winged blackbirds of my childhood. Nearly sixty years of life, with all of its diversities and social pleasure, its joys and sorrows, successes and failures, a whole changing theatre cast of characters, some still loved and on the stage, others long since slipped into the darkened wings, and I remain most entranced by the simple glories of a fruit tree and a songbird. Why should it be so? *Joy* is a dirty word in North America, and neither childhood nor old age earn any respect.

Yet somehow my escape from the pandemic was as simple as a man remembering the love he felt as a child for his mother. And that love was all about cherry trees and red-winged blackbirds. You see, I grew up in a period of economic decline in a neighbourhood filled with ruins. Within a five-minute walk from my house, I could enter any of six condemned Edwardian houses, a boarded-up movie theatre, a half-block of empty stores and an abandoned vegetable canning factory the length of a football field. Or if I preferred smaller shelters, I had my pick of rotting fishboats on the banks of the river, including a ghostly sternwheeler right out of *The Adventures of Huckleberry Finn*, and any number of rusting vehicles with missing doors and back seats clunky with empty beer bottles. Indeed, in my decrepit part of town, every yard had a junked car, a dry-docked boat and someone out of work. In that environment, often the only signs of hope came from the natural world, and I was a child blessed with the great good fortune of unstructured time spent in the tall grass and the treetops.

We lived at the end of one of our town's original streets. Back in the third-quarter of the nineteenth century, a wealthy citizen built a big house at the south end, and the north end (where we lived, a stone's throw from the mouth of the Fraser River), being part of the same extensive property, formed the orchards – pear, plum, apple and then, several decades later, cherry. By the early 1970s, most of the trees were gone, cleared away for other houses (such as our little bungalow) or fallen to rot. But the trees that remained – a dozen of them – contained that mysterious gnomic power that gives old trees their magic, particularly for children, who have a more intimate relationship with it. I can remember stroking the black trunks of some of those gnarled survivors as if they were horses' necks. And I can remember – no, I can still see, almost a half-century later – the exact knobs and knots and curves on many of those branches. In my childhood days, the branches literally meant life and death to me, for if I failed to assess their strength, if I didn't recognize by the particular physical qualities of each one exactly where I was (especially when climbing in the dark, as I often did), then my time in the tall grass below would have been long indeed. Of course, the danger wasn't nearly so great as that afforded by the hundred-foot-tall Douglas fir in the vacant lot across the street from our house, so I probably inhabited the fruit trees on instinct, which is always uncomplicated in a child. But as I spent much more time in the remnants of the old orchards – near my house but also in others scattered like charred campfires from the last century throughout the neighbourhood – my familiarity with them was greater. Of all the blackened ruins I could explore, they were the most appealing, for two key reasons: they possessed the magical ability to change and when the change happened, the singers arrived.

Spring is always splendid, of course, but spring for a child with ready access to blossoming fruit trees is something else entirely, almost a lived-in myth. And if several of those fruit trees should happen to be cherry, well, there you have all the joy and the sadness of life brought together in one dark fountain of pink and white water that flows for only two weeks, near the end of March and the beginning of April. There you have the joy of being a child who can climb to a treetop in seconds, and the sadness of an adult who hasn't even contemplated such a move in decades. There you have the beauty and generosity of the natural world, and its ephemerality too. There you have a middle-aged woman calling her youngest child in for supper, and a bedridden old woman in a nursing home who can't have visitors and whose main pleasure in life is receiving calls from her family. So life and time and the world turn us all around.

But in this time of fear and contagion, I keep myself still so that I can learn again what I had to learn in my first years, the difference between the trill of the red-winged blackbird and my mother's imitation of that sound. For that was how she called me home: by whistling the red-winged blackbird's song. A low note, a longer high note and another low note. She would open the side door and lean out and whistle, and I would climb down from a tree or leap up from the tall grass and run toward that loving music. Through the fall and winter, the system was perfect; I could hear those notes ringing out clearly from wherever I was. But in the spring, when the red-winged blackbirds began to inhabit the tops of the fruit trees, and to carry on with a kind of rapacious gaiety, I had to listen more carefully; I had to learn the difference between life and art, between the non-human and the human. That is, I began to become a poet, a man of cherry blossoms. Like Issa, the great haiku master of the early nineteenth century.

I do not pretend to understand the full significance of sakura (cherry blossom) to the Japanese and their culture, past or present, but I know a little something about trying to capture the ephemerality of life in words, and about trying to make a way through the world that is rich in freedom and unburdened by a hunger for material possessions. Issa – who translated his adopted name as the bubble in "one cup of tea," another nod to transient pleasure – endured an unhappy childhood and a roaming adult life often marred by conflict, tragedy and poverty. His mother died when he was young, and his stepmother was every bit the fierce caricature of that role found in Western fairy tales, so that Issa, who claimed to have been beaten hundreds of times a day, finally had to leave home at the age of thirteen. Unsurprisingly, for the rest of his life, he sought out both beauty and simplicity from the natural world, in the haiku tradition, and he did so with a memorable blend of good humour and melancholy. Famed for his love of small birds, insects, plants and other overlooked forms of life, he also wrote innumerable haiku referencing the cherry tree, its blossoms and shadows, its beauty that seemed to fade as quickly as the heat from a cup of tea. For Issa, the cherry tree is mostly sadness, a glorious sign of the Buddhist recognition of life's brevity.

Just being alive!
miraculous to be in
cherry blossom shadows!

Pain and suffering –
even if the old cherry
had somehow blossomed

Evening cherry
blossoms – now this day too
Enters history

It was my favourite
place for cherry blossom shade
now gone forever

So many of Issa's haiku about the cherry tree and its blossoms are weighted with melancholy; even when he expresses the miracle of being alive, he's in the shadows. But then, he was following a long tradition in which the Zen qualities of mono no aware (a sense of beauty intensified by recognition of temporality) and sabi (spiritual loneliness) were dominant. Just as significantly, his mother died when he was only two years old, and the rest of his childhood, more than unmothered, was abusive. The cherry blossom, then, symbolizes the brevity and frailty not only of all life, but of what is most beautiful and precious in life.

MY MOTHER IS STILL ALIVE, BUT WE HAVE REACHED THE END OF CHERRY blossom season, and I don't know if my own mono no aware and sabi could be any greater if I was Japanese. We had a very old Queen Anne (also called Royal Anne) cherry tree in our backyard, and its branches hung over the small firepit around which my parents, my siblings and I often sat, drinking tea and watching the sky for shooting stars. Sometimes I would be alone there with my father, and my mother would bring us each a cup of tea and then sit with us until we'd finished drinking. I can remember the surrounding cold of early April nights, the warmth of the crackling driftwood fire and – was the ghost of Issa hovering nearby? – the occasional time when a blossom, swirling down, landed in my cup of tea, and I would gently remove it with my fingertips. It seems, more and more, that the dying of the blossoms more than their brilliant life defines my memory of those long-ago springs: how the brown-tinged delicate circles stuck like dried bloodstains to the bedsheets and pillowcases on our backyard clothesline; how they gathered on my father's and brothers' black gumboots on the side steps and turned them into startling ceramic sculptures; how they sprouted on the silver sides of the salmon laid out on the grass in the side yard and seemed to be a second layer of scales and a deepening of the death in the salmon's black eyes; how they thickened on the windshield of my brother's Mustang so that he had to use his wipers to clear them away every time he backed out of the driveway; and how we always walked through them from the government wharf to the house, and back again, as if through late snowfalls, somehow hearing the red-winged blackbird's song piercing the storm, winter and spring so oddly together, Issa whispering *Haya Sabishi* (the loneliness is already there) in recognition of the Zen idea that the seed of life and the seed of death are one.

YET I WAS A MUCH-LOVED CHILD WHO SAT IN THE TREETOPS AT THE height of the blossoms' glory – why should it be so hard to recapture those intense moments? Because they were even more transitory than the blossoms' dying, or because, as we age, joy inevitably and perhaps naturally defers to loss?

But for my mother's sake, I do remember, my mother who was the last-born of fourteen children (only six of whom, due to poverty's illnesses, reached adulthood) and whose own mother died suddenly a few short months after my mother had crossed the country by train to begin her married life on the coast. How it must have shattered her young heart to decide not to return home, knowing that she could better face the future with a living and not a dead image of her mother in her consciousness. I remember, because my Irish grandmother had, as her youngest child still says, "a heart as big as all outdoors" and would, even during the leanest years of the Great Depression, sacrifice her own portions to feed the bread man and the iceman, and because my own mother's heart has always been just as large, and because my heart, by comparison, has always been so small.

"THE RIVER IS MOVING / THE BLACKBIRD MUST BE FLYING," WRITES WALLACE Stevens in "Thirteen Ways of Looking at a Blackbird," as fine a haiku-influenced sequence in English as exists. But I seek only the one way, just as Kobayashi Itaro, at the age of twenty-nine, chose the Way of Poetry (kado) and adopted the name of Issa. I can remember hundreds of red-winged blackbirds clinging to the tops of bulrushes in the salt marsh at the end of our street; I can even see their crimson bangles flash as they shifted on their unsteady perches and filled the air with song. Yet I retain no picture of a red-winged blackbird among the cherry blossoms, though they undoubtedly filled the several dozen trees in the neighbourhood. Their darkness must have made a brilliant contrast in those effulgent canopies, and the blossoms must have shivered like notes coming from those opened beaks. But I'm sure that I shared time in those treetops with the blackbirds; it is only a failure of memory that keeps the blossoms and the birds apart. Or maybe, in a dark time, poetry is asking me again to enlarge my heart, and when I do so, it is the brevity of life and the sound of a mother's love that matters more than anything.

At the end of our street, at the bottom of the fifteen-foot-high dike, a single street lamp shone. At night, in those weeks when the cherry blossoms began to die, I could stand on the sidewalk in front of our house and look down a whole block of darkness to see windswept masses of blossoms swirl across the light. It was like looking through the lens of a microscope at the beautiful and complex cells of the world.

I'm looking again now, here in this locked-down house a thousand miles away from my hometown where the cherry trees are all gone, where my childhood home has been sold and where my mother lies unvisited in a nursing home bed. I'm looking, and it isn't the past that I see, but the same inexplicable longing for the capture of life, the preserving of its most meaningful experiences, which compels me to call my mother on the phone and to ask her if she remembers how she used to call me in from play. "Not really," she says, and I can hear her mind slowly trawling through almost ten decades of sensation. Then follows a long pause. I can see the cherry blossoms coming on all around my childhood like gas lamps. I can see the one bubble in my cup of tea, feel the warmth of the fire. My sight is trained on the cells under the microscope. I want so much, like Issa, to hold on to what is most beautiful in our brief and difficult lives.

But after several more seconds, when my mother finally whistles the red-winged blackbird's song to me over the phone lines, I cannot come to her across the fields, I cannot come in from the world as darkness falls and I cannot, despite her example, and Issa's, carry the weight of dead blossoms with so much courage, grace and equanimity. All I can do is listen and remember. "My mother is whistling / the blackbird must be flying." And so the blackbird *is* flying, and so it will, with cherry blossoms on its wings, over what remains of the ruins of the ruins of my childhood and the natural world.

PART TWO

THE HERMIT'S SMOKE

Doomed for a certain term to walk the night.
— Shakespeare, *Hamlet*

She was thinking that, after all, feet are the most important part of the whole person.
— Virginia Woolf, "Street Haunting"

There are no more deserts. There are no more islands. Yet there is a need for them. In order to understand the world, one has to turn away from it on occasion. . . . But where can one find the solitude necessary to vigour, the deep breath in which the mind collects itself and courage gauges its strength?
— Albert Camus, *The Myth of Sisyphus*

I know no greater delight than the sheer delight of being alone.
It makes me realise the delicious pleasure of the moon
that she has in travelling by herself.
— D.H. Lawrence, "Delight of Being Alone"

I drew solitude over me, on the long shore.
— Robinson Jeffers, "Prelude"

TRAPPED ON THE ISLE OF DESPAIR

Crusoe was without food, without shelter, without supplies — and had never trained to live apart from the luxuries of civilization. But somehow, using only wreckage and his wit, Robinson Crusoe would have to learn to survive. Without help. Without hope of rescue.

Alone.
— back cover copy of 1989 paperback edition

I

MY FATHER, GUMBOOTED AND SKULLCAPPED, WITH A SWITCHED-OFF flashlight in hand, stood on the braided mat by the kitchen door, speaking softly to my mother. She wore her housecoat and slippers, so I knew without even looking at the clock that it was very late.

"What's happened?" I asked, surveying all the chairbacks for my coat, just in case.

My mother sighed. "Go back to bed, Tim. There isn't any fishing."

I already knew there wasn't any fishing because I knew the scheduled openings better than anyone. Once school ended in June, and before it started again in September, I phoned the Department of Fisheries and Oceans' recorded message three or four times a day. Even now, a month and a half into another school year, with dew heavy on the spiderwebs and on the pumpkins orange as salmon roe in the fields, I phoned the DFO just to hear the list of zones that had closed – Bella Coola, Bamfield, Ucluelet. The names were a sort of lullaby to the seasons I already sensed I would miss as much as I would miss my father himself one day.

Headlight beams poured through the window and slid along the wall above my parents' heads. When the beams clicked off, my parents seemed to inhabit a greater darkness than they had just a few seconds before. An engine shut off and a car door closed. There was a crunching sound as someone walked up our gravel driveway.

"Who's that?" I turned from one parent to the other. "What's going on?"

"It's Dr. Kaney," my mother said, clutching the two sides of her night-gown together at her neck. "I wonder if I should put the kettle back on. He might like a tea before you go." She looked at my father, who shook his head.

"He's a busy man. Look what time it is now," he said.

He wasn't speaking to me, but I raised my eyes to the clock on the wall anyway: 1:17.

The doctor's footsteps clumped on the wooden stairs, and I didn't hes-itate. I hurried into my room and pulled on a pair of jeans. Then, back in the kitchen, just after the door opened and the doctor's shadow fell on the braided mat, I discreetly found my coat and pulled it on. It didn't much matter to me why my father and Dr. Kaney were going out together in the early hours of the October morning, but since they obviously were, I knew that the outing involved our boat and the river.

"Good evening. How's the young scholar today?"

Dr. Kaney's slight smile seemed broad due to the fullness of his lips and his general grave demeanour. A heavyset man with remarkably bul-bous eyes and a permanent five o'clock shadow, he always reminded me of a slightly down-on-his-luck Alfred Hitchcock. Because he spoke more slowly than anyone else I knew, and because he was connected in my mind primarily with illness and boredom (the wait to be called into his office during my infrequent visits was always interminable), I both respected and feared him. The adults in my life were not professionals; in fact, most, in-cluding my parents, had not completed high school. The college certificates on the walls of Dr. Kaney's office might as well have been hieroglyphics.

But because he spoke to me as I put on my coat, and made a passing reference to my recent honours status in grade eight, my parents must have interpreted his words as an invitation. Whatever the case, no one objected as I hurriedly pulled on my boots.

"I apologize for the hour," the doctor said, "but I had a delivery tonight and have early rounds at the hospital in the morning."

"I'm a night owl anyway," my father said. "I'd just be poking a stick into a fire in the yard."

"Mrs. Maxwell is very concerned." The doctor's eyelids slid halfway over his bulging eyeballs before sliding back again. Even on waking, he must have always looked exhausted. "Otherwise I would not think to ask for your help at such an ungodly hour."

My mother, handing a brown paper bag to my father, said, "There have been many times when you've come to us in the middle of the night. When Nola had rheumatic fever."

Again, the slow, reptilian smile that did not part the lips, and a kind of half-bow. "I remember. A fever of 105. I was impressed that you had not called me sooner."

My parents, children of the Great Depression who had married during wartime, had an exaggerated respect for authority, especially medical authority, and also an individual capacity not to trouble it unless absolutely necessary.

"Be sure you have some sandwiches and tea," my mother said as the men turned to the door. "I made plenty. Harold, there's the basket too."

"Tim can grab that."

As I bent to pick it up, Dr. Kaney said, "Provisions will be more welcome than us, I'm afraid."

My parents looked quickly at each other, a glance I understood to mean, "Helen Maxwell doesn't exaggerate"; it also meant, "Tim would not be going if there was any real danger"; finally, it meant what I had by now grasped: we were going to Alf Harley's island.

Dr. Kaney tightened the belt of his beige trench coat across his stomach. His five o'clock shadow seemed an inch thicker than when he'd arrived, his jowls a little more pronounced, as if pulling the belt triggered physical changes on his face. "Shall we?" He placed his hand, hairy as a werewolf's paw, on the doorknob and, nodding good evening to my mother, opened the door and walked out. My father and I followed.

In the narrow side yard stood a large Gravenstein apple tree. The thick aroma of its last windfall rose up from the wet grass but wasn't strong enough to mask the smell of the river for long. As if the dike had burst, the river pushed its tide of mud, brine, dead fish and leaf mulch across our low-lying little town of potholed streets, straw-filled doghouses and tattered backyard gardens. The tide seemed to swing the catch of dead pheasants hanging on the black branches of the apple tree, still dripping blood because my older brother had hung them there only a few hours before, just after dusk. The tide even seemed to make the faint stars shiver.

Beyond the tree, outside the jonquil shine of the porch light, the darkness possessed a material thickness, falling in alluvial folds off the sharp edge of the invisible moon. Once we'd left the driveway, we heard, more than saw, each other. Neither my father nor the doctor bothered with small talk, and I already knew that the questions I wanted to ask would be answered soon enough, so we completed the few-minute walk to the government wharf in silence except for the doctor's harsh breathing. He was perhaps a decade older than my father, and considerably larger; we walked behind him as if tracking a wounded bear.

On the deck of my father's small gillnetter, a broad-sterned, shallow vessel designed to cope with the shifting sandbars and flowing muds and silts of the river mouth, Dr. Kaney cleared his throat as he gazed westward, downriver. I saw half of his rough, bouldery face in the match's flare and then, embarrassed by the silence throbbing above the coughing engine, I slipped into the cabin.

My father, at the wheel, held an unlit cigarette between his lips. It dangled expertly from the corner of his mouth as he peered into the dim spotlight for signs of floating logs or even just driftwood large enough to damage the propeller. The harbour channel was narrow, not more than two hundred feet from bank to bank: the town side was cluttered with wharves, net sheds, moored boats of various sizes – from long aluminum herring skiffs to high-bowed seiners; the river side just marsh grass broken intermittently by the charred candelabra of a weeping willow.

I stood beside my father, above the uncovered engine, mesmerized as always by the motion of the pistons and the fan belt, not quite sickened by the gas fumes. I wanted to shout a question above the steady noise, but somehow to do so seemed violent with the reserved doctor on board. So I just watched the wild bank of the mainland dissolve into the waving grassy point as my father, knowing the underwater layout of the sandbars, kept going when it seemed that he might turn upriver toward the north and the distant clump of ski lights on Grouse Mountain. Indeed, he almost touched the eastern bank of the first silt island before he turned the wheel and chugged along at a few knots past the graveyard of deadheads dragged into place by fishermen tired of snagging their nets on the same heavy hazards.

The tide was running out, I knew, because the deadheads all pointed downriver, like dogs straining at the leash, and we seemed to inch up the muddy bank even though the engine rattled and throbbed and I almost gagged on the fumes. Carefully, my father took his cigarette from his lips and then bowed as he backed out of the cabin and assumed a safe smoking position at the deck wheel.

For a moment, I thought we'd lost Dr. Kaney overboard. But to my surprise, he'd moved into the stern, behind the large wooden drum on which two hundred fathoms of net were wrapped, and was gazing back toward town, his hands behind his back. Somehow his two positions, the one leaning oceanward, the other landward, troubled me. It was as if, in the course of our short journey, he'd made an important decision, and one that I couldn't understand. But at least he'd carried his black medical bag with him into the stern; whatever he'd decided, at least he hadn't given up medicine.

Within five minutes we had turned down one of the broad sloughs between the islands. Three feet of mud showed between the river and the grass along each bank – occasionally the tide tore a chunk of mud off and it splashed soundlessly under the surface and the drone of our engine. I shuddered each time at the sight. Already the chill southeasterly wind had penetrated my clothing and my gloveless hands grew heavier by the second as the numbness set in. But I realized that the shuddering had a human source.

For one thing, it was strange to be out on the boat with no intention of setting a net. My father was not a recreational sort of man, and I was not old enough to be allowed to take the boat out on my own. For another thing, we never had non-family members on board. Finally, no one – and this was a fact that, at twelve, I could fathom only in the way that I could study a heron's shadow to understand flight – ever went near Alf Harley. Oh, you'd drift along his island, of course, and sometimes see the smoke rising from whatever particular grove of cottonwoods he'd dragged his boat into all those years ago, but you never saw the man. And, apparently, he never left the island either. My father, without regarding the situation as noteworthy in any way, described Alf Harley as a hermit. When I'd pressed him on the subject, during some lazy slack tide a few summers before, his answer had been brief and direct: "He doesn't like being around people, that's all. Prefers his own company."

"Doesn't he ever get lonely?"

I believe now, if I could bottle the silence that followed my question, and use my father's distant look as a label for the bottle, I could sell some sort of tonic for the human condition. But at that time, I was twenty years away from William Carlos Williams's lines "I was born to be lonely / I am best so!" and forty years away from beginning to understand them.

"I guess not," my father had finally said, gazing off along his cork line and turning his back on Alf Harley's island.

"But what about his family? Doesn't he have any?"

"A sister, I believe. Back in England. But I'm not sure."

And I knew there was no sense in pursuing the matter; I could tell from my father's tone that he had exhausted his store of information, or at least his willingness to share it.

I turned from studying the muddy bank to see Dr. Kaney's outline, just visible in the miniscule amount of mast light, still frozen in place. Beyond him, like a dirty, underwater moon, the face of the town clock hovered, the hands unclear, the hour unknown. Even time seemed to feel the deepening frost that settled over and around us.

We left one slough and slipped into another, much narrower one, perhaps forty feet wide. At the mouth of the Fraser River, some sloughs act as
channels between the half-dozen small islands, and some sloughs serve as
entryways into the islands themselves. The latter are, naturally, more secre-
tive, somehow shrouded even without overhanging foliage to obscure them.

My father cut the engine and the night came alive. Or rather, the silence deepened, even in its tricklings and creakings of current and tree
limbs. Somehow, the river drew back like an arrow on a great black bow
– all was tensile, quivering, and yet heavy with frost that seemed to come
up from the island and down from the invisible stars. Back in the random
groupings of cottonwoods and maples, their seedings a matter of river flow
and wind direction, something appeared to be watching us, as if an owl
perched on a pillar of Stonehenge gazed across the whole of England to see
a small ship approaching the coast.

My father, pike pole in hand, tested the slough's depth as we drifted,
slower and slower. Raising the long aluminum pole from the water and
swinging it back down again, he resembled a tightrope walker. But if he
fell, he would land in perhaps a dozen feet of silty water, which was alarming enough, for the current and the night air had the consistency of a La
Brea tar pit. Great fossils with massive open jaws shifted and swirled like
clouds on the river bottom and far above us. At any second, I felt I would
feel myself lifted or would see my father yanked down.

To gain my senses, I turned to the doctor. He had moved alongside the
drum, onto the side locker, half-crouched with the medical bag in his right
hand, as if ready to leap overboard. For a moment, I stared at him, horrified,
convinced that he would leap and vanish. I wanted to look away, but somehow my eyes were the stones and he was the pane of glass, and if I moved
at all, there'd be a terrific smash and the river would bear his pieces away as
easily as it shifted the tons of silt sifted down from the interior on every tide.

"This is about as far as we can go," my father said through a great
spiderweb of breath. "Tim, see if you can tie us to a big stump or log."

He bent into the cabin and turned the spotlight on the bank. Rope in hand, I waited until a massive stump emerged out of the gloom, its roots as thick as my arm and tangled like a nest of snakes. The boat barely drifted now, so I had no trouble mooring us with a double-hitch.

My father switched the spotlight off and the darkness dropped around us again. I could hear the doctor's laboured breathing as he moved up to the main deck. For the first time, I noticed the tiny red glow of a cigarette in his free hand, which explained his breathing and his occasional harsh cough that now echoed like gunshot over the island. Lonely or not, Alf Harley would almost certainly know by now that he had company.

The idea scared me even more when my father came out of the cabin with a lit, shimmering kerosene lamp in hand and announced that he would go on ahead to make sure . . . of what he didn't specify, but I understood that Alf Harley, under normal conditions, discouraged company, and since these were not normal conditions, the other dangers had to be equally worrisome.

Using a root of the stump for leverage, my father easily hoisted himself over the bank, the light shaking around him like blossoms blown off a branch. Briefly, the island dark swallowed him as he crossed a low area, and then he reappeared, twenty seconds later – or rather his light did, fluttering erratically against the tree line like a big moth doused in phosphor.

Alone with the doctor, I immediately felt awkward. As I struggled to think of something to say, however, he surprised me by reading my mind.

"Everywhere's a kind of waiting room when you really think about it. But there aren't always magazines to look at. I think, for you, it might be a good idea to practise being alone with your own thoughts." He lifted the cigarette to his mouth, drew in, then broke into a shuddering cough that rang out across the watery island. "What I mean is . . ." I could almost hear the smile, slow as his blinking, take shape in the darkness. "There's no need to talk. I'm enjoying the quiet. I hope you don't mind."

Immensely relieved, I blurted out some kind of acceptance of his terms and retreated to the bow, where I sat cross-legged, my hand touching the cold, coiled anchor chain. Alone with my thoughts, I tried, as a model student and as the son of parents who taught me to respect my elders, to practise *being* alone with my thoughts. But the self-consciousness of thinking about thinking – the kind of mental exercise that would define my midlife years, mostly to their detriment – only made me more anxious for my father's reappearance. I tried to locate the Big and Little Dippers, or even the north star, but the night sky was too cloudy or too dark – and then I wondered if the night could in fact be so dark that the stars wouldn't show through. As soon as the thought occurred to me, my father's light, like a low star determined to disprove my theory, began to move toward the boat, or else the boat began to move toward my father's light. It was so quiet and so dark that all of the normal space-time dimensions had ceased to operate. The night flowed tortuously toward dawn. An owl hooted somewhere in the vastness – two, three times – and I could almost hear the rapid panting and shivering of prey in the rushes and grasses.

I looked down into the slough and couldn't even tell its darkness apart from the night's. But the undertow moved ominously, as if composed of the final breaths and heartbeats of suicides. Desperately, I looked back up to see that my father's star had become a kerosene lantern and the outline of a man. I stood, my hand coming off the cold chain and immediately, briefly warming. By the time I'd reached the deck, both of my hands were chilled.

"There's no danger of being kept away," my father explained to Dr. Kaney. "He's in his bunk. Didn't respond when I spoke to him."

"Breathing?"

"Yes. But it doesn't sound right."

"But he's conscious?"

My father, standing three feet above us and bathed in light, possessed a frightening authority. Even so, he lowered his voice, perhaps for my sake, perhaps for the occasion's. "I don't really know if you could call it that. But his eyes are open. When I held the light up, I could see that." My father shifted the lantern and vanished for a few seconds. Then he added heavily, "But it didn't seem like he saw me even though he looked straight at me."

Dr. Kaney's cigarette slid through the dark air and sizzled when it hit the slough. He bent and picked up his black bag again. I could hear the instruments clink inside.

"Shall I take the light and go myself? You don't need to make the return trip."

My father's face turned thoughtful and even more serious. "I'd better. If he comes around, well, he'd recognize me."

Suddenly stricken at the thought of being left alone, even if I retreated into the cabin, I hurried to the stump and pulled myself onto the bank.

"I'm afraid I'm not such an athlete," the doctor said pleasantly. "You'll have to give me a hand, Harold."

A few minutes later, we started across Alf Harley's island. The ground was soft under the low grasses, muddy and silty, but not so soft we had to worry about losing our boots to the suction. My father guided us through the driftwood stumps and logs, avoiding the marshiest spots, walking slower than usual, probably on account of the doctor, whose heavy breathing was the only sound I heard as we crossed the island and came into the cottonwoods.

The six or seven trees seemed remarkably solid in the darkness – thick pillars of the air. Their few leaves shook ceaselessly, though more like returning bats. I felt watched, and not with kindness. As a fisherman's son, I had no illusions about nature's relationship to the human world; in fact, part of the love and intimacy I knew for my surroundings depended on my knowledge of my meaningless fragility within them. To be no more and no less regarded as a fish or a bird or a blackberry holding on to its last summer second was to be connected to, rather than divorced from, the environment. And yet, I was scared now, and realized that I had been from almost the time we left the harbour. And what scared me most of all was that I sensed that the fear had a uniquely human source. It was not the river, or the night and its creatures that posed any threat. It was in the doctor's solitary gazing from the stern, my father's body sinking and surfacing on the island and, now, the gillnetter that had inexplicably been dragged into the trees and unevenly propped at the base of two trunks, its hull raised on our side as we approached, with some kind of rough frame of drift lumber and rope holding the unusual habitation in place. The boat, about the size and shape of ours, had a cabin just as small, with little room sufficient for sleeping in. But what I saw I saw only in the wavering corona of light from my father's hand.

"Around here," he said to the doctor, and led the way past the stern to the port side where a large, levelled-off block of cedar provided a step up onto the deck. I wasn't asked to board, nor was I told to remain on the ground. Once my father and Dr. Kaney had boarded, I felt the eyes in the cottonwoods narrow; but much worse, I heard a voice far inside me that I'd never heard before, a voice telling me to stay where I was, alone. That choice, however, suddenly seemed no different than the other. The ground might just as easily have been deep water, but the boat, too, was made of water and offered no refuge. Finally, because I loved my father, I made the only choice I could and followed the shimmering light into the cabin.

The fetid smell almost knocked me back again. It seemed caked on the sloped interior sides of the hull in the bow where Alf Harley lay, a smell of sweat and vomit and urine and excrement. I clasped my hand to my mouth and nose and watched the giant, grotesque shadows of my father and the doctor swivel on the wood of the cramped space. Their shadows seemed to be feeding on the blanket-swaddled mass in the bunk.

The doctor's breathing slowly evened out. He opened his medical bag and removed a stethoscope and plunged it into the dark swaddling. His own material bulk slid together with his shadow and completely covered the upper half of the body in the bunk for several seconds. He asked my father to move the light closer. And the light seemed to flare up briefly, like a fire eating a gust of wind. Alf Harley's sunken eyes and unkempt beard drifted out of the gloom, then sank back under. The doctor said something in a low voice, either to himself, his patient or my father. But there was no response. I hung where I had stopped, slightly above the three men, in the narrow space between the bunk and the wheelhouse. When the doctor rose, I half expected to see blood dripping from his lips. But his face had remained the colour of his trench coat. This time, I heard what he said to my father, and the words also flared briefly before they turned irredeemably cold. "He's dying."

"I figured as much," my father said after a weighty pause.

"We'll have to get him to town."

This time, the pause was longer and heavier. "When?"

Dr. Kaney's large eyes opened and closed, as if the lamplight had shed pollen on the lids. His voice was tired. "As soon as possible. Now, if we can manage it."

"We can't." My father sounded relieved, though that didn't seem likely under the circumstances.

The doctor turned toward the bunk. "No, I don't imagine the three of us could manage. We'll have to come back. With reinforcements."

Immediately I saw eight fishermen, like pallbearers before the corpse was even a corpse, trudging across the island to the trees. And then, much worse, I saw them with their burden headed back the other way.

"How long has he got?" my father said.

"Not very. A few days, maybe a week. I'm surprised his heart has held up this long."

We all turned now, straining to hear the heartbeat through the thick flesh and heavy blankets.

"Can you give him something?" My father's voice did not soften, but I heard the tenderness in it.

The doctor stared at my father, as if his words were somehow more complex. Then he sighed. "To ease the pain, yes. But it would be better in the hospital. He'll be clean, and as comfortable as possible."

The river, the trees, the night all tensed behind me. I almost heard the words before the doctor spoke them.

"And he won't be alone."

The last word hovered in the air for several seconds until it seemed as isolated and doomed as the man in the bunk. We all remained still, waiting for the man or the word to die. But they were connected now, as if Alf Harley had, out of his semi-comatose state, summarized his condition with one communicable breath. I had never known my father's silence to be so weighted. He was a quiet man, often standing in the stern for hours while fishing, just smoking and gazing at his net curled over the grey waters, or sitting in a chair in front of a backyard fire until the embers burned to ash long after everyone in the house and the town had fallen asleep. He was also a man with no significant close relationships outside of his family. But then, men of his generation seemed above friendship somehow. My father's silence wasn't unfriendly; it was just natural for him, easy. Except it wasn't easy as he picked the lantern up by its wire handle and swung it slightly toward me so that the light splashed up to my waist.

"I can take you back now," he said.

Dr. Kaney registered the change as clearly as I did. He frowned, his lips parted, closed, opened again. "Harold," he said solemnly, "there's nothing else we can do."

"Alf has always wanted to be left alone."

"In health, yes. In strength."

"Always." My father bent as he stepped toward the wheelhouse.

I scuttled back, almost falling in my haste. Suddenly and inexplicably afraid of being noticed, I withdrew to the deck.

In a matter of seconds, the light and the two men reached me. I saw my father glance at me and hesitate.

"It could be any time," Dr. Kaney said, breathing heavily just from the move from the bow to the deck. "Or a week. I think we need to assume the latter and act accordingly."

My father said nothing.

"I can't come back until the afternoon, at the earliest." The doctor followed my father's gaze, but his expression revealed little. "We should be able to get a party together by then."

Water, perhaps from an earlier rainfall, dripped off the branches somewhere back of us. I looked hard through my breath-clouds to see if my father moved, but he remained almost perfectly still.

Through this entire conversation, I detected an unsettling lack of authority in the doctor's tone. He seemed to be asking questions even as he made statements. Now, as the silence lengthened, he looked much as he had looked standing in the stern as we approached the island. The invisible dripping water might have been slowly eroding his stillness. I was afraid for him, but I had no idea why. My father, meanwhile, wore an expression

I had seen only rarely, after he'd had an argument with my mother – his lips were tightened, his jaw was set and his eyes did not close even to blink.

"I can stay until daylight," Dr. Kaney said. His voice wasn't weak or pleading, but it lacked conviction.

"Tim," my father said, "take the light and go get the Thermos and sandwiches."

I hesitated, intuiting that I was being dismissed for my own protection. But from what threat, I couldn't say.

The doctor smiled his disturbingly slow smile. "It's always coldest before the dawn, as the saying goes. I'm afraid I'm going to need that tea."

Though I knew he meant to reassure me that all was just as it should be, I could still see Alf Harley's open eyes and hear the night's dripping water, now heavy as solder. Almost against my will, I took the shimmering lantern and set off across the wet grasses.

Every minute of the fifteen that I was away, I felt that I'd trapped a hunting owl in my chest. Yet I could not bring myself to hurry either. Speed did not seem a part of the situation, since the leaving and the returning seemed exactly the same. I might have started the boat and headed out to sea and that would have been no different than stepping up onto the cedar block, as I did, and finding my father and Dr. Kaney sitting wordlessly in the dark wheelhouse, the red tips of their cigarettes like the eyes of some stalking beast. The tension was as thick as the foul smell rising up from the bunk.

The doctor rubbed his hands together as I set the lantern down. "Ah, just in time. You see that we've chosen the little bit of warmth over the fresh air. But it isn't much warmth. Some tea will help."

My father didn't move except to raise and lower his hand that held the cigarette, so I unscrewed the Thermos and poured the slightly steaming tea into the lid.

After taking a sip, Dr. Kaney sighed before subsiding into the fraught silence. Neither thirsty nor hungry myself – but cold to the point of shivering – I kept my hands around the body of the Thermos and stared at my father.

The dawn light came slowly on. The men smoked several cigarettes down as their profiles sharpened in the grey air and my hands cooled on the Thermos. From outside came the chittering, piercing sounds of life stirring in the rushes. Below us, in the dark bunk, the life stirred intermittently – an infrequent moan, an intake of rattling breath, but never a cry or a word.

At some point in the vigil, I understood that the doctor and my father were arguing without language, but I still did not grasp the nature of the conflict. We were waiting for Alf Harley to die. If he did not die before daylight, my father would take the doctor back to town and, later in the day, a party of men would return to take Alf Harley to the hospital. It was straightforward enough. But the tension was not so easily explained. Yes, I realized that death waited nearby, but this tension had existed before we even reached the island, existed in Dr. Kaney's tired gaze from the deck and my father's first departure with the oil lantern; it existed, too, in the river's tearing of mud from the bank and in the inexorable unseen falling of an old rainfall and the thickening of the dew like silver rust on the tips of the bulrushes.

Apologetically, the doctor, now fully visible, cleared his throat. In his heavy hand, an inch of cigarette trembled. My father turned like an iron weather vane, his eyes as open as the man's in the bunk. I shuddered at the image. And the doctor's trembling climbed up his arm without quite reaching his voice. Firmly but quietly, he said, "I'll just have a last check, then."

My father only nodded.

The doctor lifted his body as if it wasn't part of him. The effort drained even more colour from his face, and now his eyelids didn't even move. He descended to the bunk just like sinking into the marsh.

All I could hear was the beating of my heart. Or perhaps it was my father's heart. I couldn't be certain in the dull, foul closeness of the wheelhouse, but the heartbeats, whosever they were, drowned out the birdsong of first light. My father's unmoving form, however, suggested somehow that his heart had stopped. When he finally raised the lit cigarette to his mouth, I had to look away, for the stick's small fire seemed to be eating my father's face to ash. We were as together and as alone as astronauts in a probe.

Ten minutes later, the doctor rose like Lazarus, grizzle thick as fresh tar on his cheeks, dark as the hollows under his eyes. He did not look at us when he spoke, and yet he was clearly speaking to someone. The words came as slowly and inevitably as the movement of his mouth and eyes.

"The hospital will not be necessary."

My father let his cigarette burn in his hand.

"We will need a party to take him off." The doctor raised his voice a notch. "There are certain protocols." Almost at the taste of the last word in his mouth, he frowned, and his voice softened again. "Of course, there's no great urgency now."

At last my father stood. He ground his cigarette against the dash, then cupped the crumpled butt in his palm. I shuddered as his flesh closed around the threads of smoke. Somehow, I expected him to take the wheel of Alf Harley's grounded boat and captain it out of the cottonwoods, off the island, off the Earth, out of the light of ordinary time altogether. But he did something even more miraculous. He thanked the doctor. It wasn't, however, the common sort of thank you exchanged between men, such as when one fisherman, helping to pull another's net off a snag, shouts "Thanks" over the growl of engines. It wasn't even the sort of thank you that a poor, uneducated man offers a wealthy, well-educated professional for services rendered and improperly compensated for. No, it was a thank you that hardly belonged to the world at all, a thank you stripped of its associations to roles and rules, a thank you that might have come out of any mouth, mine or even the closed mouth under the endlessly open eyes of the dead man in the bunk. I heard it pass by me and echo over the marshes, over the now-changing tide, out to the capacious, retreating sea.

The doctor, too, seemed to recognize the rare quality of the words. He almost tried to lean on them. His body, which had returned to his weight and his daily purpose, swayed a little in the fresh eruption of birdsong. I leaned forward myself, eager to hear the words that could follow my father's.

But Dr. Kaney suddenly resumed his place in the order of our town and all towns. He nodded. He bent to his medical bag and picked it up. He smiled his excruciatingly slow lizard's smile, and when he spoke again, it was in the same voice that I heard whenever he finally pulled open the door of the examination room and asked me how my studies were going.

"If you could take me back now, Harold, I can get started on the paperwork."

Within minutes, we had started back across the island, the doctor now in front, as no light was needed, my father a few respectful feet behind him, and myself taking up the rear. Perhaps the order was the order of age, some concession to the natural process of our mortality, and perhaps I was meant to be at the end so I could stop and turn around and imprint the final extinguishing of Alf Harley's smoke on my brain.

But I didn't stop or even look back. All my life lay ahead of me; it was dawn light and birdsong, and even if my dozen years carried an intimation of mortality within them – of Dr. Kaney's death by leukemia and my father's death by kidney failure and of my childhood by the planet's circuiting of the sun – my fate was to advance and not to retreat.

And yet, where was I going that Alf Harley, Dr. Kaney and my father hadn't already gone? Something followed our leaving across the island, but it wasn't a living creature, nor anything I could easily put a name to. Still, its intensity burned. The tide in the slough made a last desperate swallow. I cast off and anchored in one motion. And though I continued to walk in the way of the world for decades, I already bore my share of the heavy casket on my shoulder, even if youth closed my senses to all the hungers, failures and urgencies of age, even if the hermit's eyes, within my eyes, hadn't yet opened to erode the hours, one by remarkable one.

II

THE FIRST DISTINCTION TO BE MADE IS BETWEEN THE HERMIT AND THE philosopher. Not all hermits are profound thinkers; in fact, many are just damaged and hurt and unable to face other people in conventional situations. And, certainly, most profound thinkers are not hermits, but rather occasional lovers of solitude who often find their own company to be society enough. Henry David Thoreau, for example, who still stands in the popular imagination as a hermit, quite obviously wasn't one, nor does he even make extravagant claims for the degree of his solitude in *Walden*, his most celebrated work. Despite whatever misanthropic feelings he harboured for the species in general, Thoreau wasn't anti-social or even unpleasant in company. At a certain point, he simply looked around at a world of rampaging industry, poverty and quiet desperation and realized that he required a respite from it, if only to concentrate better on the philosophical and literary work he wanted to accomplish. But a respite is not necessarily positive without a concerted effort at withdrawal from worldliness. As Michel de Montaigne, another literary self-exile, writes, "Ambition, covetousness, irresolution, fear and desires do not abandon us just because we have changed our landscape . . . They often follow us into the very cloister and the schools of philosophy. Neither deserts nor holes in cliffs nor hair-shirts nor fastings can disentangle us from them."

For Thoreau and Montaigne, the whole point of solitude was to advance the mind and spirit; for a hermit like Alf Harley, who kept no books and published no writings, and who died uncelebrated and largely forgotten on an unpopulated island in the mouth of the Fraser River in the company of three other humans whose attitude toward his fate differed considerably, solitude was just easier. He had always been cripplingly shy, and the salmon fishing industry gave him an independent way of life that kept contact with others to a minimum. Once he had enough money to provide the basics for his old age, he vanished from the mainstream world, and what he thought of his decision or of life in general no one knows, or likely ever did know.

But there is every possibility that Alf Harley thought in a similar way to one of the most notorious hermits of our time, a man named Christopher Knight who spent the years 1986 to 2013 living by himself in a makeshift shelter somewhere in the woods of the same state of Maine where Thoreau famously retreated (though only for two years). Dubbed the "North Pond Hermit," Knight survived in total isolation for nearly three decades by breaking into uninhabited vacation cabins and stealing non-perishable or frozen food items, batteries, clothing and sometimes CDs (he liked to listen to music). Upon his capture, he claimed that he hadn't spoken to another person during his time in the woods, and also that he'd never been ill ("Sickness comes from people," he said). The more puzzling claim, at least to the mainstream idea of hermitage, was that he had simply entered the woods because he didn't like the world and its concerns; in other words, he wasn't a philosopher and he had no profound intellectual or spiritual reason to choose such an extended period of solitude. He wasn't even sure when he'd left the regular world behind: pressed for a specific date, he recalled that it was around the time of the Chernobyl nuclear disaster.

So, Montaigne in 1571 retreats to his estates in a crisis of melancholy over the death of his father and invents the essay form as a way to cope with grief; Thoreau goes to the woods in order to wrestle out the true nature of life; Alf Harley, sucking his paws like a starving bear or surveying the tides of the river like a self-proclaimed lord (it's impossible to say), dies without confession and his 350 pounds of solitude meet the fate that all flesh is heir to; and Christopher Knight, who spent a year in minimum-security prison for his career of petty crime, has apparently been reintegrated into regular society. According to his brother, Knight has a job and he's in contact with the authorities, but how he *feels* about his current situation is likely as unknown as how he feels about his long hermitage – obviously intelligent and sensitive, Knight just doesn't seem interested in explaining his inner life. To the mainstream world, this lack of explanation is the most confounding and maddening fact of all. If a genius wants to be alone to work out his brilliant theories, fine. If an intensely devout person wants solitude for the sake of communing with God, fine. Even if a person suffering from some terrible trauma, like a Vietnam vet buried deep in Alaska, chooses to be alone with his terror, well, that's psychologically understandable to most of us. But when an ordinary young man, albeit a shy one, spends nearly thirty years by himself for no obvious reason, suddenly Søren Kierkegaard's seventy thousand fathoms of space open up under the plank we're all standing on, and we're forced to look down – or rather in – to the nature of our own character and experience.

What is an acceptable desire for solitude and what is a mental disorder? More to the point, who decides? The poet Theodore Roethke writes, "What is madness but nobility of soul / at odds with circumstance?" But if you remove the opposing circumstances, as Christopher Knight did when his car finally ran out of gas at the edge of the Maine woods and he climbed out and just kept going, do you also remove the madness? What about the nobility of soul?

Before he disappeared into the world upon his release from prison, Knight granted an interview to a journalist named Michael Finkel, but only because Finkel had the good sense to approach the suddenly famous hermit through the molasses-slow means of a handwritten letter. In the subsequent article, published in *GQ*, of all places, no satisfying explanation is given for Knight's choice to leave the regular world (including his mother and siblings) behind, though the journalist did press for one (under delicate conditions, given his interview subject's aversion to self-analysis) and was rewarded with the following insight: "Solitude did increase my perception. But here's the tricky thing – when I applied my increased perception to myself, I lost my identity. With no audience, no one to perform for, I was just there. There was no need to define myself; I became irrelevant. The moon was the minute hand, the seasons the hour hand. I didn't even have a name. I never felt lonely. To put it romantically: I was completely free."

In our materialistic Western world where everyone is encouraged to have an image, a brand, to celebrate constantly the triumphs and even the failures of the self (not just on social media, though perhaps most dramatically there), the idea of no self at all is as alien and horrifying a condition as death, and even the most devout believers in an afterlife in our culture often abhor the thought of dying. When Knight claimed that he is no mystic and that he simply finds the modern world to be full of "speed, trivialities, and inanities," there is absolutely no doubt that, if he hadn't been caught on a sophisticated security camera in an empty cabin and then apprehended by an off-duty police officer who'd made it a personal mission to prove the North Pond Hermit's existence, Knight would still be living without human contact and very likely going to the grave without it.

Madness or nobility of soul? Both conditions, like fame, exist only in society. Without others to set a standard, there are no standards. For the record, after examination by medical experts, Knight was diagnosed with possibly a mild form of autism that combines high intelligence with an extreme sensitivity to light and sound. At one point in his first in-person interview with the journalist, Knight remarked of the human face that it's just too busy with information, an insight that seems quite brilliant when you consider the complex mainframe behind the expression of even the greatest dullard, but one that also denotes a condition that the vast majority of us do not inhabit if only to function in the world. Who can afford to find a human face a sensory overload in a digital culture where, to most of us, a human face is as slow as handwriting, walking or the breaking of dawn?

Without question, the North Pond Hermit troubles not only our high-speed, instant gratification age, but something inherent in our nature, and troubles it at a more disturbing depth than Thoreau's philosophizing. It's no surprise, therefore, that Christopher Knight dismisses Thoreau with one word: *dilettante*. Even so, the author of *Walden* did upset his equally famous contemporary Ralph Waldo Emerson, who believed that Thoreau took everything too far and who summarized the whole hermit enterprise thusly: "Very seductive are the first steps from the town to the woods, but the end is want & madness." Thoreau, however, never came close to the want-and-madness stage of self-exile, never had to wake himself deliberately at 2:00 a.m. every morning for twenty-seven harsh Maine winters because, if he hadn't done so, he would have died from the cold. Christopher Knight would have found much more relevance in essayist Miguel de Unamuno's comment that "we die of the cold and not the dark," and he would have said of Thoreau exactly what Montaigne said of Pliny the Younger and Cicero, whose withdrawal from society he described as "all verbiage and show" designed to garner acclaim.

But to mention Christopher Knight in the context of famous philosophers is to misinterpret his example completely. After all, the North Pond Hermit reserves his highest praise for the music of Lynyrd Skynyrd, and claims that he occupied much of his first decade alone listening to conservative talk radio. Henry David Thoreau he most decidedly is not, despite his admission that he spent innumerable fascinated hours charting the growth of a large mushroom on a tree. Ultimately, we must take the North Pond Hermit at his word: the last thing that bothered him about his hermitage was the lack of contact with what most of us couldn't imagine living without – other people.

William Carlos Williams wrote, "When I am alone I am happy," but that isn't the same as always wanting to be alone, nor is it the same as being unhappy around others. And Greta Garbo's famous retort to a reporter ("I want to be alone") continues to be scandalously misrepresented, for what she actually said ("I want to be *left* alone") constitutes an entirely different position, and an appropriate one when you're dealing with bothersome journalists who are likely going to misquote you.

The truth is, most of us don't willingly choose extremes of solitude, and so really don't understand what we're capable of. In this sense, hermitage holds a similar place in Western society to veganism, another alternative means of living which is widely dismissed by mainstream culture yet which, considered logically, not only makes sense but is also quite easily adopted. Every day, in a hundred subtle and not-so-subtle ways, we are sold a belief system of buying and selling whose pernicious hold on us must be constantly negotiated for the sake of our emotional, physical, moral and financial health. What if the idea that the human being is a social animal that requires other human beings is also largely an advertising gimmick? Montaigne writes, "There is nothing more unsociable than Man, and nothing more sociable: unsociable by his vice, sociable by his nature." Therefore, if vice appears to be in the ascendancy, hermitage might just be a sane choice. It might be necessary, that is, in an unhealthy society, to avoid people in order to like them at all. Such a paradox is decidedly uncomfortable, but Western life, for all of its privileged wealth, is uncomfortable in many ways.

At the very least, there can be little doubt that Western culture sells us our gregariousness even as its technologies encourage our isolation, which isn't the same condition as solitude. By now, it's an old chestnut to point out that Facebook and Twitter and Instagram and other forms of social media generally increase feelings of loneliness and depression: the lives of others, caught in digitized images of joy or unhappiness, do little to foster a sense of community or sociability. As for Montaigne's idea that nothing is more unsociable than man, well, that observation, over 450 years of human civilization later, remains anathema to almost every system that tries to sell you something, whether it be a political belief, a new truck or a green funeral for your rapidly dematerializing self.

The salient point is, hermitage isn't a money-maker, so it must be the choice of kooks and losers, or philosophers and the devout, which, let's be frank, are synonyms in our culture for kooks and losers. Thomas Merton sums up the mainstream opinion of the hermit clearly and succinctly: "The hermit has a very real place in a world like ours that has degraded the human person and lost all respect for solitude. But in such a world, the vocation of the hermit is more terrible than ever. In the eyes of our world, the hermit is nothing but a failure – we have absolutely no use for him, no place for him." But if the vocation of the hermit is genuine, if the desire not to engage with other people is sincere, then why would the hermit be concerned about his usefulness? That is to say, isn't a hermit's place precisely to have no place except what he carves out of the casual violence, banality and chaos that surround him? If the creation of that place is "terrible" for society, surely that isn't the hermit's business. In fact, the hermit's only business is to have no business with society, including its opinions of hermitage.

But Merton was an orphan who grew up to devote his life to a patriarchal concept of God. Therefore, he saw hermitage only within a specifically spiritual context. But what about the secular human who, worn out with the fast pace and extravagant wastefulness of capitalism, not to mention the narcissism of the Digital Age, wants simply to disengage from all the noise and violence and trivial distractions? What about the average, reasonably healthy person who just decides he doesn't want to play the same game that most others seem intent on, or have been trapped into, playing?

I'm an ordinary fifty-five-year-old white Canadian male with an increasing appetite for solitude and a desperate desire to hold on to a sense of wonder. Or at least I believe so – who's to say what's ordinary? But for the sake of argument, here's all the ways in which I represent my demographic group: married with children, and paying off a mortgage, I do work that requires a computer, begrudgingly accept politicians and banks as necessary evils, and need to watch my weight for cardiovascular reasons. I also have a few regular acquaintances but no close friends, feel the weight of responsibility and carry it, sometimes leading to stress and poor sleep, and look back on the past with much fondness but also several genuine regrets.

What stands out? Perhaps having no close friends. Is that still representative of middle-aged and elderly men? Friendlessness was certainly common amongst the men of my father's generation, and I suspect that little has changed. Significantly, Montaigne's own melancholia was also triggered as much by the death of his close friend at the age of thirty-two, but that was a friendship, according to Montaigne, of the kind that occurs between men only every few centuries. The twenty-first-century man, like the sixteenth-century man before him, is largely dependent on women (often one woman) for friendship.

I'll be even more blunt: if I were to die tomorrow, my absence likely wouldn't be felt in any meaningful way by anyone outside the members of my immediate family. Yet I am not personally unpleasant or lacking in ordinary social graces; most people who know me would describe me as a nice fellow. I'm at ease around children, respectful of the elderly and adept at the routine small talk that forms the bulk of human intercourse. When I walk the dog in the river valley, and another dog walker stops and enquires after the age of my pet or comments on his thick coat, I make the appropriate response. When I go to the barber for a haircut, I can discuss the weather or the state of the economy, if not with enthusiasm at least with social aplomb. Yet I don't really engage with anyone outside of my family on a deeply emotional level.

This idea of my actual isolation staggered me, for I am not a cold or distant person. And it occurred to me at about the same time that I first heard of my contemporary Christopher Knight and his almost thirty years of solitude in the Maine woods. What had I accomplished, as a social being, during all those years that Knight hadn't also accomplished by living as a hermit? Sure, I had met hundreds of people, and even rather liked most of them, and I had conducted tens of thousands of conversations largely dealing with the same half-dozen subjects (the weather, sports, politics, literature, the environment, family); I had published twenty books and performed over a hundred public readings; and I had taught hundreds of students how to improve their writing and reading skills. In short, I had been a normal participant in the ordinary channels of life. But what exactly did all this normalcy mean if it only led to friendlessness at fifty-five and a growing desire to retreat from the world?

More to the point, what was I going to do for the rest of my life? How was I going to cope in society if my desire for an anchor-hold, a medieval hermitage, continued to grow? In what direction lay my greatest chance at recovering a sense of wonder?

The more I thought about Christopher Knight and his experience, the more I recognized, with a kind of panic, a fraternal self. In that recognition came a plumbing of the past that stirred up the ghost of Alf Harley, his smoke and his ultimate fate that cold October morning, a fate that grows more complex whenever I try to stare it down. How could the trip I made with my father and Dr. Kaney have lain dormant so long in my memory? After all, a man died in the bunk of his beached gillnetter and, though I hadn't witnessed the death or indeed the corpse, I had been there. No doubt, at the time, the event was just one of hundreds of miraculous experiences that youth holds out to us – the most extraordinary happenings, to a child, are often banal. But why did the significance of that hermit-death take so long to reach me?

In Flannery O'Connor's short story "Everything That Rises Must Converge," a cheerful, racist and deluded mother berates her young adult son for his cynical attitude. In the words of O'Connor's third-person narrator, "She said he didn't yet know a thing about 'life,' that he hadn't even entered the real world – when already he was as disenchanted with it as a man of fifty."

Disenchantment. Was it the inevitable fate of my age and sex? An idealist for decades, I had reached my sixth decade having lost almost all faith in what my culture had taught me since birth: I didn't believe in any god, nationhood had clearly been sacrificed to global corporate control and the idea of winning and losing was an obvious delusion when one inhabits a mortal frame that will inevitably cease to exist. Even my long-held belief in the goodness of the individual human was wavering under the unbearable weight of that belief's irrelevance: What did individual goodness matter in a world run by and for the greedy on a planet rapidly being destroyed for profit?

But disenchantment with the world isn't necessarily a path to isolation. After all, to live with minimal contact with society, even for a short period, is a major undertaking, with multiple unknown consequences, such as . . . Well, I finally realized that there was only one way to find out. The memory of Alf Harley, logically enough, pointed the way.

I decided to return to his island and to stay there, for as long as I could manage and, to be honest, for as long as I could handle. I didn't expect to secrete myself away for months, or even weeks. First of all, I couldn't. As a husband, the father of three adolescents and the son of a ninety-year-old mother, I bore responsibilities that couldn't be shirked indefinitely. Besides, even a week without human contact, without technology, a week with a campfire, minimal shelter and the flow of the Fraser River would give me a taste of the hermit experience, perhaps enough to clarify the rest of my life, one way or the other. I would either come out of the solitude wanting more of the same, or I would emerge with an insatiable desire to reconnect with all my high school classmates on Facebook. In any case, the conversion rate regarding hermitage would turn Thoreau's two years outside of nineteenth-century hustle and bustle into about a week outside of the twenty-first-century rat race – so those seven days, if I could manage them, would be an eternity. But whether I could manage even that amount of solitude remained to be seen (and heard and felt).

I decided to bring just one book with me, the ultimate desert island book because it is about nothing less than being shipwrecked on a desert island: Daniel Defoe's *Robinson Crusoe*. And if such a thing as the spirit exists, I would have ample opportunity to commune with the shades of Alf Harley, my father, Dr. Kaney and my own young self – the four of us around the heavy ashes of a mortal fire, feeling the chill in the embers.

BUT I WASN'T DELUDED ABOUT THE DIFFICULTIES THAT LAY AHEAD. IN fact, over the past two decades, I had become such an urban creature that I almost sympathized with that old witticism "I am at two with nature." Nor could I legitimately claim an hour in a used bookshop followed by a coffee in a nearby café as solitude, especially considering that I lived with a spouse, three teenagers and a golden retriever whose need for exercise daily put me into small-talk contact with other dog owners.

Yet I had been a Huck Finn type of boy (or at least a Tom Sawyer type) alongside a great river, and I had fished for salmon on that same river up until the age of thirty: my body was one vast storehouse of sensory experience in nature. Even in the midst of a busy urban existence, I found times to be outside, relatively alone, watching for coyotes on the trails of the North Saskatchewan River Valley or just gazing up at the different phases of the moon. Once, in fact, I had been walking home late one winter evening when I came upon no fewer than six coyotes on the trail (two adults and four youngsters). At that moment, I realized exactly how "at two with nature" I really was, for I didn't know what to expect from the coyote pack, or even if an accumulation of coyotes is called a pack. Would they attack? If they were hungry enough? How would I fight them off? The largest animal slowly walked toward me (weren't they supposed to be shy of humans?) while the others slipped into the trees. I tried to out-strategize whatever strategy the coyotes were putting into action, but nothing came to mind; I just kept walking, perhaps recalling that old chestnut about not showing any fear. The large advance coyote eventually turned off the trail, and only re-emerged once I had gone fifty feet past him. The others remained hidden, no doubt in order to snicker at my ignorance.

In a sense, the modern coyote has been forced more and more to make the opposite journey to the one I had in mind. The trickster figure of several Indigenous cultures has, like so much of rural Canada over the past three decades, moved into the urban maelstrom in order to survive. If I was planning the reverse – heading to an unpopulated childhood island – what kind and degree of survival did my intentions entail? Was I somehow tricking myself?

The question is a key one, for we live in an age where the marketing of the self and the self's development has reached a fever pitch. Everyone is seeking to fill a spiritual emptiness or meet a deep psychological need, or so it seems. Even those people who choose the hermit life often appear to be no more than Christopher Knight's dilettantes, hermits of half-measures.

For example, in my preparations for a limited solitude, I discovered *Raven's Bread*, a quarterly newsletter for hermits put out by two eremites (Christian hermits) living together on a secluded mountain slope northwest of Asheville, North Carolina. Yes, *together.* Married hermits. With two border collies and a white cat named Merlin. Paul and Karen Fredette, in fact, "minister to hermits worldwide" through their newsletter, and they also offer resources and guidance at their website.

Marriage? The Internet? This wasn't my idea of solitude or isolation at all. Of course, I realized that some marriages can be intensely lonely and that the online world is hardly the paradise of human communication it's marketed to be, but still, I couldn't quite accept the daily interaction with others – "Hi, Honey, how was the hermiting today? We've got ten new followers on Twitter!" – as a legitimate hermit experience. It reminded me of the Monty Python skit in which Eric Idle and Michael Palin, as two hermits living on the same mountain, gossip about the interior decorating of their caves. "Oh, you must try bracken," Palin says at one point.

Nevertheless, out of a spirit of fairness, I ordered a copy of the Fredettes' book *Consider the Ravens: On Contemporary Hermit Life* in order to do a more thorough investigation. Awaiting its arrival, I decided to test my own limits of withdrawal from sensory overload.

DEEP WINTER IN EDMONTON, THE MOST NORTHERLY CITY IN NORTH America with a population of over a million people, can be forbidding, desolate and long. Temperatures with wind chill often dip below -40°C, and snowfall has been known to start in September and last until May (and, on rare occasions, even June). But the deep winter can also be beautiful, especially for someone seeking solitude. To go outside on a severely cold night at the start of a new year is to celebrate absence: absence of sound, absence of people, sometimes even absence of feeling in your extremities.

I left the house an hour after midnight, with no particular destination in mind. I merely wanted to experience the stillness that comes with such extreme cold. Immediately, I felt the sharpness of the wind on my face and watched a cloud of my own breath flow behind me like thrown water. Within minutes, I had tears in my eyes and had to remove my glasses so I could dab away the moisture and clear my sight. As soon as I put my glasses back on, I became aware of two things: the apocalyptic emptiness of the neighbourhood, and the startling size of the full moon. Somehow the two things seemed related, as if the moon had transferred its barren landscape to the Earth. The recent and still fresh snow, several feet deep on the lawns and rooftops of my neighbours' properties, only added to the illusion. Uneasily, I kept my eyes on the moon as I seemed to walk across its surface.

The only sound I heard – my boots crunching the thin layer of snow that the plows had left behind on the street – was alarmingly loud. I looked down at the grey-black striations on the pavement, half-convinced that I was crushing clamshells with each step. But eventually I grew used to the sound and returned my attention to the moon.

It was much larger and brighter than normal, what is known as a supermoon, a full moon at its closest orbit around the Earth. Its size, in fact, stopped my progress, almost seemed to call out to me. After all, what is more solitary than the moon? The sun, perhaps, though its heat detracts from the association of loneliness. Also our own planet. As Walter de la Mare says of the Earth in *Desert Islands and Robinson Crusoe*, "Is not this great globe itself a celestial solitary?" From that question, it seems only logical to ruminate on our own solitude, as de la Mare does thusly, "Flesh is flesh and bone is bone, and only by insight and by divination can we pierce inward to the citadel of the mind and soul."

Such is our fate on our familiar great globe. In any case, where celestial bodies are concerned, the sun cannot be walked on, and the Earth has been trod by billions. As for the moon, its paradoxical proximity and distance, its history since the summer of 1969 and the Apollo 11 mission, deepens its solitude. We have touched its surface, but we have lost interest in the achievement; we have lived most of our species' existence relying on its light, but now we rarely notice the illumination; we once saw the moon as a glorious dream, but now we require a second habitable planet to satisfy our imaginations and, perhaps, to preserve our kind.

Yet there shone the moon in the southern sky, one dim star to its left, a vague constellation to its lower right, and the craters across its middle like partially healed black eyes. I felt sorry for it; the moon, despite its undeniable majesty, seemed abandoned. The more I stared at it, the more I began to feel sorry for myself, to doubt the wisdom of my growing hunger for solitude. The cold around me suddenly became the cold of space.

I tried to shake off the feeling, to focus on my surroundings. The branches of the great elms along our street seemed brittle as icicles; even the chimney smoke blown sideways by the wind looked as if it could snap in two. Suddenly a terrific echoing sound, as if the tectonic plates of the darkness had shifted, broke the silence. I recognized the sound after several seconds. It was the shunting of boxcars in the rail yards several miles away.

I walked on. After ten minutes, I had seen no people, nor even heard a car or a siren, though I live close to the city centre, to two major traffic arteries. Just as unsettling, I encountered no animals – no scavenging coyote, no jackrabbit moving like an *Alice in Wonderland* chess piece into and out of a street lamp's glow. The cold closed around me, but only my feet felt numb, even through my Blundstones and two pairs of wool socks.

Again, the sound of my walking and the numb heaviness of my step turned me back to the moon. I almost felt guilty for trying to ignore it. But I couldn't for long. How could I? A fisherman's son, and later a fisherman myself, I knew intimately the friendship of that lunar light, knew the security and comfort it gave on a dark and fast-running river. More than that, I was a child of the Space Age, five years old and on the Fraser River with my father that July day when Neil Armstrong took his famous small step and giant leap.

How strange it was to think that the bootprints of Armstrong and of the eleven other humans who walked on the moon after him still marked its surface. Because there is no atmosphere on the moon, no wind and rain, no erosive action, the bootprints of the astronauts will never disappear. I looked down and behind me. Even just seconds after I had stopped, all signs of my progress were so faint as to be invisible; I left no discernible impression on the frozen street. Looking back at the moon, I tried to recall what I knew of its surface. Wasn't it colder there than on the Earth? Permanently cold? Or would it be like the Earth, warm or cold depending on its relationship to the sun? How could there be any bootprints at all if the surface was frozen-solid rock?

I realized then that what I knew of the moon was the stuff of mythology not fact, including my fisherman's belief that a ring around the moon meant that the salmon would be on the move. Then I understood, with a shiver of intuition, that I really knew nothing substantial about human nature either, perhaps least of all my own. Dostoevsky, in his classic short work of alienation, *Notes from Underground*, addresses this point directly: "In every man's memory there are things he won't reveal to others, except, perhaps, to friends. And there are things he won't reveal even to friends, only, perhaps, to himself, and then, too, in secret. And finally, there are things he is afraid to reveal even to himself, and every decent man has quite an accumulation of them. In fact, the more decent the man, the more of them he has stored up."

The moon I could learn about through books, but human nature, especially in regards to the relationship between solitude and community? Only partially so, because each person's experience of this dynamic must be more individual than it is universal. Was it likely, for instance, that I would ever feel about my fellow beings and life itself the way that Montaigne felt, or Thoreau, or Dostoevsky? What about Christopher Knight, my contemporary, who walked into the Maine woods the same year that I left university and vanished into the dying culture of the west coast salmon fishery? (According to Finkel, Knight's favourite book is *Notes from Underground*.) What he carried into those woods – experiences, memories, tastes – was certainly different from what I carried at twenty-two, and what I carried then perhaps has only a small relation to what I am carrying now. We aren't one person through time, no matter how much we focus on and celebrate the self.

I had begun to walk again and soon reached some woods on the upper edge of the North Saskatchewan River Valley. The moonlight brightly illuminated a winding footpath through the scrub poplar, birch and criss-crossing windfall and deadfall that I had taken many times. It was only a short passage, perhaps two hundred yards, and ended at a flight of wooden steps dropping fifty feet to the broader paved valley trail below.

Standing there in the full moon's glow, thinking about Christopher Knight, I recalled something from the book that Finkel eventually published about the North Pond Hermit. Knight (ironically, given his name) feared nothing during his hermitage as much as he feared a full moon. In his own words, he had to deal constantly with the "moon question." Considering that his hermitage, expertly hidden as it was behind a great boulder and under much dense foliage, was so close to some cabins that he could often hear people talking, Knight couldn't take chances by foraging in moonlight. He required a deeper darkness, just as he had required a deeper something when he stood, as I stood now, at the entrance to some woods.

Here were Robert Frost's two roads diverging in a yellow wood, even though this forest was Brothers Grimm–black and the road only a single trail. Without question, I was at a crossroads, on the verge of taking the road less travelled, just as Knight had done. But I didn't have to make a decision yet; in fact, I was still exploring, still more in the human world than out of it. Even so, I hesitated, almost as if I was Knight in 1986, the nuclear flames of Chernobyl far back over my shoulder and a seductive, dangerous stillness somewhere in the mysterious and ancient hush of the trees. Somehow, to go along the trail now, as I had done hundreds of times before, seemed like a commitment to a different trail entirely.

The moonlight fell heavier, turned the snow to white solder. I almost laughed at my unwillingness to move, but then I realized the situation wasn't funny. I wasn't a young man; to withdraw now from community, even for a short time, would be decisive in the same way that choosing to have children had been decisive. Once started on the journey, I suspected that I wouldn't turn back. Or if I did, I doubted that the return would be as easy.

Finally, without even being conscious of the decision, I entered the woods. Miles away, the night's first siren began to keen, but the trail soon narrowed and closed off the sound at its throat. A minute later, I stopped again, letting my heartbeat echo my halted footsteps. Over that familiar sound, I eventually heard another, a kind of furious wingbeat twenty yards off the trail to my left.

Though the moonlight was obscured by the clustering branches and windfallen skinny trunks of earlier winter storms, I soon identified the sound. In fact, I'd heard it before, in the daytime, a week earlier. Strange that I hadn't connected the sound to my recent introspection; even stranger that I hadn't connected it to Christopher Knight until now.

What I heard was the flapping of a blue nylon tarp that some homeless person seeking any kind of rude shelter had hastily and poorly tied to a few scraggly birches. The river valley, especially in the summer and fall, contains many such improvised camps, and I had on several occasions come upon city workers clearing them out, dragging away the sodden blankets and garbage and tarps accumulated over the more temperate months. My neighbourhood, in fact, serves as a natural corridor between the city's destitute downtown areas and the fashionable Whyte Avenue strip where the panhandling opportunities can be optimized. Hundreds of times over the years I have encountered Edmonton's disenfranchised class pushing shopping carts along our back alley in search of refundable plastic, and occasionally I've seen one of the itinerant campers slipping through the trees. Like anyone, I don't generally philosophize about these common urban interactions, but of late I'd begun to wonder about my freedom in relation to my "down-and-out" fellow citizens. In particular, were their lives less stressful than my own?

I doubted it. After all, I had read Lars Eighner's notorious account of his life as a Dumpster diver (in his book, *Travels with Lizbeth: Three Years on the Road and on the Streets*, which deals extensively with homelessness), and had been shocked by the rigours of his schedule and the anxiety of his search for shelter. As for Christopher Knight, the obsessive attention to detail and planning that his hidden life of breaking and entering demanded was considerably more involved and panic-inducing than the average rat-race urban dweller's. His claims that he was "completely free," on the evidence, are only a hollow romantic boast. And yet, beyond the reasons for choosing a derelict and itinerant life, which include, of course, addictions and fleeing from abusive pasts, there must be at least some compensatory moments of freedom and relief.

But surely not at -40°C with a few thin blankets and a hanging nylon tarp for shelter. I stood at the skinny side trail made by perhaps one or two people's footsteps and listened. Nothing. Just the flapping sound, which followed an irregular pattern. I stood there for two minutes, my feet getting colder, the moisture in my eyes heavy as ink. But I heard no indrawn breath, no rippling snore: nothing to indicate another human presence. A person sleeping rough under such conditions would almost certainly die of hypothermia, which was why Christopher Knight, during the harshest Maine winter nights, forced himself to stay awake, to walk circles around his enclosure. I heard no one moving about, and yet I had to be sure. Just a little closer . . .

I took a few steps along the footpath and stopped. My instinct to leave well enough alone and my instinct to investigate were at odds, at the same odds as my life. Why should I investigate if not because of empathy, a concern for others? Why should I move on if not because of the desire to escape all human entanglements?

Solitude, which seems simple enough in the abstract, had to be much more complex in the concrete reality. I walked another dozen or so steps until the flapping of the tarp sounded like the beating fear in my chest. Close enough to see, in the fractured moonlight, a scatter of sweaters and shirts, a couple of plastic pop bottles and, most poignantly, a bottle of shampoo. But no sleeping or crouching human form. Whoever had sheltered here had been wise enough to seek a warmer camp, at least during these killing temperatures.

Relieved, I walked quickly back to the main trail and straight out of the woods. It was almost as if I feared the possibilities of my own future. Had I come upon that most disturbing of all camps, the forlorn limits of the heart? Time alone – as time always is, even though we attend it – would tell.

Walking back home, my feet as heavy on the moon-drenched snow as Neil Armstrong's boots before he escaped Earth's atmosphere, I resolved to investigate solitude, at least for the rest of the winter, in a more comfortable manner: through books, questions and a few small experiments.

I DIDN'T WANT TO START WITH THE RELIGIOUS SOLITARIES FOR THE obvious reason that the search for a deeper communion with God doesn't interest a non-believer. But when I did a little research, I soon learned that most atheists justify their position by emphasizing not only the here and now but also the primacy of human relationships. On a website called The Friendly Atheist, most respondents answering the question "Do atheists ever get lonely?" stress the importance of other people, as if the choice is either God or society. Of course, loneliness isn't the same as solitude, but since so much of the latter involves a religious retreat from the world, not much about atheism and solitude appears to have been written, for the likely reason that atheists are, in the main, defensive about being stereotyped as misanthropes (hence the name of the above website). The writing about solitude that might come from atheists is rarely identified as such: that is, many writers, if they don't talk about God, substitute nature or art. But if you celebrate nature, you might just be a pantheist (another form of theist), and if you celebrate art, you've merely bought into a human manifestation of creator power.

Anthony Storr, in his widely praised 1988 study of solitude and creativity (ironically given the highly uncreative title of *Solitude* – it's amazing how many books on solitude simply use that word for a title, as if the word is its own solitary marooned on Title Island), argues that some people are simply geniuses who function quite cheerfully on their own and require little interaction with others to achieve happiness. Citing Kafka, Beethoven, Kant, Jung, Beatrix Potter and a whole host of other writers, philosophers, musicians and psychiatrists, Storr justifies isolation as a necessary path to creative accomplishment. Even overlooking the fact that many, if not all, of these creative individuals had damaged childhoods and therefore sought isolation as much out of social terror as inspiration, I couldn't celebrate what Storr sees as a successful overcoming of circumstances.

In brief, I was no longer romantic about artistic creation, and could no longer see its special kind of solitude as noble and selfless. Having lived as a writer for the majority of my adult life, I knew from the inside just how much artists, especially males, justify selfishness as an essential but worthy means to an end. While I was grateful for the books of many solitaries, I wasn't about to deify literary solitude; I wasn't going to substitute my own creativity or anyone else's for God. After all, I was an atheist, which can be defined as someone who is anti the belief in a creator power to which one owes homage and obedience. What did I owe to any writer? Nothing. But I would give time to read them. What did I owe to my own writing impulse? Also nothing, but I would give time to write. Tempting as it is, for an artist, to believe in a magnanimous isolation, I knew too much about the ego to buy into the romance and mythology. The following call to solitude by the acclaimed Canadian-born minimalist painter Agnes Martin, for example, is the sort of call that conscience wouldn't let me heed:

> We have been very strenuously conditioned against solitude. To be alone is considered to be a grievous and dangerous condition. So I beg you to recall in detail any times when you were alone and discover your exact response at those times.
>
> I suggest to artists that you take every opportunity of being alone, that you give up having pets and unnecessary companions.

My problem with this kind of creative summons to solitude is directly addressed by the Italian poet and novelist Cesare Pavese. "A man is never completely alone in the world," he writes. "At the worst, he has the company of a boy, a youth, and by and by a grown man – the one he used to be." The American writer Paul Auster, more recently, argued that a person's language, memories and even their concept of isolation – in fact every thought in their head – arises out of their connection with others.

Even if I instinctively agreed with Pavese and Auster, I don't really know if they were right. After all, only by experiencing the kind of isolation that mainstream Western culture relentlessly lobbies against can a person begin to understand his or her own personal capacity for solitude and the results that might come from it.

I soon discovered that my atheism, along with my unromantic attitude toward the creation of art, placed me in a unique position. The philosopher William James, for example, refers to one of his colleague's students in this way: "He believes in No-God, and he worships Him." In other words, atheism, being a belief system of anti-belief, is itself a form of religion. An interesting idea, but a flawed one. As Paul Cliteur writes in the journal *Philosophy Now*, "Atheism is not a religion, but the *absence* of religion. In particular, atheism is atheism."

Not being a philosopher, I resisted going down these rabbit holes of logic. Instead, I realized that, where solitude was concerned, I needed to both broaden my horizons and also to limit them. One step at a time needed to be my path. So, because it was winter, I settled in to read *Alone*, Admiral Richard E. Byrd's account of his four-and-a-half-month isolation at Antarctica in 1934. And because Robinson Crusoe, as I recalled from my boyhood reading, had lived in a cave, I sought to mitigate the male influence by also reading Vicki Mackenzie's *A Cave in the Snow: A Western Woman's Quest for Enlightenment*, her biography of Tenzin Palmo, a Western woman who became a Buddhist nun and spent twelve years living alone in a cave high in the Himalayas. A man obsessed with recording data for science and a woman driven to achieve spiritual enlightenment: these two poles of human solitude seemed like appropriate bookends for my own exploration.

AMERICAN PILOT, NAVAL OFFICER AND EXPLORER RICHARD E. BYRD WAS a man's man in a patriarchal culture. Brave to the point of repeatedly defying death, ultra-rational, patriotic, with a conventional spirituality that saw the cosmos and all its orderly workings as undoubtedly the product of one supreme guiding intelligence (someone much like Richard Byrd himself, in fact), he lived an adult life that moved between lecturing to raise funds to go exploring in the name of science and exploring. In the opening pages of *Alone*, he travels to extreme lengths to distance himself from his emotions, to make clear to his readers (most of whom he would expect to be powerful men who might finance his future ventures) that he's not the sort of mush-headed fellow who's about to let something as irrational and dangerous as feelings get in the way of his purpose.

> My other books have been factual, impersonal narratives of my expeditions and flights. This book, on the other hand, is the story of an experience which was in considerable part subjective. I very nearly died before it was over. And, since my sufferings bulked so large in it and since a man's instinct is to keep such things to himself, I did not see how I could write about Advance Base and still escape making an unseemly show of my feelings. . . . The whole business was so intimate in memory that I doubted that I could approach it with the proper detachment. . . .
> . . . I appreciated that I should be obliged to discuss matters of personal moment in a way that would be distasteful.

The admiral really shouldn't have worried so much, because *Alone* is definitely seemly, detached and tasteful in every conventional sense that matters. Indeed, I soon grew bored with the discussions of enterprise, teamwork, national destiny and meteorological data. All I was interested in *was* the emotion, or at least some insights into the nature of severe isolation. Byrd does provide them, and his writing occasionally rises to the challenge, but how much one wishes that Thoreau might have made the expedition instead!

Still, Byrd did spend four and a half months alone (though with almost daily radio contact with his home base) at one end of the Earth under extreme conditions – the temperatures often dropped seventy degrees below freezing, the long nights were as black "as the dark side of the moon" and he nearly died from the fumes of his faultily ventilated heating system (a stove). More interestingly, his willingness to take these risks, against the advice of most of his colleagues, wasn't just down to science. Byrd wanted to "sink roots into some replenishing philosophy," to escape all the gregariousness and fanfare that came with being a globe-trotting lecturer and fundraiser: "Out there on the South Polar barrier, in cold and darkness as complete as that of the Pleistocene, I should have time to catch up, to study and think and listen to the phonograph; and, for maybe seven months, remote from all but the simplest distractions, I should be able to live exactly as I chose, obedient to no necessities but those imposed by wind and night and cold, and to no man's laws but my own."

Here was *Robinson Crusoe* over two hundred years later, except on a remote crevasse-ridden glacier instead of a tropical island. The same faith in industry and enterprise, the same nationalism and religion, the same colonizing instinct and, equally so, the same impressive ingenuity, courage and perseverance. Without question, Richard Byrd, an educated and intelligent man, would have read Defoe's great work in his boyhood.

For an American male who came of age in America's century, the reckless bravado and mercantile imagination of Crusoe was nothing short of inspirational. To be a law unto oneself – the dream that Byrd claims exists deep in every man – still dominates popular representations of masculinity (Hollywood action-adventure movies, for example). Though I wasn't interested in that sort of aggressive solitude, something in me did rise to the possibilities of extreme change, something in me did agree with Byrd's "contention that no man can hope to be completely free who lingers within reach of familiar habits and urgencies."

But when does one know that he's no longer within reach? It might take a highly financed expedition of hundreds of men and tons of equipment, or it might take a great deal less than that. In any case, *Alone* only sprang to life for me in occasional passages toward the end, after Byrd has nearly died from asphyxiation and been rescued by other members of his team. At these moments, he admits to questioning everything he has ever striven for: "We men of action who serve science serve only a reflection in a mirror," and "I was a fool, lost on a fool's errand."

Ultimately, though, his lyrical expressions of faith, somewhat akin to Thoreau's and Emerson's, left me as cold as the Arctic nights. I just couldn't believe all of that mystical stuff about man never being alone because of some Divine Intelligence that pervades the cosmos and creates a universal harmony.

EVEN THOUGH I TRIED TO AVOID THESE SORTS OF SPIRITUAL PLATITUDES, finding no comfort in them whatsoever because I had never been aware of any such intelligence, they seem to be unavoidable when one researches solitude. But Buddhists, as far as my limited knowledge told me, didn't believe in external creator intelligences. Perhaps *A Cave in the Snow*, then, would be more grounded. It certainly had to be less concerned with matters of destiny.

As it turned out, the story of Tenzin Palmo, a Buddhist nun who began life as Diane Perry in London's East End in 1943, was more mystical than *Alone* and, surprisingly, even more concerned with personal destiny. Diane's father, a fishmonger and war veteran who'd been gassed, died when she was only two, but the nun named Tenzin Palmo claimed that she'd had an idyllic childhood anyway. Oddly, this idyll involved a series of illnesses that left her so enfeebled that doctors and teachers advised that she should never take up any physically taxing work. Born with the base of her spine twisted inwards – an excruciatingly painful condition – she also nearly died from meningitis, suffered a mystery ailment that kept her hospitalized for months at a time and three times a year would become completely debilitated with high fevers and intense headaches. As a result of all these setbacks, she spent a great deal of time alone, and often would "just wander around the streets, floating above everything, looking down on people for a change, instead of always looking up at them."

Before long, Diane Perry was on the path to becoming that rarest of creatures: a Western woman who would achieve yogi status, enlightenment, omniscience – "the highest state of evolution humankind could ever achieve."

From giving up a swinging young womanhood in hip-and-happening early sixties London (she became quite good-looking, dated often and found work as a librarian) to living alone in a cave thirteen thousand feet up in the Himalayas, Diane Perry/Tenzin Palmo certainly travelled an unorthodox journey. As a little girl, she had always been attracted to Asian people and Eastern religions and had never felt completely at ease in Western society, so when she discovered Buddhism, everything suddenly made sense: she was reincarnated. Consequently, she felt a magnetic pull to a different life altogether. Renouncing the world and all of its material and physical attractions, she entered a Buddhist nunnery in northern India, shaved off her chestnut curls, learned to speak Tibetan, met her guru some years later and finally, with his blessing, retreated into her cave hermitage, living there from the age of thirty-three to forty-five.

Now we come to the crux of the matter. By any measurement, twelve years in a space measuring ten feet wide by six feet deep, thirteen thousand feet above sea level (about one thousand feet higher than Mount Robson in the Rockies) and several hours of treacherous hiking away from any semblance of community meets the definition of solitude. Tenzin Palmo longed for this kind of isolation in order to devote her entire energy and time to profound and prolonged meditation and not to record data for science, but the hardships she endured and the ambition she harboured were very similar to Admiral Byrd's. He went alone to Advance Base against the wishes of his team, while she had to talk her hiking companions into letting her enter her retreat; he suffered through intense cold, ultimately having to confront the possibility of either dying from hypothermia or asphyxiation, while she was almost buried alive when an avalanche covered her cave entrance (she eventually dug her way out); he often found it difficult to feed himself due to weakness, while she almost starved one winter because the person in the nearest village responsible for bringing up her supplies didn't make the trip; he had his belief in cosmic harmony confirmed, while she claimed to be nothing but grateful for the opportunity to deepen her inward spiritual journey.

Despite the great risks, the near-death experiences, the discomfort, both explorers enjoyed the isolation. For Tenzin Palmo, it was a rare opportunity as a woman to feel safe and free, far from the unwanted interferences of men. So rare and refreshing, in fact, that she wasn't at all bothered by the presence of wild animals (wolves, bears) or, indeed, more mysterious presences: "The first year that I was there I discovered these huge footprints outside the cave. They were much bigger than a man's but looked similar to a human's with an instep. You could see all the toes but they also had claws. It looked like a human print with claws." Was this evidence of the mythical yeti? Tenzin Palmo never saw the footprints again, but she didn't see why such a creature, which the Tibetans have a name for and which even lamas often talk about, shouldn't exist.

OVERALL, TENZIN PALMO'S HERMITAGE EXPERIENCE WAS INSTRUCTIVE, and indeed groundbreaking for a woman in the male-dominated Buddhist faith. As a result, when she finally left her Himalayan cave, she became, in effect, a female version of Richard Byrd, going on the lecture and work-shop circuit in an effort to raise funds (in her case, to start a nunnery for Tibetan Buddhist nuns). Ironically, her hermitage eventually resulted in a globe-trotting worldliness of the kind familiarly found in the Western society that she had so willingly renounced.

So what, ultimately, did twelve years of isolation teach her? In short, a greater emotional detachment ("In my opinion there's so much more to life than relationships") and a greater awareness that "the nature of our existence is beyond thought and emotions, that it is incredibly vast and inter-connected with all other beings." For Tenzin Palmo, our basic problem stems from an ignorant dualism in which we create a sense of an "I" with everything else being a "Non I." For this former Cockney who has achieved more enlighten-ment than any other Buddhist female, "The reason we are not Enlightened is because we are lazy. . . . There's no other reason. We do not bother to bring ourselves back to the present because we're too fascinated by the games the mind is playing. If one genuinely thinks about Renunciation it is not a giving up of external things like money, leaving home or one's family. That's easy. Genuine renunciation is giving up our fond thoughts, all our delight in memories, hopes and daydreams, our mental chatter."

Easy to leave one's family? Well, Tenzin Palmo did receive a letter in her cave telling her that her mother was dying of cancer back in England, and Tenzin Palmo chose not to go home (she couldn't step off her spiritual path even if she developed cancer herself, apparently). I find it unpalatable and, frankly, damaged, to desire a spirituality that basically sets you up as more enlightened than others so that you never have to do the much harder work of forging and maintaining messy human relationships. Living in Advance Base in the Antarctic and living in a cave in the Himalayas were obviously unique experiences involving physical suffering and requiring great reserves of mental stamina, but since neither period of isolation actually resulted in significant change, then what exactly was the point?

I already knew I wasn't an explorer or a Buddhist, and so I came away from reading *Alone* and *A Cave in the Snow* much as I had gone in: confused about the call of solitude. Perhaps my own journey was unlike any other? Perhaps there is no such thing as a hermit type? In my case, I was mostly wanting to avoid social media and humdrum small talk, to escape the celebrity and leadership/teamwork cultures, not my "delight in memories, hopes and daydreams." While I shared Richard Byrd's desire to read and listen to music and Tenzin Palmo's desire to sit calmly without having my thoughts interrupted, I certainly didn't relish near-death challenges at the bottom or top of the Earth.

Happily, these two books of solitude did have the salutary effect of making my moonlit winter walks a little warmer. In fact, for a short time, they made all of my walks, including others that I made for research purposes, more congenial.

THE OLD STRATHCONA DISTRICT IS ONE OF EDMONTON'S MOST POPULAR entertainment and shopping areas, a four- or five-block strip of bars, cafés, restaurants and trendy shops selling vintage clothing and vinyl albums. In January's severe cold, however, popularity is rather a misnomer. I often walked along the icy and treacherous Whyte Avenue sidewalks to buy groceries at an organic food store, and sometimes didn't pass more than one or two other pedestrians. In my current state of consciousness, of course, this isolation was appealing, but I was still faced with the noise and general busyness of urban existence – just the steady vehicle traffic alone kept my Spidey-senses at maximum intensity.

Then I saw the sign, one of those folding sandwich boards that business-es off the main strip set up to attract potential customers. This particular sign advertised something called the Float House. Below the name was the intriguing phrase *Experience Nothing*, followed by an arrow and the words *23 steps this way*. Attached to the board – happily for someone both inquisitive and reluctant to speak to another human – were a number of small brochures. Each one showed the same image under the words *Experience Nothing*: a prone white figure of an anonymous male, his whole profile outlined in light blue, as if he lay suspended in water that didn't threaten to drown him.

As much disturbed as intrigued – experiencing nothing, to an atheist, is basically a description of what occurs after death – I nonetheless plucked off a brochure with my gloved hand, stuck it in my backpack and scurried off to get my groceries and then retreat to a warm and quiet corner of a café.

"What is floating?" the brochure asked rhetorically. Apparently, it's lying in an enclosed tank of warm water so filled with Epsom salts (850 pounds of it) that you lie with your ears just below the surface. Because the water is kept at a constant temperature of thirty-four degrees Celsius (skin receptor neu-tral), "you lose track of where your body ends and where the water begins."

I looked at the floating white man again. He resembled nothing so much as a chalk corpse, or a traffic-light figure that had been struck by a car. I looked once more, honestly trying to see the blissful rest that the brochure promised as a result of reduced sensory input. But I saw only the reduced sensory input that Jay Gatsby must have experienced while floating around on a pneumatic mattress after suffering a fatal gunshot wound. Then Philip Larkin's bluntly direct poem about death, "Aubade," floated into my mind. The poet's interrogation of his fear of dying explicitly references the horror of not feeling, of not experiencing:

no sight, no sound,
No touch or taste or smell, nothing to think with,
Nothing to love or link with,
The anaesthetic from which none come round.

Yet the brochure promised that floating is "likely to be the most relaxing thing you've ever experienced"; that in the enclosed and insulated tank the mind is free to explore thoughts without distraction. Could this be a brief experience of wu-wei, the ancient Daoist philosophy of acting without acting, of unselfconsciousness, in which one learns to move at ease through the open spaces of life? Maybe. But the figure floating on the Epsom salts made me skeptical. After all, they call it the Dead Sea for a reason.

Sure enough, North American efficiency and busyness, our philosophy of "Just do it!," expressed itself clearly on the remaining pages of the brochure. Floating for just an hour and a half could help me "to cut strokes off [my] golf game, develop complex scientific theories, learn new languages, and draft whole portions of books." Though, in fairness, physiological and psychological benefits were also emphasized. But the final selling point, that floating "has the ability to deeply aid and impact anyone who sets forth into the warm, cozy, silky blackness," naturally sounded like a return to the womb to me.

It was below minus forty outside in the mean streets of Edmonton. I could hear my wife's optimistic voice warning me against "contempt prior to investigation." Perhaps the "warm, cozy, silky blackness" for ninety minutes, which is just the length of a soccer game and not nearly so strenuous, would give me some small insight into Christopher Knight's stargazing, relaxed moments in his bunker. Perhaps that insight would prepare me, even in just a tiny way, for my brief hermitage on Alf Harley's island.

I looked at the front of the brochure again. *Experience Nothing.* As I stared at the white figure, he grew bigger, heavier, wider, and he began to sink, except now the waters weren't warm; they were autumn cold and not silky black at all. Nor was the night in which several silent fishermen stood on the muddy bank and lowered the 350 pounds of dead hermit into the Fraser's erosive current.

After a moment of such powerful and hopefully inaccurate sensory intake, I rallied, took a sip of my skin-receptor neutral coffee and vowed to be brave. Faint heart never won fair solitude. I decided to book a session, knowing full well that my greatest concern wasn't the claustrophobia or the silence or the need to shave strokes off par, but rather the no-longer simple human interaction of meeting and talking with a stranger. More and more, these ordinary social exchanges were becoming a challenge, though I believed I could muster up the gregariousness to run the gamut of the Float House tank attendant. As long as he wasn't named Lance and wearing a necklace of crystals . . .

MEANWHILE, I HAD BEGUN TO SEE THE MOON AS MY ONE TRUE COMPANION in solitude. Domestically, I carried on much as before – joking with my two teenaged sons and daughter, planning routine tasks of shopping and bill paying with my wife, talking to the dog as if he really could understand me – and professionally I still stood in front of university writing students and lectured to them about the need for conflict, rising tension and resolution. But I wanted nothing more than to find the moon and stare at it in silent camaraderie. We seemed locked into the same orbit of uselessness. Bizarrely, I began to imagine my trip to the Float House as a kind of Apollo training mission: Would I pass the antigravity test? Even more bizarrely, I started to fantasize about rocketing not only out of the noisy, busy, memory-destroying Digital Age but also out of my own life and familiar sense of self. Neil Armstrong had met Christopher Knight and they both clutched copies of *Robinson Crusoe* in their hands.

I booked a floating session (online, without having to talk to anyone) and then, the day before, cancelled it. Weeks passed. January remained frozen and bitter, redeemed only by lunar spectacles. On the last day of the month, in particular, a second full moon occurred – a second full moon in the same month is called a blue moon – but this blue moon was also a blood moon (occurring during a total lunar eclipse) and a supermoon (larger because of the moon's closeness to Earth). A super blue blood moon had not been seen in North America in 150 years, and obviously wouldn't be seen again in my lifetime. I had a feeling that the universe was trying to tell me something, but there was too much noise and distraction for me to hear.

So I deactivated all social media networks and stopped watching television. Never having owned a cellphone, I did all I could to avoid seeing others staring at them, which meant I minimized contact with almost everyone, including my own children. Once free of any unavoidable daily duties, I found quiet places to read and to muse. The minus forty nights continued, and I made the same walk to the flapping tent in the woods, a shelter I had come to regard as the dark sibling of the Float House – somehow, I couldn't bring myself to lie down in either.

Increasingly, I was turning into a dangerous combination of Melville's Bartleby the scrivener and Dostoevsky's Underground Man, two fictional urban residents of the nineteenth century and progenitors of modern alienation. Like Bartleby, I preferred not to do anything; like the Underground Man, I lived with self-consciousness as a kind of toxic sickness.

The face of the moon, rather than Facebook, now occupied my leisure hours. Curiously, the lunar eclipse itself didn't much interest me, as I wanted the familiar old friend of the moon that I had known all my life, the Apollo moon, the moon of my childhood and my salmon fishing years. I began to do a little more research, into both the moon and solitude. As it happens, my journey wasn't even on a unique trajectory. Over three hundred years earlier, Daniel Defoe, author of *Robinson Crusoe*, had even published a fantasy about travelling to the moon.

The Consolidator: Or, Memoirs of Sundry Transactions from the World in the Moon appeared in 1705, seventeen years before Crusoe, and, quite frankly, no one other than academics specializing in the eighteenth century ever reads it. The book is basically a satire of politics and society in which Defoe's narrator travels to the moon in a feather-covered rocket ship and meets a race of advanced Lunarians who, regarding the Earth as their own moon, routinely visit it. The narrator is given a pair of special glasses through which the advanced Lunarian civilization can observe the iniquities and absurdities of human life and governments. To say that this fantastic tale makes for dry reading is to say that the story of Robinson Crusoe fires the human imagination. But just think of the power and influence of the moon over eighteenth-century pre-electricity London; it's no wonder that many long-dead authors besides Defoe speculated about the moon and about the possibility of another civilization existing on it. Nor is it surprising to connect Defoe's moon traveller with his much more famous shipwrecked sailor: the moon, a desert isle and the wisdom that accumulates from reaching such remote destinations forms a pleasing trinity.

All I had, alas, was a less mysterious moon, an urban-surrounded silt island in the Fraser River and no particular prospects of instructive wisdom. But who could say? No more fantastic and perhaps frightening journey is possible than each person's descent into greater solitude and fuller consciousness.

While in the eighteenth-century literature section of the University of Alberta library (also a very solitary place, not surprisingly), I happened upon the 1741 edition of a book published in 1637. The former had the type of delightfully long title that publishers favoured in the eighteenth century: *The city-hermit or, the life of Henry Welby, Esq; who liv'd at his house in Grub-Street, forty-four years, and, in that space, was never seen by any: and there died, (Oct. 29, 1636) aged eighty-four.* Forty-four years! Sixteen more than Christopher Knight, and Henry Welby, Esq., didn't even have the benefit that apparently comes to human beings from living in the silence and serenity of the natural world. Given that Christopher Knight's fondest memories of his hermitage involved floating in a borrowed canoe on a lake and stargazing, the complete absence of any outdoor reveries for Henry Welby suggests that he must have had other ways to cope with his extended isolation. According to the text, these ways were exactly two: prayer and scholarship. Mr. Welby, as it turns out, ordered every single book that appeared, in England or on the continent, making him a kind of low-profile Samuel Johnson, the celebrated author of the early eighteenth century who once claimed that he had read every book ever written.

In the case of Mr. Welby, his capacity for withdrawal from society had a lot to do with reading but also with his faith in the Christian God. As one of the multiple contributors to this long-titled book puts it, "He died living, that he might live dying; his life was a perpetual death, that his Death might bring him to an eternal life; who accounted himself no better than a Glow-worm here on Earth, that he might hereafter shine a most glorious Saint in Heaven."

The paradox of living in dying, that two-sided coin, was rather neatly reflected in the chronology of Henry Welby's mortal existence. He lived, as the text neatly summarizes, "Fourscore and four Years, half in the World, and half from the World," a description that only made me think of the moon again, with its dark side and its light side. But no one, except the long-dead Henry Welby, really knows which half of his life, on his un-attended deathbed, he actually preferred: his privileged youth travelling around on the continent and later living as a man of means on the family estate, or his midlife and old age of absolute seclusion.

In any case, there's no denying that he withdrew from the world to an astonishing degree, and right in the middle of a populated city. Being a gentleman of considerable means, he was able to arrange his domestic matters in such a way that when food was about to be brought to him, he retired into a neighbouring room, only re-emerging to eat once the servants had gone. But even with his books and his God, the solitude must have been a trial. The authors of this strange little book mince no words when commenting on Welby's accomplishment:

> Now, as touching the Solitude of his Life, to spend so many summers and winters in one small or narrow Room, dividing himself not only from the Society of Men, but debarring himself from the Benefit of the fresh and comfortable Air; not to walk, or to confer with any Man, which might short-en the Tediousness of Night, or mitigate the Prolixness of the Day. What Retirement could be more? Or what Restriction greater? In my Opinion, it far surpasses all the Vestals and Votaries, all the Anchorites and Hermits, which have been memorized in any History.

It possibly surpasses the North Pond Hermit as well, except Henry Welby's guarantee of food and warm shelter takes a certain stoic edge off his isolation. Even so, I doubt that Christopher Knight would call the old gentleman a dilettante. Forty-four years alone is pretty hard to dismiss, even if you do have a fat purse and several servants.

But two hermits, like two roads in a yellow wood, also diverge. First of all, Knight was a thief who had to steal to survive; Welby had so much money that he was famous for making charitable donations. Second, and more interesting to me, Knight had no particularly dramatic or epiphanic moment that led to his decision to cast society away; Welby, by contrast, had the kind of epiphany that comes from having a gun pointed at your face. And not by some random criminal lurking in the Grub Street shadows either, but by his own brother! Welby's younger brother "drew a Pistol, charged with a double Bullet, from his Side, and presented upon the elder, which only gave Fire, but, by the miraculous Providence of God, no farther Report." Welby the Elder then disarmed his sibling, retired to his chamber and checked the gun to see if there were actually any bullets in it. There were.

The end result? According to his biographers, only one choice was possible to prevent further violence: "His Affection so far and so deeply wounded him, that since, where he expected the Love of a Brother, he had found the Malice of an Enemy, since he could not enjoy his Face with Safety, he would ever after deny the Sight of his own Face to all Men whatsoever." The logic here is rather nonsensical, but logic and human emotion are almost sworn enemies. It's clear, however, that shock and horror drove Henry Welby into retirement, while the trivialities of ordinary American life compelled Christopher Knight's decision (or so he explained, not very convincingly, almost three decades later). In this regard, Knight is much like Thoreau, who once wrote, "It is impossible for me to be interested in what interests men generally."

But the hermits of Grub Street and North Pond emerge together into the same clearing on the most important point: they preferred solitude to company. Knight, after being caught and put in minimum security prison, couldn't bear being around others, those myriad faces full of confusing information. As for Welby, who dodged a sibling's double bullets to spend half of his life out of the world, *"Nunquam minus solus, quam cum solus*: He was never better accompanied, or less alone, than when alone."

The moon's two-sidedness seemed a relief to me after such paradoxes. Facts – such as the air temperature on the surface of the moon dropping to -183°C at night and climbing to 106°C during the day – struck me as both calming and consoling. But a full moon – even a super blue blood moon – eventually wanes, new phases occur, and the newness of a new moon, like the newness in any human life, can't be seen right away. Still, I kept walking on the frozen dark side of consciousness, waiting to float, diving deeper into the history of hermits and solitude, and into my own capacity for whatever newness I was moving toward.

ONE DAY, THE POSTAL CARRIER DELIVERED A COPY OF *CONSIDER THE Ravens: On Contemporary Hermit Life*, by Paul A. Fredette and Karen Karper Fredette. I dropped into it like a shell that a raven drops in an effort to crack it open.

A few hours later, I re-emerged, having forced myself to stay with the authors despite their relentless religiosity. Is there no one, I wondered as I sighed heavily after yet another reference to indwelling with God, who chooses a solitary path without wanting to pray endlessly to some fantasy figure? I didn't believe in the hereafter; I believed in the present, which is apparently what a hermit's life is supposed to entail, at least according to this book. Much is made about not worrying and not fearing, about living in the moment, about being mindful. For example, the author references the famous story told by the popular Buddhist monk Thich Nhat Hanh in which a guest to his house offered to wash the dishes after a meal. The monk says,

> Go ahead, but if you wash the dishes, you must know the way to wash them. . . .
>
> . . . The first is to wash the dishes in order to have clean dishes, and the second is to wash the dishes in order to wash the dishes.

With the greatest of respect, I had to disagree. "The miracle of life while standing at the sink" seemed as preposterous to me as experiencing nothing. Yes, of course, I got the point, but even though I hate washing the dishes, I was more than capable of mindfulness at other times, just as many people are. A person can also work a job they don't particularly like and still enjoy plenty of mindfulness in their leisure hours.

But I have to admit that I was already suspicious of the whole married Mark Zuckerberg kind of hermit that the authors of *Consider the Ravens* found acceptable. Particularly amusing to me was the following passage, which I considered reading aloud to my gregarious wife: "Another arrangement exists where only one spouse is drawn to solitude. If the partner understands and supports this desire, a loving, workable lifestyle can be developed which allows the solitary spouse to devote the majority of his or her time to prayer and silence while the other takes care of the necessary activities which modern life requires."

"Hey, honey," I imagined calling out, "I'm going to meditate for a while. You might want to wash all the dishes in the sink. But be sure you're washing them when you wash them." Of course, human history is basically the history of men doing things while women take "care of the necessary activities which modern life requires," so, in the end, my amusement faded rather quickly.

In any case, the title's reference to the following biblical passage tended to sum up my whole problem with at least the Christian ideal of living a simple solitary life: "Consider the ravens; they do not sow; they do not reap; they have neither cellar nor barn – yet God feeds them. How much more important you are than one of these!" While I might think that my own life is more meaningful to me than a bird's life, and while I would likely kill an animal to save a fellow human, I've never been under the delusion that our species has some sort of special birthright to lord it over all other creatures. But then, as I say, I wasn't a religious seeker after a spiritual solitude. I had no desire to "be buried with Christ," like the medieval anchorites, or to do any kind of penance. Overall, the hermit life, as described by the married author-hermits of North Carolina, sounded earnest, dour and, frankly, broken rather than whole.

But *Consider the Ravens* does contain some useful wisdom and inter-esting information regardless. In fact, enough wisdom and information to keep me from straying off the solitude path entirely, especially a tidbit such as "Islands around the world apparently appeal to hermits." This quota-tion was particularly apt in my case, of course, but I was still deep into northern Alberta's winter, and besides, my little silt islands weren't the tropical type that constitute Edmontonians' daydreams in January. In fact, when I thought of Alf Harley's island in relation to *Consider the Ravens*, I saw loneliness and death more than spiritual awakening; I heard the river and the daybreak pipings of birds in the marsh rather than tiny digital explosions. (Yes, modern hermits can apparently unwind from long spells of prayer by playing video games. Even the stoical Christopher Knight stole hand-held Nintendo games to while away the hours.) The comfort of the current solitary, at least of the Christian type, suggests that the book should be properly titled *Consider the Ray-Bans*.

But bad puns aside, I had no real interest in mocking anyone else's call to greater quiet and reflection. By my age, I understood that every human carries a unique kind of baggage, much of it more haunting or at least more challenging than mine. And certainly the authors of *Consider the Ravens* were sincere in their desire to escape the trivialities, noise, violence and material obsessions of Western culture. I just didn't think that they were talking about real solitude.

Not surprisingly, however, they made multiple references to every mod-ern religious solitary's favourite author: Thomas Merton, a Trappist monk and the author largely responsible for the mid-twentieth century's resurgent interest in hermit life. Merton, to my relief, appeared to recognize the true nature of solitude, at least as it relates to Alf Harley, Christopher Knight and thousands of others who have withdrawn from society. The Fredettes' book includes this intriguing Merton sentence: "The call to perfect solitude is a call to suffering, to darkness, and to annihilation." I made a mental note to read more of Merton's writings on solitude before I returned once more to my late-night walks under the indifferent moon.

TIME PASSED. I DID WHAT MY FAMILIAR LIFE REQUIRED, INCLUDING washing the dishes, but I had an uncanny sense that I had vanished from the world. Instead of going to cafés, where I usually chatted with the staff or else encountered a neighbour, I chose to stay home. No longer on screens, except to take a peek at email, I became blissfully unaware of the goings-on of the greater world, events that had never given me anything more than disquiet of some kind. Because my wife communicated with our three teenagers by cellphone texts, I stopped answering the landline, and used it only to call my elderly mother. Day by day, I *was* withdrawing, but I still had no idea where the path was leading me. As for sensory deprivation, I was far too in love with coffee, music and books to walk that diverging road. Almost hilariously, I still couldn't bring myself to experience something as simple as a float in a tank of Epsom salts.

Instead, I took longer walks, usually between 1:00 a.m. and 3:00 a.m.; the loss of feeling in my extremities due to the frigid temperatures about the only sensory deprivation I was prepared to accept. Somehow, even within a family within a large city, I was erasing my steps in the world. I wasn't unique, however. When the authors of *Consider the Ravens* sent out a survey to hermits (yes, I know . . .), they were "continually surprised to receive new subscriptions from denizens in the 'canyons' of New York City, proving that genuine solitude can be found in one of the busiest metropolises in the world."

Perhaps. But what appears to be genuine solitude might be loneliness, isolation and depression instead. As John D. Barbour points out in *The Value of Solitude: The Ethics and Spirituality of Aloneness in Autobiography*, "Solitude is often confused with related concepts such as loneliness, isolation, alienation, and privacy, and these ideas are often blurred . . . solitude itself is not an emotion but a condition. The state of being disengaged from other people may be accompanied by various emotions or by none at all." In her book *The Lonely City: Adventures in the Art of Being Alone*, Olivia Laing goes so far as to suggest that the emotional hell of urban social disengagement is more harrowing because the proximity of so many other human beings ought to, but doesn't, dispel a sense of isolation. "You can be lonely anywhere," she writes, "but there is a particular flavour to the loneliness that comes from living in a city, surrounded by millions of people."

Of course, the Digital Age didn't create urban alienation. Bartleby the scrivener and Dostoevsky's Underground Man make a strong case for the nineteenth-century version of the problem, as do the aptly titled Robinson poems of the vanishing poet Weldon Kees, who either jumped off the Golden Gate Bridge in 1955 or else withdrew into Mexico, a plan that he often mentioned to friends. A few of those friends even claimed to have seen Kees in Mexico City decades later, though it's more likely that they saw only what their hopeful imaginations inspired. After all, Kees, who has been described as the world's bleakest poet, routinely walked to the Golden Gate Bridge to stand at the railing and gaze into the fog. The last person who ever heard from him, the film critic Pauline Kael, said that he phoned her and, in a despairing voice, asked the most hauntingly human question there is: "What are *you* going through?"

Had I substituted the moon and a flapping nylon tarp for a bridge and a thickening fog? No. I wasn't an unhappy man whose spirit was unravelling under the onslaught of financial struggles and personal setbacks (Kees's marriage had ended less than a year before his disappearance). What brought me back to Kees was the name he gave to his most memorable poetic character. What else should an alienated, self-marooned post–World Wars urban isolate be called but Robinson? Little wonder, then, that Malcolm Cowley wrote the following descriptive blurb for Kees's final book of poems: "These are poems about Robinson, the average popular, despondent man, shipwrecked by middle life and cast away on a waterless island. They are felt poems about unfeeling and liquid poems about the dry heart of an era. In his own voice, recognizable in every line, the poet speaks for us all."

Consider this portrait of Robinson in the city, and note how the physical proximity that Olivia Laing mentions is no relief at all, but is instead a compounding of the misery:

Robinson walking in the Park, admiring the elephant.
Robinson buying the *Tribune*, Robinson buying the *Times*, Robinson
Saying, "Hello. Yes, this is Robinson. Sunday
At five? I'd love to. Pretty well. And you?"
Robinson alone at Longchamps, staring at the wall.

Robinson afraid, drunk, sobbing Robinson
In bed with a Mrs. Morse. Robinson at home;
Decisions: Toynbee or luminol? Where the sun
Shines, Robinson in flowered trunks, eyes toward
The breakers. Where the night ends, Robinson in East Side bars.

There is a strong sense throughout Kees's entire work that other people, while they might not be Sartre's hell, are certainly no great help either. If one is like Thoreau, disinterested in what interests men generally, can there be any other fate besides loneliness? Can solitude, in fact, be a comfortable and preferable condition?

Not for Kees's Robinson. Perhaps Jay Gatsby, in his much wealthier urban isolation, trembling under the stars as he stares at the famous green light across the waters of Long Island Sound, experiences a kind of ecstasy that not even his old love can rival. But Robinson, when he isn't at the zoo or sobbing in bed with a Mrs. Morse, finds no comfort in his domestic hermitage. Here again, almost contemporaneous with Thomas Merton, is that suffering, darkness and annihilation that the Trappist monk describes as real solitude. But most disturbing to me, in my own solitary journey, was Robinson's relationship to moonlight:

These are the rooms of Robinson.
Bleached, wan, and colorless this light, as though
All the blurred daybreaks of the spring
Found an asylum here, perhaps for Robinson alone,

Who sleeps. Were there more music sifted through the floors
And moonlight of a different kind,
He might awake to hear the news at ten,
Which will be shocking, moderately.

This sleep is from exhaustion, but his old desire
To die like this has known a lessening.
Now there is only this coldness that he has to wear.
But not in sleep. – Observant scholar, traveller,

Or uncouth bearded figure squatting in a cave,
A keen-eyed sniper on the barricades,
A heretic in catacombs, a famed roué,
A beggar on the streets, the confidant of Popes –

All these are Robinson in sleep, who mumbles as he turns,
"There is something in this madhouse that I symbolize –
This city – nightmare – black –"
                                    He wakes in sweat
To the terrible moonlight and what might be
Silence. It drones like wires far beyond the roofs,
And the long curtains blow into the room.

"Uncouth bearded figure squatting in a cave." That line certainly suggests that the poet had Robinson Crusoe in mind, but it was the nightmare city, the restless sleep under the terrible moonlight and the droning silence that made my hands tremble as I laid my copy of *The Collected Poems of Weldon Kees* on my desk. There was no creature comfort in such isolation, no relentless lover to seduce the spirit back to ecstasy. Yet I couldn't stop rereading the poem. What did Kees mean by "moonlight of a different kind"? Was that the moonlight I experienced each night on my solitary walking reveries, or was I in some sort of danger by not recognizing the peril in my lunar obsession?

Reading the final two Robinson poems only made matters worse. In "Relating to Robinson," the poet-narrator sees the isolated figure as a terrifying doppelgänger leading him to annihilation, and in "Robinson," it is the absence of Kees's persona that constitutes the terror:

The pages in the books are blank,
The books that Robinson has read. That is his favourite chair
Or where the chair would be if Robinson were here.

The reader is forcefully reminded of the isolated sailor whose story clearly seems to be at least a partial inspiration for Kees's muse: "Robinson alone provides the image Robinsonian."

Several hundred years on from Henry Welby's self-exile, but here again was that curious two-sidedness, Tenzin Palmo's troubling duality, that dark and light side of the moon, summarized in the Latin phrase *Nunquam minus solus, quam cum solus*, which translates as "He was never better accompanied, or less alone, than when alone." Except, of course, without the comfort of religion, Kees's Robinson can only look into a mirror that "reflects nothing at all." Maybe that mirror was the same as the screens of all those earbudded urban isolates sitting in cafés and gazing into their cellphones and laptops. Or maybe the blank mirror could also be the full moon. In any case, the more I read, the harder it was to remain sanguine about my growing solitude. Even if I had intended to find God, and I certainly didn't, could solitude ever be anything but a glimpse of death?

When I finally delved into the writings and life of Thomas Merton, and discovered how often he wished to "disappear," and how "So I will disappear" were among the last words he spoke on the day he was found electrocuted in his room in Bangkok, I couldn't separate him, God or no God, from Weldon Kees and his longing to vanish. The authors of *Consider the Ravens* at least recognize the dangers of a solitary life, asking if a taste for it might be a sign of psychosis, a major depression or the cliché of a midlife crisis that requires change for change's sake.

Good questions, but then the authors provide a wholly unsatisfying answer: "The one thing that we are most certain about is that there is an aching void at our center." Does it really have to be so profoundly wound-based, this longing for solitude? Perhaps for some. But I didn't feel an aching void, nor was I in recovery from trauma. I also knew that I wasn't just looking to meditate for an hour a day so that I could return fully energized to managing my stock portfolio. The stakes were exactly these: to spend the majority of my time alone in the last decades of my life, or to spend the majority of that time with others. Try as I might, I couldn't laugh the situation away.

BY NOW, I KNEW THAT CHRISTOPHER KNIGHT WASN'T A HERMIT AT ALL. In the book that Finkel eventually published about him (*The Stranger in the Woods: The Extraordinary Story of the Last True Hermit*), the search for God barely even comes up. Clearly, Knight was a recluse not a hermit. Even though dictionary definitions of these words often use them interchangeably, the fact remains that someone who withdraws from the world largely out of a distaste for society and without any particular God or spiritual path in mind is a recluse. But the definitions didn't matter to me as much as the vanishing did. Knight, Richard Byrd, Tenzin Palmo, Henry Welby, Thoreau, Montaigne, Weldon Kees, Thomas Merton and Alf Harley: to varying degrees, they all stepped out of the current of ordinary life. To what end? Were they really better off than if they had stayed in the current?

In one of his most characteristically enigmatic short stories, Nathaniel Hawthorne explores what happens when a person excuses himself from his own life without actually committing suicide. The protagonist of "Wakefield" decides one day that he will not return to his home and wife in the centre of London, but will instead take up lodgings the next street over without informing anyone of his decision. For the next twenty years, Wakefield – wearing a reddish wig and image-altering clothes – hides from his old life and periodically catches glimpses of his "widow" when he's out walking alone late at night. In the first few days after making his startling decision, however, he almost gives up the idea.

> Habit – for he is a man of habits – takes him by the hand, and guides him, wholly unaware, to his own door, where, just at the critical moment, he is aroused by the scraping of his foot upon the step. Wakefield! whither are you going?
>
> At that instant, his fate was turning on the pivot. Little dreaming of the doom to which his first backward step devotes him, he hurries away, breathless with agitation.

"Wonderful escape!" Hawthorne has his character think, as Wakefield rushes away, unaware that a "great moral change has been effected." The die has definitely been cast, and Wakefield, ordinary and vain as he is, adopts his disguise and soon slides into his new routine: "It is accomplished. Wakefield is another man. The new system being now established, a retrograde movement to the old would be almost as difficult as the step that placed him in his unparalleled position."

One small step for man, one giant collapse into inhumanity. Or, in Hawthorne's words, "It is perilous to make a chasm in human affections; not that they gape so long and wide, but so quickly close again!" Wakefield keeps to his new habits for ten years (that familiar halfway mark reminiscent of Henry Welby) without incident, but then, a scene! He suddenly comes face to face with his wife in a crowded marketplace and, terrified, runs to his lodgings and bolts the door: "All the miserable strangeness of his life is revealed to him at a glance; and he cries out, passionately, 'Wakefield! Wakefield! You are mad!'"

Now Hawthorne turns up the heat, suggesting that his character could not even claim the distinction of being a hermit: "He had contrived, or rather he had happened, to dissever himself from the world – to vanish – to give up his place and privileges with living men, without being admitted among the dead. The life of a hermit is nowise parallel to his. He was in the bustle of the city, as of old; but the crowd swept by, and saw him not."

Finally, after twenty years, which Hawthorne claims would "appear, in the retrospect, scarcely longer than the week," Wakefield walks past the dwelling he still considers his own. It is a gusty and rainy autumn night, and he suddenly feels an overwhelming desire to return to the warmth and love of his old domestic hearth. With the same crafty grin on his face that he wore twenty years earlier upon his disappearance, Wakefield crosses the threshold.

So ends the tale, except for Hawthorne's final reflection, which yet again brings up that haunting power of our potential choices: "Amid the seeming confusion of our mysterious world, individuals are so nicely adjusted to a system, and systems to one another, and to a whole, that, by stepping aside for a moment, a man exposes himself to a fearful risk of losing his place forever. Like Wakefield, he may become, as it were, the Outcast of the Universe."

Just by stepping aside for a moment, a man can lose his place forever. Here were my stakes exactly, which are everyone's stakes. Was it any wonder that my footfalls were so heavy on the frozen ground?

And yet, it's possible that a stepping aside might ultimately be banal rather than tragic, as happens to Dashiell Hammett's character Flitcraft in *The Maltese Falcon*. Like Wakefield, Flitcraft decides suddenly to abandon his familiar married-with-children middle-class life, except he leaves not only the small town in 1920s Washington state but also the country. After several years of being "vanished," however, he is spotted in a Seattle crowd by his wife, who hires the detective Sam Spade to track him down. When Spade locates the delinquent husband, he learns that Flitcraft has remarried and taken up what is, in almost every respect, the exact life he left behind years before. Fascinatingly, Flitcraft's explanation for his behaviour might have been penned by Hawthorne just as well as Hammett. One day, as he's walking along the street near a construction site, a beam falls from above and misses Flitcraft by inches. The event shocks him. He had always been a man "in step with his surroundings," but after the near-accident, Flitcraft's attitude changed dramatically. As Spade explains, "What disturbed him was the discovery that in sensibly ordering his affairs he had got out of step, and not into step, with life. He said he knew before he had gone twenty feet from the fallen beam that he would never know peace until he had adjusted himself to this new glimpse of life. By the time he had eaten his luncheon he had found his means of adjustment. Life could be ended at random for him by a falling beam: he would change his life at random by simply going away."

When Flitcraft returned to Washington after wandering around for a few years, he settled into what was essentially his old life without even seeming to care that he had almost become Hawthorne's "Outcast of the Universe," merely by taking a step aside. Again, in the words of the enigmatic detective Sam Spade: "He wasn't sorry for what he had done. It seemed reasonable enough to him. I don't think he even knew he had settled back naturally into the same groove . . . But that's the part of it I always liked. He adjusted himself to beams falling, and then no more of them fell, and he adjusted himself to them not falling."

What I took from these two fictional stories of vanishing was that the human heart is itself a system, albeit a chaotic one, and that we are always in danger of stepping aside from common sympathies. After all, even the "fact-based" story of Christopher Knight (many people in Maine doubt the veracity of his hermitage story) is a painful underlining of how the self can take precedence over all other considerations. At twenty years old, Knight vanished from the world of systems just as if he had committed suicide, and he didn't let his parents or his siblings know about his decision. For twenty-seven years! He claimed that there was too much risk of being captured if he confided in anyone. He also said that, of all the members of his family, he missed his younger sister the most, a younger sister with Down syndrome, because she was closest to him in age. This younger sister, who, according to the neighbours of the obsessively private Knight family, no one had seen in decades, must have missed her older brother terribly. Yet Christopher Knight could not act by putting others' feelings ahead of his own. Is this normal egocentrism, or a sign of mental illness? The question hangs over all the romantic speculation surrounding the North Pond Hermit's seclusion, and largely remains unanswered. It seems that a stepping away from the familiar path, whether fictitious or real, inevitably ends in a resolution whose threshold we are not invited to cross. Hawthorne and Hammett leave Wakefield and Flitcraft in a kind of unplumbable stasis – we simply don't know the end of their stories beyond the page. Nor do we know the ultimate fate of the definitely real Christopher Knight. Finkel leaves him back at his mother's house where he is perhaps pondering suicide and where he is most certainly longing for the solitude that he lost when the off-duty police officer captured him burgling a cabin for the thousandth time. North Pond Hermit, whither are you going?

After twenty-seven years of extraordinary solitude, how can conventional life measure up? Perhaps Wakefield stays with his wife until death, and perhaps Flitcraft has to adjust to another falling beam, but either way, the next choice seems oddly banal even if it might be haunting. Christopher Knight, once a remarkable hermit, is now just another lonely and broken human in our apocalyptic millennium.

Alexander Selkirk, the real-life castaway whose story Defoe likely used to create Robinson Crusoe, had his fifteen pre-Warhol minutes of fame in London society in the early part of the eighteenth century, but then the world moved on from him and he was left alone with his marooned memories and hardscrabble financial existence.

While it's unlikely that the American poet Elizabeth Bishop drew on Selkirk's fate for her poetic imagining of Robinson Crusoe's life after his island solitude, it's clear that she knew right down to the bone the weight of ordinary existence relative to those rare human moments of intense significance. In her late poem "Crusoe in England," Crusoe narrates his own story, continuing on past explanations of his emotional and practical challenges while marooned to a final summation of his post-rescue years as boring, in large part because the living soul has dribbled out of material objects. Looking at a knife on his shelf, he recalls how intensely he used to implore its blade not to break, while now his eyes merely rest on the knife and pass on.

THE AIR MUST BE RIGHT OUT OF CHRISTOPHER KNIGHT'S BALLOON TOO. After the keen knife's edge of existence, how can the dull blade be borne with equanimity? Buzz Aldrin, the second most famous Apollo astronaut, the man who followed Armstrong onto the lunar surface, once wrote of his post-Apollo life, "I had been to the moon. What could I possibly do next? I suffered from what the poets call 'the melancholy of all things done.' Without some new goal, I was aimless." The living soul of life, it seems, is always in danger of dribbling away, even if your glory days didn't involve tropical islands, Himalayan caves or deep space.

But how, then, to respond? If I was suffering from a kind of inevitable melancholy that comes with advancing age, was my draw to solitude a healthy or a dangerous temptation? From my ongoing moon research, I already knew that Buzz Aldrin eventually returned full-force to the public eye, that his pop culture status as the inspiration for Buzz Lightyear in Disney's *Toy Story* reflected an eager, outgoing person who, despite his battles with clinical depression and alcohol, embraced his rather curious celebrity as the world's most famous runner-up astronaut.

But I still couldn't escape those first solitary human steps on the moon. In fact, as the winter cold continued, and my night walks grew longer, I seemed to hear Armstrong's steps come from behind me, as if in pursuit. Atheist I might have been, but a few lines from Francis Thompson's famous religious poem, "The Hound of Heaven," came to mind:

> Up vistaed hopes I sped;
> And shot, precipitated,
> Adown Titanic glooms of chasmed fears,
> From those strong Feet that followed, followed after.

I wasn't a Victorian Christian being pursued by God, but for a man born in 1964 whose childhood eyes widened with wonder at the Apollo 11 mission, I figured that Neil Armstrong probably came as close as any human ever has to the glory of a divine being. That I knew almost nothing about Armstrong's life after space shocked me a bit, so I set out to rectify the situation. Meanwhile, I orbited my usual life, trying not to isolate myself too quickly, for fear that, like a hasty diver, I might get sick and not be able to reach the surface again.

"Oh you always loved the astronauts," my mother said when I told her over the phone that I had become obsessed with the moon. (I wasn't going to tell her about the call to solitude, as I didn't want to worry her.) "Don't you remember all the toys you had? I remember I brought some little plastic astronauts home from the drugstore one time. You played with them every day for years. Used to take them into the bathtub too. They were just little plastic things. It was funny how much you loved them."

After I got off the landline, I went and leaned back on the couch, lost in memories. Do you recall the start of *Citizen Kane*, when Orson Welles as the old William Randolph Hearst character, is dying, all alone, and he whispers "Rosebud"? Well, I was having my own precariat-class Rosebud moment. That is, I could clearly see one of those little plastic figures – a red one, with a helmet and an air hose. I could see it floating in the bathtub. I could see my hand above it like a little planet. The vision was both wonderful and unnerving. Between that bathtub and the Float House, between a capsule and a coffin, lay every human being's remarkable journey. Did it have to descend into darkness before the darkness closed in? Francis Thompson asks,

> Whether man's heart or life it be which yields
>   Thee harvest, must Thy harvest-fields
> Be dunged with rotten death?

Elizabeth Bishop's poem about Robinson Crusoe certainly suggests that the answer is a frightening yes, for the closing lines refer to Friday's death by measles some seventeen years before.

But surely even in the face of death, perhaps especially at that time, we can choose to pull on the helmet of our solitude and prepare for liftoff. As Césare Vallejo writes,

> I will die in Paris, on a rainy day,
> on some day I can already remember.
> I will die in Paris – and I don't step aside –
> perhaps on a Thursday, as today is Thursday, in autumn.

Friday. Thursday. One small step, or not, to the side of life. For a person drawn to solitude, the matter is a weighty one, and possibly the only matter at all once a certain age is reached.

Yet I wasn't an unhappy man. In fact, it was my very happiness and love of life that wouldn't let me live in blissful disregard of mortality, of those pursuing steps that might just as well have come down off the moon for all I had ever understood of them. But I wasn't going to stand still to be caught. A greater or lesser solitude – either option was a reaction against death, against the experience of nothing. So I did what a man of the twenty-first century would do: I looked on eBay and found those exact little plastic 1960s astronauts that I had played with in the dirt of the Fraser River delta earth almost a half-century earlier. I even found a trio of the little figures in their unopened plastic wrapping for sale. The original price? Ten cents.

The asking price? Twenty-five dollars plus shipping. Well, I thought, that's a cheap cost for an Apollo mission. So I made the purchase.

As the astronauts travelled toward me, I arrived at the sad and rather reclusive moonscape of the elderly Neil Armstrong. Almost the first sentence I read about him – and most of the sentences are unrelenting authorized hagiography – took up a defensive position. In one of the hundreds of *Life* magazine books and articles on the space race (*Life* had an exclusive arrangement with NASA), I came across this odd comment: "Armstrong hardly turned into a hermit in his astronaut afterlife, and there's no question but that he was proud of what he – and his many associates – had accomplished."

Already I knew that where there's hermit smoke there's hermit fire. Hadn't I seen the effects of Alf Harley's burning driftwood years before I visited his island and felt, rather than saw, his dying solitude? That the word *hermit* immediately orbited the words *astronaut afterlife* told me a story that, within a few days of research, no amount of rah-rah official biography could cover up. The first man to walk on the moon was private to the point of invisibility, even within his own marriage. To say he was emotionally distant is an immense understatement. Seven years before Apollo 11, for example, when his two-year-old daughter died of a brain tumour, Armstrong reacted by returning to work within two days. Over time, his first wife could no longer bear her famous husband's shutting down, which included his unwillingness to talk about his grief, citing "years of emotional distance" when she filed for divorce in 1989.

Ironically, it was Armstrong's reserved demeanour, his unflappable cool under pressure, his apparent predictability, which might critically be called blandness, that led NASA to choose him as the first man to walk on the moon over the more openly ambitious and attention-seeking Buzz Aldrin. Even in 1923, long before the space race, D.H. Lawrence identified this quintessential American blend of impersonality and technological genius:

Even the winged skeleton of your bleached ideal
Is not so frightening as that clean smooth
Automaton of your uprisen self,
Machine American.

In a very real way, Armstrong represented the American Everyman ideal of his time and place: conventional, manly in terms of physical courage, intelligent but not a genius, generically attractive in a conservative, clean-cut way, silent. Add all of these attributes together and the one word NASA came up with was *safe*. Neil Armstrong wouldn't cause any trouble. As Thomas Mallon put it in a 2005 *New Yorker* article, "a short-haired dominating blandness seemed to go with the job."

Except, of course, Armstrong took that quality so far that he ended up being, if not trouble, then at least no real help to the space agency. After Apollo 11, NASA wanted him to be little more than a glorified salesman for their programs, setting him up in Washington in a nice office with a view of the Capitol, but it soon became obvious that the first moonwalker had other ideas. As early as 1971, a mere two years after leaving the bootprints that made him a celebrity, Mr. Middle America returned to Ohio, bought a dairy farm, took up a teaching position a half-hour away at the University of Cincinnati and, as far as the media were concerned, vanished. He gave almost no interviews over the next several decades, becoming a kind of interstellar J.D. Salinger.

But the reticence was much more involved than just shunning the media. Armstrong rarely talked about his astronaut days with anyone – it's possible he didn't even mention the moon to his immediate family. Why should he? As he said on the few occasions when he was willing to say anything about the Apollo 11 mission, he had a job to do and he did it. No waxing poetic on the accomplishment at all. In fact, his first wife said that he carried considerable guilt for all the attention he received, knowing as he did how many thousands of unsung heroes behind the scenes had made his momentous small step possible. Why he should he take all the credit? A commendable humility, perhaps, but hardly an attitude that NASA would be able to convert into a bigger budget. More to the point, it was an attitude that seemed, well, inhuman in some ways, ungenerous, certainly not in the spirit of optimistic exploration. But then, Armstrong was only giving his country what they originally wanted: a man who wouldn't make a fuss, not when his daughter died, not when he had to abort a docking mission at the last moment to save himself and a fellow astronaut, and not when he came back to Earth after walking on the moon. He was nothing if not true to himself: private to the point of invisibility even when physically present.

I BEGAN TO CHANGE MY ROUTINE, AS IF MOON-HAUNTED, JUST BACK FROM a landing. After cancelling one class, I cancelled another. Then, like the corporate Armstrong, unable to shrug off my responsibilities completely, I returned to work. But I didn't lecture. Instead, I gave in-class writing assignments, staring out at the young faces in front of me, each as inscrutable as the moon. I made excuses not to meet acquaintances for coffee, and, because of the late hours I was keeping, I slept on the couch in the living room. I told myself that I was being considerate of my wife, a light sleeper with a full-time job, but the truth was that I could now watch the moon in the southern sky outside the living room window as I drifted off to sleep. The solitude I had begun to enter somehow seemed less solitary and alarming when accompanied by one of humanity's most faithful companions. The moon's cold glow dimly lit the ocean-swell boughs of the giant blue spruce in our yard, casting shadows like huge moving Rorschach blots that I didn't even try to decipher. Most nights, the last image I saw before losing ordinary waking consciousness was the moon through branches like a glass ball in seaweed. Most mornings, I woke feeling lost, uncertain of who or where I was, eager to get through the required tasks of the day only so that I could return to my post-midnight walks, even though they were as disturbing as they were comforting. I seemed to have entered another world without fully leaving the familiar one – like Hawthorne's Wakefield.

Hawthorne, in fact, was often on my mind. He set many of his "romances" (most of which I had first read as a very young man) in the woods during moonlit hours, and even began his most famous work, *The Scarlet Letter*, by describing the effect of moonlight on the objects in a room:

All these details, so completely seen, are so spiritualized by the unusual light, that they seem to lose their actual substance and become things of intellect. Nothing is too small or too trifling to undergo this change and acquire dignity thereby. A child's shoe; the doll, seated in her wicker carriage; the hobby-horse; – whatever, in a word, has been used or played with, during the day, is now invested with a quality of strangeness and remoteness, though still almost as vividly present as by daylight. Thus, therefore, the floor of our familiar room has become a neutral territory, somewhere between the real world and fairy-land, where the Actual and the Imaginary may meet, and each imbue itself with the nature of the other.

But it was again the poet Elizabeth Bishop who captured my experience perfectly. In "The Man-Moth" she writes of a strange subterranean creature, a 1940s American female version of Dostoevsky's Underground Man, who crawls up from the earth in order to squeeze himself through the hole of the moon. Drawn by its light, the Man-Moth, like the astronauts, "trembles, but must investigate as high as he can climb." Always failing to reach his goal, he returns to "the pale subways of cement he calls his home," where he rides the subways all night, facing the wrong way, unsure of "the rate at which he travels backwards." (I was reminded of how the Apollo astronauts travelled upside down, with their feet toward the moon.) In this curious ephemeral Hawthornian world of the Actual and the Imaginary, the Man-Moth "dream[s] recurrent dreams" and fears "the third rail, the unbroken draught of poison" that runs outside the subway window. Finally, the poet brings us face to face with her strange creation, at once making our eyes and his as strange as any unvisited planets:

> If you catch him
> hold up a flashlight to his eye. It's all dark pupil,
> an entire night itself, whose haired horizon tightens
> as he stares back, and closes up the eye. Then from the lids
> one tear, his only possession, like the bee's sting, slips.

The Man-Moth (Bishop was inspired by a newspaper misprint of *mammoth*) can't be anything other than solitary in his strange nightly journey, and is, in fact, an early Bishop representation of the kind of melancholy isolation she would explore decades later in "Crusoe in England." It was an isolation she knew well herself, having been orphaned as a little girl (albeit not technically, for though her father died, her mother lived for decades in an insane asylum) and then spending much of her life travelling, as if seeking, like the Man-Moth, some way to avoid that deadly third rail (Bishop did struggle with alcoholism for much of her life). Poetry, her only possession, saved her, in the reading and the writing of it, just as a search for God saved that other solitary orphan, Bishop's contemporary, Thomas Merton.

But it was the Man-Moth's relationship to the moon that struck me. I too understood the unsettling reality of too much moonlight. I could feel it, even in the middle of the day, erasing my outlines – vanishing me. As Walter Benjamin writes, "The light pouring down from the moon is of little value in the arena of our daily existence. The area that it uncertainly illuminates seems to belong to a counter earth or a contiguous one."

Drawn as I was to the moon, I was a twenty-first-century realist and man of science. I knew that it was a lifeless rock and not some sort of succubus; I knew that it had been walked on by twelve humans between 1969 and 1972 and that those humans had left plastic bags of their ex-crement, as well as plenty of other junk, on the surface; I knew that the world of progress wanted to return to the moon only to mine its natural resources for profit; and I knew that the "terrible moonlight" wasn't even its own light but just a reflection of the sun's brilliance. In fact, I soon learned enough about the moon, scientifically, to adopt Neil Armstrong's utilitarian attitude toward it.

I learned that the most accepted theory of the Earth-moon relationship posits that a giant planetoid hurtled into the Earth 4.6 billion years ago, setting off a series of earthquakes and speeding up our world's rotation to its current once-every-twenty-four-hours schedule; and I learned that that planetoid, on impact, drove its mineral core, mostly iron, deep into the Earth, before spinning off, a mere fragment of its original bulk, to be cap-tured in Earth's orbit as our familiar legendary moon, a sort of counter or contiguous Earth, to use Walter Benjamin's terminology. I learned that the moon, having no atmosphere, is under constant bombardment by various sizes of space matter, thereby explaining the large craters on its surface visible from the Earth with the naked eye. I also learned that the moon is a quarter of a million miles away, that it exerts a terrestrial influence on even as small a body of water as a cup of tea, and that it is in synchronous rotation with the Earth, meaning that we only ever see one side of it. Within a short period, I knew the highlights of the science about the moon. I also knew that the science was its least interesting or important aspect, that the mythology and romance of Earth's only satellite added a companion awe to our own divided selves, the yin and yang of pain and pleasure to our human condition. Either way, on the science or the mythology side, the moon was of little concern to most people.

And yet, its very abandonment by the indifferent screen-seduced humans that surrounded me made it – hang the science! – my brother in solitude, though, it must be said, a dangerous, unpredictable sibling, its visible craters like several marks on the forehead of Cain. Armstrong and Aldrin might have landed the *Eagle* on the Sea of Tranquility, but that didn't provide me with any particular equilibrium when I exchanged the warmth and electric light of my house for the arctic cold and moonlight of my solitary walks in the woods.

After all, the moon's usual winter colour was of that disquieting bone-white that Herman Melville, in one of the most celebrated chapters of *Moby-Dick*, "The Whiteness of the Whale," describes as terrifying, the very opposite of innocence and goodness:

> Is it that by its indefiniteness it shadows forth the heartless voids and immensities of the universe, and thus stabs us from behind with the thought of annihilation, when beholding the white depths of the milky way? Or is it, that as in essence whiteness is not so much a colour as the visible absence of colour, and at the same time the concrete of all colours; is it for these reasons that there is such a dumb blankness, full of meaning, in a wide landscape of snows – a colourless, all-colour of atheism from which we shrink?

Curiously, though Melville's Ishmael mentions white fields and white seas, polar bears and great white sharks, even albino humans as appalling, he doesn't single out the solitary moon. But perhaps he includes it in his final few sentences of the chapter, when he turns to "the mystical cosmetic which produces every one of [Nature's] hues, the great principle of light [that] forever remains white or colourless in itself, and if operating without medium upon matter, would touch all objects, even tulips and roses, with its own blank tinge – pondering all this, the palsied universe lies before us a leper; and like wilful travellers in Lapland, who refuse to wear coloured and colouring glasses upon their eyes, so the wretched infidel gazes himself blind at the monumental white shroud that wraps all the prospect around him."

Was I wretched and gazing myself blind? I didn't think so. At least not yet. As for Melville (who was, incidentally, a close friend of Hawthorne), he was something of a Neil Armstrong himself, having achieved early fame with his first two romances of the South Seas, and then withdrawing further and further into himself because he refused to give the public what they wanted. By the time of his death in 1891, the author of *Moby-Dick*, a man who had been as brave an explorer of human limits as any astronaut, was completely forgotten. And Ishmael, the narrator of Melville's great novel, named for the Biblical character in Genesis who would be "a wild ass of a man, his hand against everyone and everyone's hand against him"? He is picked up by another whaling ship after the terrifying splashdown of the *Pequod*. The only survivor of the final battle with Moby-Dick, he becomes, like Thomas Merton, Elizabeth Bishop and so many others, just "another orphan."

Perhaps, because of the moon, which in one Hindu creation myth is considered the centre of human consciousness, my thoughts became Melville-feverish and began to run wildly along that third rail that Bishop's Man-Moth could see outside the subway window. I wasn't losing my grip on reality, but I was losing my interest in it. Meanwhile, my readings in the orphaned Merton didn't help:

> The solitary is a man who has made a decision strong enough to be proved by the wilderness: that is to say, by death. . . .
> . . . Even the desire for solitude must be supernatural if it is to be effective and if it is supernatural it will probably also be a contradiction of many of our own plans and desires.

And in the next chapter: "The solitary is necessarily a man who does what he wants to do. In fact, he has nothing else to do. That is why his vocation is both dangerous and despised."

But Merton is also quick to point out that solitude as a mere brief interval in a busy life (as in ninety minutes in a flotation tank or seven days in a meditation retreat) is not a meaningful solitude. I had fallen somewhere in between, living hours of solitude each night but also maintaining my place in the world, a kind of Jekyll and Hyde of consciousness. The mental effects were both unnerving and delicious. I began to see doubleness and paradox everywhere: the moon as a barren rock only visible because of the sun; Thomas Merton, the seeker after God's light, killed in a hotel room by man's electricity; Henry Welby never better accompanied, or less alone, than when alone.

One night, after the cloud cover of the past few days had finally cleared and a three-quarter moon cast sufficient light on my path, I stopped halfway across a four-lane paved bridge seventy feet above the Mill Creek Ravine and stared down through the treetops at the serpent-winding ice. At 3:00 a.m., no traffic passed behind me, yet I could hear the familiar low throb of the urban grid and soundscape, a noise that, according to recent studies, raises our blood pressure even when we're not conscious of the decibels. A few miles away, on the northern horizon, the great vertical beehives of Edmonton's skyscrapers blazed their electricity against the moonlight. I looked down, thrilling myself with the vertigo, with the knowledge of, but not the longing for, the ease of an irreparable and permanent vanishing. Then I saw something in the combined bridge light and moon glow that made me draw back.

Fifty feet up in the black branches of a poplar standing alone on the creek bank dangled several pieces of footwear, some in pairs, some in singles, all hanging by their laces. Because the night was windless, the running shoes and winter boots didn't move, but were frozen in the air, as if in arrested steps. Straining my eyes, I counted thirteen shoes in all, then immediately intensified my gaze to avoid the number. Atheist or not, I have never seen any good reason to play around with old superstitions – if there were thirteen people at the Last Supper, and if the downtown skyscrapers had no thirteenth floors as a result, I wasn't eager to tempt Fate, even if I didn't exactly believe in it.

But thirteen shoes were all I could see, thirteen soundless steps. It didn't matter that I almost immediately knew why the footwear hung from the branches. I had been a boy and a teenager – I had thrown a pair of laced-together sneakers into the air to dangle them from telephone wires. Obviously, some group of young people had chosen this one tree to play a non-digital game of manual dexterity. Or maybe this game had several players over a number of years. What most struck me, after the initial sighting and counting, was that the shoes were so high up in the tree that it might have been just as easy to toss them onto the branches from above, from the bridge railing, almost exactly where I stood.

Anxiously, I looked along the sidewalk in both directions. No one. It was the middle of the night, still very cold. The grid humming all around me suddenly sounded like a predatory animal. My heart began to take quicker steps. I looked down at my feet. An even stranger vertigo – an epiphanic awareness of life as a certain number of steps immediately erased upon death – made me shiver. One day, I would be into those final thirteen steps, and so would everyone else, my wife and children included. Then the grid seemed to raise its decibel level. I turned, half-convinced that the moon had cleared its throat to remind me of what I had almost forgotten. The dark smear of craters peeled off those dangling human shoes, seemed a print of them, as if we had all walked in space once those two Apollo astronauts touched down and descended the *Eagle*'s ladder.

Except that my steps, and yours, and everyone else's save a dozen humans, several of whom were already dead, would no longer exist in time or space. The idea disturbed me, but in both directions at once. To leave no trace, or to leave a permanent trace. I heard Neil Armstrong whisper over my shoulder the sadly mysterious words he'd spoken in one of his rare interviews. When asked what he thought about his footprints remaining visible on the lunar surface for eons, he replied, "I wish somebody would go up there and clean them up."

The words hovered in my visible breath as if I had spoken them, then dropped off the bridge. Still, the shoes didn't move. And the words made no sound as they landed on the ice of the creek. From my position, I couldn't see the nylon tarp flapping a half-mile away, but I thought of it, and of Christopher Knight, his obsessive efforts to leave no tracks. Neil Armstrong was dead, and Knight was alive: I wondered if the North Pond Hermit, in his terrifying re-entry into the toxic atmosphere of quotidian time, wished that his twenty-seven years of footprints – thousands upon thousands of them – had become visible in his woods almost as solitary as the moon.

My legs felt heavy when I finally moved away from the railing. When I took my eyes off those thirteen shoes hanging like executions, each step felt as momentous as those staring down from 250,000 miles away. But impermanent, without particular resonance for my kind, though perhaps with an even greater meaning in their insignificance.

Awake in a city of a million people, more aware of their fate, as well as my own, than I had ever been, I couldn't embrace this kind of solitude as a gift, I couldn't agree with Merton who wrote, "The further I advance into solitude the more clearly I see the goodness of all things." But if I couldn't see goodness, I could see, at least, a form of dark and compelling magic. Christ had to remove his sandals, and Hitler his boots. The hands that touched the straps and laces made an icy cupping around the Earth and moon as I made my heavy and trackless way home.

THAT NIGHT, I COULDN'T FALL ASLEEP. MY HEART PACED IN MY CHEST AND I tortured myself by counting each step, half-afraid that I was into the final thirteen. Foolish, yes, but consciousness is like that for anyone who tries to honour it. Philip Larkin, who explains the horror of apprehended death so vividly in "Aubade," could nonetheless dismiss childhood as one long boredom. But at what other period of life can an intelligent human live fully and honestly without feeling that encroaching black shadow? From adolescence on, in varying degrees, a sensitive human (and why be concerned with any other kind?) knows who his most faithful companion is, knows that the white bone of the moon is Yorick's skull held aloft by Hamlet. Yes, yes, it isn't anything of the sort. It is a barren rock that reflects sunlight, a cosmic dump site degraded by science and industry, just like the Earth.

But Neil Armstrong is dead and his footprints remain. He took thirteen final steps on the Earth, but the steps he took over a two-and-a-half-hour period on July 20, 1969, walk right over his terrestrial journey. As I lay on the couch, away from my wife's side, fancies of even greater strangeness came to me. What had happened to Armstrong's body? In particular, to his feet? If it was true, as Richard Nixon declaimed on the deck of the *Hornet*, the ship that brought the Apollo 11 astronauts back from their splashdown eighty miles off the Hawaiian Islands, that "this is the greatest week in the history of the world since the Creation," should Neil Armstrong's feet be simply turned to ashes? Galileo, the father of modern astronomy, is today so honoured that a severed middle finger from his right hand is preserved beneath a bubble of glass in the Museo Galileo, in Florence. Withered and twisted and still pointing upwards, like God's digit in Michelange-lo's painting, Galileo's finger has achieved the status of a holy relic. But what Galileo pointed toward was the heavens that Armstrong actually journeyed to and walked upon. Surely his feet deserved a more permanent and glorious tribute. The boots, no doubt, are prominently displayed in a NASA museum, but how individual and personal are a pair of space boots compared to the flesh and bone slipped into them?

I tried to settle my thoughts and my nerves. My heart only walked faster. The nearly full moon tangled in the branches watched me, as usual, without emotion. I felt numb in all my extremities. And then, in that most mysterious of processes that defies all of man's systems, my brain shifted from one state to another, and I was gone again from the world that we call real.

EXHAUSTED THE NEXT MORNING, I AVOIDED MARKING STUDENT WRITING and returned to the scene of last night's haunting vision. Perhaps, in my (literal) lunacy, I had imagined the shoe-tree. I decided to go down into the ravine to the base of the poplar along the creek bank. The footing was a little treacherous, being some distance off the path, and I wasn't at my sharpest, but I finally reached the spot.

Oddly, a rough red woollen blanket lay at the base of the tree, not quite wrapping around it as in a nursery, but a few feet away like a dried splash of blood. I looked up into the branches. Sure enough, there hung the shoes, though they looked quite different in the sunlight and from below. A slight breeze swung them a few inches from side to side, as if an invisible presence was gently breathing in the proximate air. Far above, the hum of traffic rose and fell, yet I still felt the eerie sensation of being as alone as I had been six hours before. I almost expected to see myself looking down from the railing and finding no one on the ground.

As the traffic noise briefly subsided, I looked at the blanket again. It wasn't frozen stiff or covered in snow, so it couldn't have been on the ground very long. But who would have come here recently? And why? I looked up into the branches so quickly that I almost lost my balance. Eleven, twelve, thirteen. The same number of shoes. Black and purple, yellow, dull green: they were more ordinary in the sunlight, as everything is. Yet it would not have been easy to loop them so high around the branches. Hardly a marvel of human ingenuity, but from a certain perspective, we don't need rockets and other planetary bodies to give us a disorienting sense of wonder. The red blanket worried me. How had it come there? We had had snow in the night. My own footprints stretched away behind me, but no others were visible. Maybe the blanket had been dropped off the bridge between my two visits.

The problem was a small one, but it seemed connected to everything else I was going through. Besides, I felt a frisson of pleasure as I stood by the tree, perplexed. Just as Dostoevsky's Underground Man explains how we will keep tonguing a sore tooth just for the pleasure of the pain, just as Philip Larkin argues that feeling nothing is the worst fate of all, I told myself that every ordinary detail of my life had been invested with meaning. That is to say, though I stood in sunlight, I walked beneath the moon.

FOR PROFESSIONAL REASONS, I STILL HAD TO CHECK EMAIL. ONE MORNING, desultorily scanning my inbox, I learned from a cousin that my favourite aunt had died after a fall and a rapid decline in hospital at the age of ninety-three. Her husband, one of my father's younger brothers, had predeceased her by a decade. The two had made a lovely couple, full of affection for each other, full of good humour and kindness. My uncle, a beekeeper and salmon fisherman, had fought in the liberation of Europe in WW II and had seen close friends killed; the experience had given him a refreshingly cavalier and open-minded attitude toward the rest of his life. He once told me that he felt that he owed it to his fallen comrades to enjoy all the things that they had had stolen from them. My aunt, who fished alongside her husband and did her fair share of the work, was just as gentle upon the earth and equally light in spirit, sheltering always the small girl inside of her who had learned to swim in Boundary Bay, just a few miles from my hometown of Ladner.

I stared at the computer screen, unable to move time forward. Death, the great isolation, had laid its bony hands on both of my shoulders. Experience nothing, I mouthed to the unfriendly air, feeling again that uncanny paradoxical sense of floating and heaviness that comes with grief.

Naturally, thinking of my aunt and uncle, I then thought of my own parents. My father had died five years before his younger brother, in 2001, but my mother was still alive, still in the family home in her ninety-second year. An urn with my father's ashes waited in the cedar hope chest in her bedroom for that time when her own ashes would be mingled with them and then spread on the waters of the Fraser. I suspected that two urns of ashes, one for my aunt and one for my uncle, would now wait for a proper time of ceremony, even perhaps of a similar kind. We are, after all, a coastal family, people of the river tides and the salty ocean winds.

Three urns of ashes for three people I had loved dearly. Was my desire for withdrawal, for a deeper, richer experience of every moment, akin to my uncle's commitment to the young men who had died nearly seventy-five years ago? Or was it a form of selfishness and cowardice, an anti-human and wrong-headed, wrong-hearted attempt to engage with that most dangerous, unpredictable and yet intimately familiar animal of which I could not fully renounce myself?

One thing was becoming increasingly clear: a certain kind of romanticism and privilege accompanied almost every work on solitude that I had yet encountered. Why, for example, should Thomas Merton's humourless wrestling with God, or anyone else's, be of such importance? Why should Henry David Thoreau's preference for the natural world be so deified and his basic misanthropy so accepted? Why should almost every new book published on the subjects of silence, loneliness, solitude and isolation be written by white urban professionals who seemed to just want a few days free of Twitter and of climbing the career ladder?

It was little wonder that Alf Harley and the Apollo astronauts brought me back to earth: the former unknown, uncelebrated and experiencing a hard death; the latter heroic and famous, and almost universally confronting a slide into depression and meaninglessness after their missions had been completed. That echo of a splash that woke me from my sleep on several nights perhaps wasn't Alf Harley's 350 pounds dropping into the Fraser, but rather the splashdown in the middle of the ocean for each of the returning Apollo capsules. No doubt the sound was both events, or simply a slight rise in the sonic amplification of my own central nervous system.

Regardless, I knew that my particular journey was my own but that it was also freighted with the chill of that long-ago October and the even more enigmatic chill of deep space. And Christopher Knight stood right in the middle of all that cold and dark, perhaps stood there now, as I did, tracking the phases of the moon and wondering what his future held. For the North Pond Hermit, I would be a dilettante, nothing more than Jem sneaking up to the nightmare loneliness of Boo Radley and touching the side of that incomprehensible shelter.

But I wasn't playing games, nor were Merton or Thoreau. I wasn't a journalist looking for a good story on a currently marketable subject; I wanted to know what I could protect of a self and a time that were dying, maybe of a self and a time that had to die. The journey meant growth, but whether away from or toward others still remained in the balance.

I stood up from the computer, put on my winter layers, and like a bee who had taken on too much pollen, I took my excess of memories out under the binding arbitration of the changing and changeless moon.

BY THIS TIME, I HAD PLUNGED DEEPER INTO THE WRITTEN HISTORY OF solitude, had found, as a result of my fascination with Neil Armstrong's permanent bootprints and Christopher Knight's terror at leaving his footprints on the earth, Thoreau's essay "Walking" and Jean-Jacques Rousseau's *The Reveries of the Solitary Walker*. Without a conscious effort, I was fighting to retain my common humanity by seeking the fellowship of my brothers in isolation. Put another way, I was walking through print and trying to see if the tracks could provide a direction.

As it turned out, "Walking" is as much about thinking and living as about any movement of the material body. For Thoreau, a man most famous for staying put for two years, equated the capacity for walking long distances alone – at least four hours every day, recording upwards of twenty miles each time – to a capacity for freedom and independent thought. The sedentary man is, in short, a slave to systems, a domesticated and therefore uninspiring creature. It astonished Thoreau that the mass of men seem content to endure their days without throwing off their fetters and going for a long walk, ideally in the auroral light and toward the west, the direction of newness. "Two or three hours' walking," he says, "will carry me to as strange a country as I expect ever to see."

Walking, in other words, isn't about exercising the body: "The walking of which I speak has nothing in it akin to taking exercise, as it is called, as the sick take medicine at stated hours – as the swinging of dumb-bells or chairs; but is itself the enterprise and adventure of the day." On the contrary, going for a walk is the equivalent of a well-adjusted and healthy suicide, in the sense that civilization and all its discontents become meaningless to a true saunterer (a word "beautifully derived 'from idle people who roved about the country, in the Middle Ages, and asked charity, under the pretense of going *à la Sainte Terre*,' to the Holy Land, till the children exclaimed, 'There goes a *Sainte-Terrer*,'" a Saunterer, a Holy-Lander"). But the extremity of Thoreau's position is best captured in sentences such as the following: "If you are ready to leave father and mother, and brother and sister, and wife and child and friends, and never see them again – if you have paid your debts, and made your will, and settled all your affairs, and are a free man, then you are ready for a walk."

By this standard, who in his right mind would go for a walk? Perhaps you had to be out of your right mind, at least as society is concerned. But what about the human affections? Using the above sentence as a measure, it's clear that Neil Armstrong was ready for a moonwalk and that Christopher Knight was ready for the Maine woods. As for me, I was, appropriately enough, caught between. I was prepared to leave a great deal behind – ambition, work, social media and almost all other people except for family – but what sort of Holy Land could I find if I wasn't willing to go the whole Thoreauvian distance? He writes, "Our expeditions are but tours, and come round again at evening to the old hearth-side from which we set out. Half the walk is but retracing our steps."

The old divide and doubleness again, the sun and the moon, going out to go inward, Henry Welby hunkered down in his house for half his life, all of us needing to lose ourselves to find ourselves. But while I could appreciate Thoreau's point – that a walk without a conscious desire for fresh perception is no walk at all – I felt, if not exactly like a tourist visiting some brochured version of myself, at least less certain of my intentions than the redoubtable misanthrope of New England.

I had higher hopes for Rousseau, if only because I quickly discovered that he had been responsible in a significant way for raising *Robinson Crusoe* to classic status. In *Emile*, to be specific, Rousseau cites Defoe's book as an essential component of a well-rounded education, which doubtless meant that the French author had some sympathy for the whole idea of solitude.

The beginning of *Reveries of the Solitary Walker* only confirms the fact: "I am now alone on earth, no longer having any brother, neighbour, friend, or society other than myself . . . But I, detached from them and from everything, what am I? That is what remains for me to seek." Envisioned as a series of ten meditations based on ten different walks during which the philosopher re-examined the events of his life, *Reveries of the Solitary Walker* faltered at the final few steps, with reveries eight and nine never revised and reverie ten unfinished due to its author's death. But I didn't have to read long into this most intimate book, which some describe as a memoir, to realize that Rousseau's urgent interest in his own past eerily mirrored my own:

> The leisurely moments of my daily walks have often been filled with charming periods of contemplation which I regret having forgotten. I will set down in writing those which still come to me . . .
> . . . Reading them will recall the delight I enjoy in writing them and causing the past to be born again for me will, so to speak, double my existence.

Again, that curious doubling and halving that so often emerges in any work on solitude also appears in Rousseau. Yet his situation, in fact, had little relationship to mine in a worldly sense. Rousseau was a famous author whose revolutionary ideas about politics, religion, education and society had made him some powerful enemies and led to his nomadic exile. I was an obscure writer whose books had made little impression on even my country's literary society, let alone its larger culture. At any time, Rousseau might have been imprisoned or even executed for his philosophies; I was only in danger of being unread. Yet there were some points of contact between us when it came to the nature of existence itself.

I was particularly caught up by a paragraph in the "Fifth Walk" that might have been written today, and if so, would likely make zero impact on the multi-billion-dollar wellness industry:

> Everything on earth is in a state of constant flux. Nothing keeps the same, fixed shape, and our affections, which are attached to external things, like them necessarily pass away and change. Always beyond or behind us, they

remind us of the past which is no longer or anticipate the future which is often not to be: there is nothing solid in them for the heart to become attached to. Thus the pleasure that we enjoy in this world is almost always transitory; I suspect it is impossible to find any lasting happiness at all.

Rousseau's happiness, such as it was, bloomed most spectacularly in one place thirteen years before he died: an island in the middle of a Swiss lake. This is not surprising in a man who so greatly appreciated *Robinson Crusoe*, even if Rousseau's island contained a steward and his family and servants. On the Île Saint-Pierre, the philosopher often went out alone on walks through the verdant meadows or rowed himself around the lake, perfectly content to do nothing at all: "Everything I did during my stay there was in fact nothing more than the delicious and necessary pastime of a man dedicated to idleness."

How unlike the four-hundred-thousand-member team of NASA, how unlike the North Pond Hermit slipping through the woods to steal from cabins, how unlike Thoreau writing *Walden* and, most cuttingly of all, how unlike me going out each night, unable to sit quietly alone in a room. But Rousseau isn't talking about an unthinking, sedentary kind of life: "The idleness I like," he writes in book 12 of his *Confessions*, "is not that of the lounger, who sits there, arms crossed, wholly inert, and who no more thinks than he acts. It is at once that of the child, who is always in motion and always doing nothing."

But here again returns that problem of words often being no more than pretty cover for human heartache and failing. Between 1746 and 1751, Rousseau placed in a foundlings' hospital the five children he had had with his lifelong companion Thérèse Levasseur, an act that even in the eighteenth century struck others as indefensible. Then again, Rousseau, like so many writers who touch on solitude, didn't exactly have a stable upbringing: his mother died a few days after he was born; his only sibling, a brother, ran away from home; and his father, forced to leave Geneva or else be imprisoned due to a quarrel he had with a French captain, left him in the care of relatives when he was just ten. At thirteen, apprenticed to an engraver, Rousseau had to run away because his master was violent and tyrannical. He eventually found domestic calm and parental guidance with an older woman who, ultimately, made her young charge her lover.

While all of this took place in the eighteenth century, the fact that we can still find meaning in Rousseau's writing suggests that what he learned of human nature relates to what we know of the damage that can be done to the psyche in childhood. Yet Rousseau's early life, not to mention Neil Armstrong's or Christopher Knight's, isn't palatable to our mythmaking tastes.

But to return to the subject of walking: in truth, Rousseau doesn't describe it in his *Reveries* in the same detail that Thoreau does in his one essay, but both men insist that a long solo walk in nature creates a merging of the self with the universe that simply doesn't occur otherwise.

I hadn't exactly felt the blissfulness of that mystic union on my moonlit walks, but I had begun to sense the mysterious and oddly appealing doubleness of existence, the way that a growing desire for solitude inevitably leads one along a path to a different world, a world which, though contiguous, is nonetheless remote from the usual course of reality. Rousseau's word *reverie*, in fact, comes from the Latin *vagari* (to wander about), and denotes a state of heightened sensibility and inner pleasure, freed from social constraints, in which the mind enjoys seeing ideas floating along haphazardly. In that sense, I approached a reverie each night, but to what ultimate purpose? I wasn't a child, constantly in motion while doing nothing, but I felt like a foundling of the universe, drifting nightly on the same cold circuit, the umbilical plugged into a technological mainframe that could, like Merton's whirring fan, short-circuit my life altogether.

Despite my reading, I couldn't dismiss one overarching fact: a person didn't have to be orphaned or even unhappy to want to withdraw from the world.

IN 1857, CHARLES DICKENS WASN'T EXACTLY TRYING TO WITHDRAW FROM other people when he went on a series of thirty-mile all-night walks between his two London residences, but he was unhappy. To be specific, the forty-five-year-old world-famous novelist was battling an insomnia brought on by the guilt he felt over his affair with an eighteen-year-old actress. Wanting to leave his wife of twenty years, but unable to take the step, Dickens found that he could sleep only after he had walked all night through the great city, taking in all the surreal, lonesome and sometimes unsettling sights. The result of these rambling nocturnal experiences became one of Dickens's most popular personal essays, "Night Walks."

I read the essay early one evening and then, inspired by the sheer physical energy that went into this small (at least for Dickens) literary production, I extended my own nocturnal ramble that night. A few hundred yards beyond the shoe-tree, and another thirty yards down to the bottom of the ravine, I reached a curiously out-of-place structure, one of only two outdoor public swimming pools in Edmonton. As sad and lonely in deep winter as the city zoo, the Mill Creek Ravine pool was, of course, completely empty, its doors bolted shut, its concession stand shuttered, the lifeguard chair bereft of a lifeguard. From shallow end to deep end, from three feet to ten feet, the bone-white concrete bottom, flickering with shadows of branches made by the full moon's light, resembled nothing so much as the surface of that very moon.

I stood outside the high barbed-wire fencing near the deep end, trying to imagine a man or woman poised on the end of the diving board. But it was no use. I couldn't think my way out of the arctic cold; my imagination couldn't transcend its flesh long enough to enter a different season. But perhaps I wasn't close enough; perhaps, if I stood on that shimmering lunar surface, the faint smell of chlorine, like Proust's taste of the dipped madeleine, might catapult me into the full aqua folds of midsummer.

As I contemplated the barbed wire, estimating the likelihood of my success in climbing over without injuring myself, I felt again that unreal and exhilarating absence of other humans. No one was down here at 2:00 a.m. walking their dog; no one was skulking about, plotting some nefarious act. It was too cold for thieves and killers. Dickens's London could not have made a greater contrast. Of course, even in the mid-nineteenth century, that city in the early morning hours was a quiet and otherworldly place in relation to its daytime bustle. And Dickens masterfully captures the eerie atmosphere, writing of the river's awful look, of its reflected lights that seem to "originate deep in the water, as if the spectres of suicides were holding them to show where they went down." In a dripping rain, he walks past prisons and mental institutions, speculating on the forlorn lives inside. He contemplates the great dead in Westminster Abbey and he enters one of the theatres and walks upon the stage from where he regards the orchestra pit as "a great grave dug for a time of pestilence." The whole time, however, he is keen to have his solitude lifted by human company. Unfortunately, the humans he does encounter are often more disturbing than the prisons and empty theatres:

> Suddenly, a thing that in a moment more I should have trodden upon without seeing, rose up at my feet with a cry of loneliness and houselessness . . . the like of which I never heard. We then stood face to face looking at one another, frightened by one another. The creature was like a beetle-browed hair-lipped youth of twenty, and it had a loose bundle of rags on, which it held together with one of its hands. It shivered from head to foot, and its teeth chattered, and as it stared at me – persecutor, devil, ghost, whatever it thought me – it made with its whining mouth as if it were snapping at me, like a worried dog. Intending to give this ugly object money, I put out my hand to stay it – for it recoiled as it whined and snapped – and laid my hand upon its shoulder. Instantly, it twisted out of its garment, like the young man in the New Testament, and left me standing alone with its rags in my hand.

Later, seeking shelter in a coffee room in the Covent Garden Market, the proprietor still half-asleep, Dickens twice witnessed a bizarre cadaverous red-faced man enter, proceed to remove a large meat pudding from under his hat and, being given a pint of hot tea, a large knife, and a fork and plate, stab the pudding with the knife and tear it asunder with his fingers. The man's speech was even more disturbing than his behaviour: "On the second occasion of my seeing him, he said huskily to the man of sleep, 'Am I red tonight?' 'You are,' he uncompromisingly answered. 'My mother,' said the spectre, 'was a red-faced woman that liked drink, and I looked at her hard when she laid in her coffin, and I took the complexion.'"

Despite these unsettling encounters and his own unsettled state of mind (some critics believe he was suffering from bipolar disorder), Dickens never loses the human touch, never seems to consider solitude as an attractive option. Always, in "Night Walks," he gives the impression that there is a brighter, vividly peopled world just around the corner, a world that he intends to return to once his strange period of "Dry Rot" (a condition that comes upon men when they have been "living a little too hard") has passed. In the meantime, however, "the wild moon and clouds were as restless as an evil conscience in a tumbled bed, and the very shadow of the immensity of London seemed to lie oppressively upon the river."

After a ten-minute clamber, during which I tore one of my gloves, I succeeded in taking my own Dry Rot out into the middle of the dry swimming pool. Once there, I suddenly felt motionless and yet weirdly and speedily transported. Where was I? My breath poured out, white as the concrete below me and as the moon's surface a quarter of a million miles away. As I looked up, I looked down. As I looked down, I looked up. There was no smell of chlorine, only snow and ice and faint woodsmoke. The surface I stood on curved toward a horizon I couldn't see, while the moon was as small as the cold meat pudding torn asunder by Dickens's spectral friend. Suddenly I felt so dizzy that I thought I'd collapse. In a panic, I wondered if everything had been leading to this – a heart attack brought on by anxiety and lack of sleep. What a terrible find I would be, a drowned man in a dry pool in the middle of winter, his final steps making no sense to anyone, least of all his dead self.

Exhaling, I tried to make light of the situation. But here I was, in 2018, no different in kind than Dickens on the bare stage of a darkened theatre in 1857. The mind and the heart of midlife in conflict had brought us both to a point of stark contrast from which we would have to walk out alone. Dickens re-entered society, published perhaps his greatest novel (*Great Expectations*) and eventually died from a stroke at the age of fifty-eight. As for the problem that caused his insomnia, he separated from his wife but did not divorce her, choosing to set his young mistress up in her own home where he would visit her until his early death. That is, he neither left his wife (with whom he'd had ten children) nor gave up his mistress, a solution of the type that likely still occurs to famous and wealthy men.

Meanwhile, I considered only the barbed-wire fence and my dizziness. The solution to the problem that sent me out on my own night walks seemed more elusive than Dickens's solution to his problem. What was I to do – set my heart up in one house and my mind in another? Touch the human world of rags in brotherhood while recoiling from the touch? In any case, Dickens wasn't choosing between two women; he was choosing between two different imaginative versions of himself. So was I. Maybe that's always the choice we face – Christopher Knight driving in his Subaru to Florida and back, Neil Armstrong flying to the moon and back, Alf Harley dying in a boat that never went on the water and me, perhaps, completely alone in a public swimming pool and suffering a heart attack.

Easy, now. Easy. I recalibrated. I told myself, You're on the Earth not the moon, you're tired and confused not dying, you're an explorer of the possibilities of solitude not a solitary. Yet when I made my way, slowly and carefully, out of the white pit I had dug with fancy, I carried the moonlight like chalk on my shoulders and hair, and I looked twenty years older than I was, the ghost of myself that every old man is in relation to the craters and canyons of his lived time.

3:28 PM EST
YOUR ITEM IS ON ITS WAY.
We are writing to inform you that your recent GSP item has shipped from the Global Shipping Center. You should receive additional automated updates regarding delivery status.
Lot of 3 Red, White, and Blue MPC Plastic Spacemen Astronauts 2" in original package.
Thank you for being an eBay customer.
The Global Shipping Program Team.

Too tired to do anything else, I stared at the above email for much longer than it took to read it. My late, late Apollo mission had liftoff. Apollo 18. Thirty-five dollars US total price. And not a soul but me and an indifferent sales team somewhere on the planet paid any attention. I wondered if this

Apollo 18 mission would take longer than Apollo 11, which lasted seven days. And what would the mini-Armstrong, mini-Aldrin and mini-Collins find when they arrived in lunar orbit and saw my white, exhausted and sleep-cratered face? Aldrin's first words when he stepped on the moon were "Beautiful. Beautiful." and "Magnificent desolation." He was a military man and not a poet, but over the years, through his alcoholism and clinical depression, I wondered if he ever realized that he was describing himself, the world of every human arrival at the moment of self-consciousness.

But what exactly was that self? Where did it originate? The more I found out about the Apollo 11 astronauts – and Neil Armstrong in particular – the more they started to resemble the North Pond Hermit. (It certainly didn't discourage me from this line of thinking when I discovered that Armstrong's second marriage was to a woman named Carol Held Knight.) Besides having decidedly unpalatable families whose idea of domestic warmth resembled nothing so much as a kind of boot camp, besides having fathers who were obviously emotionally withholding and controlling, and besides being described by others as "ordinary," Neil Armstrong and Christopher Knight shared one thing above all others: they preferred their own company to anyone else's, and in that preference, they had to suffer.

In *Quiet: The Power of Introverts in a World that Can't Stop Talking*, Susan Cain points out that North American society aggressively markets and buys into the "Extrovert Ideal – the omnipresent belief that the ideal self is gregarious, alpha, and comfortable in the spotlight." Cain adds a few other traits to the extrovert profile: "prefers action to contemplation, risk-taking to heed-taking, certainty to doubt." The extrovert also "favors quick decisions, even at the risk of being wrong." According to Cain, "Introverts living under the Extrovert Ideal are like women in a man's world, discounted because of a trait that goes to the core of who they are." The Extrovert Ideal, of course, is perfect for a world built around industry, enterprise and profit, a world that the ambulatory Thoreau knew so well that it made him retreat from it in order to retain his health. Here he is, in the middle of the nineteenth century, on the subject of business: "This world is a place of business. What an infinite bustle! I am awakened almost every night by the panting of the locomotive. It interrupts my dreams. There is no Sabbath. It would be glorious to see mankind at leisure for once. It is nothing but work, work, work. . . . I think that there is nothing, not even crime, more opposed to poetry, to philosophy, ay, to life itself, than this incessant *business*."

The Extrovert Ideal and the central importance of business are more firmly entrenched in Western society than they were in Thoreau's day, and anyone who takes up his pen against them will make even less of an impact than Thoreau did. A year prior to my moonlit musings, I attended the high school commencement of my eldest son and had to sit through a two-hour encomium on leadership, teamwork and industry, while nary a word was spared for the deep human benefits of working alone or for working with a purpose other than advancing material/technological progress. But in that crowd of graduating teenagers sat more than a few Christopher Knights alongside their NASA-bound classmates, and even among the NASA-bound there must have been a few reclusive Neil Armstrongs. In any case, a person attracted to such questionable solaces as nature and solitude can't expect much help from society, a fact Thoreau understood so deeply that he opened "Walking" with the following paragraph: "I wish to speak a word for Nature, for absolute freedom and wildness, as contrasted with a freedom and culture merely civil – to regard man as an inhabitant, or a part and parcel of Nature, rather than a member of society. I wish to make an extreme statement, if so I may make an emphatic one, for there are enough champions of civilization: the minister and the school-committee and every one of you will take care of that." Of course, even ministers and high school principals, like the rest of us, constitute some blend of extroversion and introversion; it's just, where civilization is concerned, what we choose to wear publicly is the Extrovert mask.

Now, no one would ever argue that Armstrong and Knight didn't exhibit masculine qualities that are widely celebrated in our society: the ability to need no one else, to remain silent even to the point of being "emotionally unavailable," to be impressively resourceful under difficult circumstances, to shun the world's attention as ultimately unseemly and of little worth. Of course, looking at the Extrovert Ideal, it's easy to think of Armstrong – a fighter pilot and space traveller who escaped death on several occasions while flying due to quick thinking that might well have turned out badly – as an alpha male supreme. Obviously, there's a big difference between climbing out of a capsule a quarter of a million miles from home and stepping onto the moon while the whole world watches and stepping out of a Subaru in the Maine woods about two hundred miles from home after driving alone down to Florida with no one, not even your family, knowing where you are. By our culture's standards, Armstrong was a big success, a hero, married with children; Christopher Knight, on the other hand, was a failure, a nobody, a loner who'd likely never even held hands with a woman. But both men, after achieving what few humans could even conceive of achieving, downplayed their accomplishments, wanting only for the world to go away. Neil Armstrong after NASA and Christopher Knight after his hermitage were essentially the same man at the core, though the comparison is anathema to our extroverted culture.

Yet I could see Armstrong behind the glass of the small trailer in which the Apollo 11 astronauts were quarantined for three weeks (in case they'd brought back any lunar bugs). And I could see Knight behind the glass of the visiting room in the minimum security prison where Finkel interviewed him as Knight looked out at the inquisitive world with the same bewilderment and distaste. If you're the first man on the moon, of course, fame will never leave you alone and you must constantly fight it off. Decades after Apollo 11, for example, Armstrong had to endure the following bizarre incident.

In 2005, a barber in Lebanon, Ohio, who cut the famous astronaut's hair once a month was approached by a collector who offered to pay three thousand dollars for a small bag of the swept-up hair clippings. After the deal was made, when Armstrong got wind of it, he had his lawyers threaten legal action, citing an Ohio law that protects the privacy of celebrities. The resultant media attention scared off the reclusive first man on the moon, so he didn't proceed with the legal threat, asking only that his hair be returned (if possible) or that a three-thousand-dollar donation be made to a charitable organization of Armstrong's choice. Meanwhile, the bag of hair was purchased by a collector named John Reznikoff, who owns the largest collection of celebrity hair in the world (including snippets from Albert Einstein, Marilyn Monroe, Abraham Lincoln and Napoleon Bonaparte). Currently, online, a person can buy a single strand of Armstrong's hair mounted on a card beside the astronaut's photo for £399, or thirty-seven strands in a Ziploc bag for $500 US directly from the dealer who made the original purchase from the small-town Ohio barber. Some people in the celebrity-collecting world estimate that the original bag of hair, with each clipping sold separately, could be worth several million dollars. The mind boggles.

Learning of this bizarre incident, I immediately wondered if Neil Armstrong ever had need of a podiatrist to trim his toenails, and if so, how much might a toenail clipping off one of those famous feet be worth? But it also struck me as odd that such a private man would want to go to a barber once a month. I couldn't even bring myself to go twice a year out of dread of the painful small talk. Then again, leaning back in the barber chair, perhaps Armstrong imagined he was moon-bound in a rocket again, out of reach of all the celebrity seekers, and not even really forced to communicate with his fellow astronauts. Indeed, Michael Collins, who mentions in his biography that the Apollo 11 crew didn't ever share "thoughts and feelings," found his captain so enigmatic that he resorted to astrology (unsuccessfully) to try to figure him out. But where the subject of fame was concerned, one other salient point occurred to me: the wealthy collector of celebrity hair probably didn't bother with a strand off Christopher Knight's head.

In any case, the North Pond Hermit's fame was much more fleeting. First of all, as Thomas Merton and many others explain, most solitaries are a threat to the rest of us, a silent condemnation of our failures, trivialities and concessions to the norm, and so we don't like to dwell on them. Second, there's nothing wondrous or awe-inspiring about a voluntary solitude in the woods: it's *interesting*, but hardly comparable to walking on the moon.

Even so, while Knight's fame lasted (he did receive the usual marriage proposal that most serial killers receive in prison), he had to fight off the world's expectations of his hermit-self just as the Apollo 11 astronauts had to endlessly face the unanswerable question of what it felt like to go to the moon. If Finkel's book tells us anything about its subject, it tells us that Knight strongly resisted every hermit stereotype, even while in his hermit-age. Pointedly, he refused to look the part, actually shaving his head twice a year and keeping himself clean-shaven as a way *not* to look like a hermit in case he encountered someone in the woods. Obviously, those hair clippings stuck to a card beside a picture of a hermit shack wouldn't make anyone rich, but Knight, despite his immense isolation, still had to contend with the expectations of others. So much so, in fact, that he finally succumbed to society's wishes and let his hair and beard grow after he was incarcerated. If everybody wants a hermit, he seemed to say, might as well give them a hermit, and then perhaps they'll lose interest and leave mc alone.

Armstrong couldn't give anything to make the world lose interest, but he tried. Oh, how he tried. In fact, the way he constructed his privacy after Apollo 11 is just as remarkable an achievement as the moonwalk itself. After all, as an astronaut, he had a job to do, a job in which he was supported by a massive economic, political and social infrastructure. As he said in a rare interview, "There was work to be done. The checklists were all over us. We weren't there to meditate." From his perspective, the flying and the engineering were easy, a matter of training and flipping switches (the control board had 477 of them). But what training did he have to deal with the unrelenting demands of fame? Of barbers selling his hair to collectors? None. And he certainly wasn't supported in his efforts to find any either. A mostly silent man who was laconic when he did speak, Armstrong endured the exhausting world tour that followed the three-week-long quarantine. Visiting twenty-five countries in forty-five days, making speeches and meeting dignitaries, might not have been as much of a shock to the system as Christopher Knight's re-entry from absolute solitude to the mainstream world, but it was a bigger shock than going from the Earth's orbit to the moon's and back again.

But most of us have to make a living. Armstrong became "a modest college lecturer" in his home state of Ohio, actually closing the classroom door in the faces of reporters on his first day. Knight, to his great regret and shame ("My parents didn't raise me to be a thief," he said) might very well have set a world record for break and enters, committing thousands over his twenty-seven-year hermitage. To put it bluntly, capitalism requires extroversion, at least until you have sufficient money to withdraw from the world enough to suit your taste.

Christopher Knight bypassed thirty years of employment (he never paid taxes, obviously), but few would choose the manner in which he protected his flesh. Many, no doubt, facing the same introvert's wrestling with an extrovert's world, commit suicide, take to drugs and alcohol, find some version of God or simply just tough it out as best they can, bearing the hideous office parties and group work and small talk, dropping off cells the way Apollo's Saturn rocket dropped its stages. And no, it didn't help me – it's simply not human nature – to think of all the human beings worse off than I was. That kind of solace is for the saintly, and I was nowhere near sainthood.

I had to work, and my work meant meeting hundreds of strangers every few months (university teaching) and travelling to give readings and interviews (publishing books). Over three decades, my atmosphere, if you will, had thinned. I was on the path to biological destruction and, like the human race, I couldn't see any clear solution. But I did know one thing, and I knew it in whatever air I had remaining: the moon was an introvert. When I walked out between one and four in the morning – and especially toward the end of that time – I had, even in a large city, what Christopher Knight had in his hermitage: a rare freedom from the demands of the human condition. The poet William Stafford, imprisoned as a conscientious objector during WW II, explained that he always got up at 3:00 a.m. to write because "even the captors have to sleep sometime." The human species, in other words, vanishes for a few hours each twenty-four-hour period, just as Michael Collins, the Apollo 11 astronaut who didn't descend to the lunar surface in the *Eagle*, vanished briefly on the other side of the moon as he orbited in the *Columbia*.

But how long could I keep up the schedule? I wasn't Christopher Knight. I was a husband, a father and a worker. I needed to function, not just exist, in the full-on extroversion of the sun, regardless of the dangers of burning up on re-entry. Yet I couldn't sleep comfortably through the moon's phases as I once did. Almost every night, I heard the footsteps on the lunar surface that summoned me to make my own on the frozen earth. For as many nights as I could stand before I crashed, I heeded that summons. But then the pattern would establish itself again. The situation was untenable, but I could no longer see my *real* life as my life, or, even more troubling, I was finding that "the core of who I was" could no longer keep up the pretenses necessary to function in the actual world.

So I allowed myself to be distracted by my obsession. Like Charles Dickens, I walked out after midnight and I returned before dawn. If I was lucky, I slept four solid hours most nights; often, I wasn't that lucky, and so I had to fuel up on caffeine to get through the blinding days.

In my sleep-deprived state, I began to see Alf Harley's island as a combination of the moon and a hermitage in the woods. I even started thinking of my boyhood self, my father and Dr. Kaney as Apollo 11 astronauts, except we had arrived at our destination to find the man in the moon on his deathbed. And that man was as blank-faced and unaccommodating as Neil Armstrong and Christopher Knight. I couldn't read the dying expression, but, more and more, I was afraid that what I'd finally see there would be my own face of magnificent desolation.

By the middle of February, I was still walking on a moonlit valley trail in Edmonton, but I was leaving footprints on a small silt island in the Fraser River. The moon, meanwhile, shone down on both worlds. The shoe-tree's hanging footwear blended with my childhood games of hangman, when only some of the letters had been guessed and only some of the hanging figure embodied. I was the missing limbs and the missing letters, peg-legged Ahab trying to explain to the gregarious Starbuck his reasons for hating the white whale, as the moon, like one of Emily Dickinson's white dresses, swept across the attic bedroom of the world.

MOON SCRIBBLINGS: LATE WINTER

"How long must it take before I cease to be known as a spaceman?" Armstrong asked a reporter seven years after coming home.

One morning, as my daughter was getting ready to leave for school, I told her about the shoe-tree. She said that dangling shoes apparently indicate a meeting place for drug deals. I didn't ask her how she knew that, too preoccupied with questioning the innocence of my childhood memories.

At the end of a four-page obituary article on Armstrong, these sentences: "He married, secondly, in 1994, Carol Knight, who survives him with two sons of his first marriage. A daughter predeceased him." The story of Neil Armstrong, and of the twentieth-century code of masculinity, lies in the blunt afterthought of that last sentence.

Christopher Knight admitted to Michael Finkel that there were times during his hermitage when he wept. But he offered no further details.

In 1927, Charles Lindbergh became the first pilot to fly non-stop and alone across the Atlantic Ocean, a feat that made him internationally famous. After watching the Apollo 11 mission on TV, Lindbergh, who was nicknamed the Lone Eagle, sent a congratulatory letter to Michael Collins, saying that he understood exactly how difficult it was for him to orbit around the moon all by himself.

> I watched every minute of the walk-out [onto the moon], and certainly it was of indescribable interest. But it seems to me you had an experience of in some ways greater profundity – the hours you spent orbiting the moon alone, and with more time for contemplation. . . .
> . . . There is a quality of aloneness that those who have not experienced it cannot know – to be alone and then to return to one's fellow men once more. You have experienced an aloneness unknown to man before.

Lindbergh goes on to say that he feels closer to Collins than the other two Apollo 11 astronauts because of this.

Whether one would want to be close to Lindbergh – a legendary reclusive and cruel practical joker who, many people now believe, was likely involved in the kidnapping and murder of his own child – is another story. In any case, Collins preferred to emphasize the positive when it came to his Apollo 11 solitude: "Radio contact with the Earth abruptly cuts off at the instant I disappear behind the moon. I am alone now, truly alone, and absolutely isolated from any known life. I am it. If a count were taken, the score would be three billion plus two over on the other side of the moon, and one plus God only knows what on this side. I feel this powerfully – not as a fear or loneliness – but as awareness, anticipation, satisfaction, confidence, almost exultation. I like the feeling."

Whereas Neil Armstrong went for a monthly trim, I avoided the barbershop completely and let my hair and my beard grow out, just as Christopher Knight did in prison. Under the moonlight, I became the world's most slowly transforming werewolf.

In her book on introverts, Susan Cain writes about the modern horror known as group think and teamwork. NASA is the very embodiment of this horror. According to *Team Moon: How 400,000 People Landed Apollo 11 on the Moon*, by Catherine Thimmesh, everyone involved in the project saw themselves as part of the Lunar Team, the greatest team ever assembled.

"We knew darn well," said one of the computer support people, "that each of us was a very, very small part of a huge jigsaw puzzle that the country was trying desperately to put together."

"Wherever is the crowd is a common denominator of stench," wrote Friedrich Nietzsche.

From *Team Moon*:

> And of course the boots, like the suits themselves, went through seemingly endless rounds of testing. Since walking was the primary goal, an ankle convolute was necessary to allow for ankle extension and flexion – the natural movements made by the foot when walking.
>
> "I spent a lot of time walking on a treadmill. And they tried out lots of combinations of convolutes and various pulleys with ropes and cables – while they photographed just the action of my ankles and feet," remembered Richard Ellis, test subject.

From *The Stranger in the Woods*:

"He knew, in many cases, the precise number of steps required to reach a cabin."

"It is impossible to move through snow without making tracks, and Knight was obsessive about not leaving a print."

"No matter what he tried, he couldn't keep his feet warm."

"Every step was calculated, every movement. He clearly took the same steps all the time, year after year, decade after decade."

According to *Team Moon*, the American space program – from Mercury to Gemini to Apollos 7, 8, 9 and 10 – was "a series of steps."

In Zen Buddhism, the following analogy: Imagine someone is trying to show you the moon by pointing to it. Your True Mind is the moon (naturally bright, has enlightenment naturally); the finger is the Teachings (dark, lacks enlightenment). The finger points directly to the moon so that you can see the moon for yourself, directly. Similarly, the Buddha's teachings (dharma) point directly to your true mind (your Buddha nature). If someone points to the moon, don't just look at the finger because: you'll miss the moon; you'll think the finger is the moon; and you won't know what is naturally bright (has enlightenment) versus what is naturally dark (lacks enlightenment).

If I had gone on a field trip for one of Neil Armstrong's classes and watched his finger, like Galileo's shrivelled digit, point to the sky, I would not have seen his finger or the moon. Just as, night after night, walking in the woods, when I look past my trembling finger at the moon, I'm looking down at my feet.

Walt McCandless was a rocket scientist who worked for NASA, but his son, Christopher, is considerably more famous because of his disappearance and eventual death in the Alaskan wilderness, a story popularized in a book and film called *Into the Wild*. A sort of latter-day poor man's version of Thoreau and the reclusive mountain naturalist John Muir, Chris McCandless was a troubled young man who took up a nomadic life of simplicity as a way to escape familial and societal demands to become as accomplished as his father. That father, according to Chris's sister and stepsisters, routinely beat and choked Chris's mother – Walt also impregnated his first wife while already having had children (including Chris) with his second wife, a fact unknown to Chris until he was an adult. This domestic narrative, as sad and pathetic as many in the NASA family circle (and, by extension, the American family circle), explains a great deal about Chris's behaviour, though many readers and watchers of *Into the Wild* prefer to speculate on the nature and purpose of Chris McCandless's tragic fate from a more philosophical point of view. For me, and for his siblings, he had an awful childhood with a violent father and everything he did was a reaction against that past.

But other people point to passages Chris wrote in his journal and letters for inspiration. Here's a representative one: "The very basic core of a man's living spirit is his passion for adventure. The joy of life comes from our encounters with new experiences, and hence there is no greater joy than to have an endlessly changing horizon, for each day to have a new and different sun."

It's no coincidence that he focused on the sun when his father worked for the great team so powerfully associated with the moon. Beyond that, I think of Christopher McCandless, dead at twenty-four, and Christopher Knight, blinking into an off-duty cop's flashlight at forty-seven, as different phases of the same person. Even if the former wanted continually changing experience and the latter wanted a permanent condition of stillness in one place, both were damaged before they set out and their stories are heart-breakingly sad.

A father has a terrible power. Is my thirst for solitude a form of violence? I hear my children moving about in the dim shadows of my consciousness, leaving footprints that I can't follow before they're quickly erased.

Speaking with my mother on the phone one night, almost falling asleep, I hear her say, "Everything is fine. I feel great. But I'm having some trouble with my feet. They're all swollen. Doctor says it's from too much fluid and that I need to walk more."

There are twenty-six bones in the human foot. A quarter of all the bones in the human body are in the feet. With these bony appendages, the average human who lives to be eighty years old will take 216,262,500 steps in a lifetime, averaging between seven thousand and eight thousand steps a day (about 3.7 miles). That is, the average eighty-year-old will have walked 110,000 miles, or five times around the Earth at the equator. All of this information comes from a website called Moon Joggers.

My youngest son stays home sick from school. Spends the day watching TV. I join him at one point and he's watching an episode of *The Twilight Zone* on a channel called ME TV (ME is short for *Memorable*). In the episode, titled "The Lonely," Jack Warden plays Corry, a convicted criminal who's sent to an uninhabited asteroid nine million miles from Earth to serve out his sentence. After four and a half years, he eagerly awaits the supply ship from Earth. The sympathetic captain, knowing of the prisoner's terrible isolation, breaks the rules by bringing him a surprise present: a female robot companion. Offended and appalled at first, the prisoner eventually forms a deep bond with the robot; in fact, he falls in love with her. When his sentence has been served, however, and the ship comes to take him back to Earth, there's not enough room for the robot. But when the captain explains that he must leave the robot behind, Corry can't bring himself to do so. Left with no choice, the captain takes out his gun and shoots the robot in the face, exposing all the wires beneath the metallic skin. "It's like a bad dream," the captain says to Corry, "a nightmare. When you wake up, you'll be back on Earth. You'll be home." Then Rod Sterling's voice signs off with the following summary: "On a microscopic piece of sand that floats through space is a fragment of a man's life. Left to rust is the place he lived in and the machines he used. Without use they will disintegrate from the wind and sand and the years that act upon them. All of Mr. Corry's machines, including the one made in his image, kept alive by love, but now obsolete . . . in the Twilight Zone."

Once Armstrong and Aldrin left the moon and reunited with Collins and the *Columbia* in lunar orbit, the *Eagle* was sent off into its own lunar orbit, revolving around the moon for over three years before it finally crashed, a used machine, into the dust and craters.

According to the Urban Dictionary, hanging shoes from telephone wires and branches indicates either a meeting place for a drug deal or an attempt to express the pointlessness of life. To my relief, many people online say that it's just a fun game for bored kids. Poignantly, one person, who moved constantly in his childhood, said that he always tossed a pair of old sneakers over the wires as a way to say to the world "Don't forget me." Less poignantly, others said that taking someone's expensive Nikes and tossing them was a common form of bullying.

It appears that the astronauts' footprints might not remain visible on the moon for as long as first believed. Due to the constant barrage of space matter crashing into the moon and kicking up the ground-concrete-like dust, the years will eventually cover up Armstrong's iconic tracks. No doubt he would be pleased.

The sun is thirty thousand times brighter than the moon. The unit of measurement used to determine this comparison? The foot-candle. Direct sunlight produces between five thousand and ten thousand foot-candles, while direct moonlight produces 0.02 foot-candles.

The famously reclusive French writer Marcel Proust spent the last three years of his life in his bedroom, which he had had lined with cork to deafen the noises of bustling Paris. A black raincoat was laid at the end of his bed, just in case he wanted to go out in the middle of the night. But mostly he stayed in, working feverishly to complete his masterpiece, *In Search of Lost Time*. A hypochondriac and highly strung, Proust, near the end of his life, was dogged by a fear that an old friend had attacked him in his about-to-be-published posthumous memoirs. The title of that book? *Les Pas effacés*. Or in English, *Footsteps Rubbed Out*.

According to legend, the ancient Chinese poet Li Po drowned while trying to embrace the moon's reflection in a river.

The poet T.S. Eliot worked unhappily at a bank in London in the years after WW I. His office – or his cave, as he called it – was underground. He would look up through thick squares of green glass at pavement that was filtered in a watery light and upon which, as one visitor remarked, "hammered all but incessantly the heels of the passers-by." Flowing with the crowd of commuters over London Bridge day after day, Eliot came up with the line, "I had not thought death had undone so many."

In 1986, the year that Christopher Knight left the world behind, the brutal dictator of the Philippines, Ferdinand Marcos, was forced out of office and had to flee the country. His wife, known for her opulent and lavish lifestyle, left 2,700 pairs of shoes behind in the palace. Later, she was quoted as saying, "They went into my closets looking for skeletons, but thank God, all they found were shoes, beautiful shoes."

Buzz Aldrin lobbied hard, with his father's help, to be the first man to walk on the moon. With quiet, unflappable resolve, Armstrong kept the honour, claiming that it had been decided by the NASA higher-ups and that the astronauts should just follow orders. When both men were on the surface of the moon, Armstrong took several clear images of Aldrin but Buzz Lightyear took none of his captain. Some suggest that Aldrin took no pictures out of spite, though he has constantly denied the charge. Armstrong, never much for the cameras, didn't seem to care.

But one iconic and striking image of Armstrong on the moon was captured – ironically, he took it himself. He appears as a reflection in Aldrin's visor. Li Po, whither are you going?

The remains of the first man on the moon were cremated and buried at sea. The fifty-two bones in his feet, burned to ash and tiny fragments, now lie on our planet as far from the moon as possible.

THE TEMPERATURE WARMED AS THE FULL MOON APPROACHED. AFTER three consecutive nights with the thermometer dropping no lower than minus five, my solitary walks changed. I now entered the woods with some trepidation, like Christopher Knight on a thieving raid, or like any woman at any hour. Suddenly, the presence of other humans felt palpable, and the feeling wasn't welcome. The number of sirens in the distance – even the amount of traffic noise coming from the nearest major thoroughfares

– increased. I couldn't shake the notion that the moon, noticing the change, shrank into itself, becoming smaller despite moving toward fullness. And yet, oddly, the darkness was brighter, as if some small switch had been flipped on behind the trees.

One night, as I turned off the paved road and slipped along the footpath, I was convinced that I wasn't alone. Halfway to the blue tarp, I stopped and listened, expecting a patter of footsteps to quickly cease behind me. Instead, I heard only the creaking in the crowded skeletal boughs, like the sound of wind in a ship's rigging. When I turned and looked back, it was as if I could see straight over the horizon, as if I stood on the earth exactly as I had stood nights earlier on the bridge above the shoe-tree. I experienced that same sense of vertigo, though now it expanded to include more than my own nervous system. Even the trees swayed off-balance. I half-expected the Earth itself to rise and take up a position beside the moon, emphasizing the disorienting doubleness I'd been aware of for over a month. Then, turning back to the woods, I saw it.

On the skinny path leading to the blue tarp, about thirty feet in, a black shape hung from a branch. At first, thinking it a person, I tensed, my body poised for flight. But the shape didn't move. As I stared at it, I saw that it was some kind of coat – long, long-sleeved, unbuttoned, its bottom edge about four feet off the ground. Sleep-deprived as I was, prone to the fancies generally born in moonlight, the coat struck me as belonging to one of the bodies whose shoes dangled off the branches a half-mile away. I could feel it from my toes to my scalp: dangerous human presence. How removed from it I had been, how insulated.

Common sense told me that one of the homeless campers had probably just checked in at the tarp, inspecting it as a possible place of refuge for the coming spring and summer. But if so, why hang a coat in the trees? The image was ominous rather than domestic. Unnerved, I backed away, deciding to take the other road, the one skirting the neighbourhood and leading over the traffic bridge. Like a child who had spooked himself for pleasure, I sensed the coat following me, unfolding itself like the wings of a giant bat. But beneath those wings, beating faster than my own, was the hunting, voracious human heart, more terrible than any creature. Increasing my pace, I burst from the woods like a madman. Any other nocturnal walker would be convinced that I posed a great danger – and how could I say, in all truth, that I didn't?

The moon seemed to pull away from me as I passed some houses, the low-key Moravian Church with its modest steeple and finally one of the city's small brick electrical buildings. My own breath sounded like my pursuer's. Except I wasn't being pursued. In fact, when I reached the bridge and began to walk along its sidewalk, the person coming from the opposite direction, the first person I had encountered at night since my walks began, seemed merely to be my reflection in the moon's visor.

Of course, it wasn't me, or even the disembodied coat flying at me from another direction. No, it was worse – it was another person. Such an ordinary thing, yet the deeper one descends into solitude, the more fraught with meaning the ordinary becomes. Already I knew this, and already I knew that it was the great threat to my life. How does a man live after walking on the moon? How does a man reintegrate into society after twenty-seven years alone? How does anyone approach the random and erratic consciousness of another human?

I held my breath. My chest tightened. My steps grew heavier, but I couldn't simply stand still and let the person approach me. To my left, to the north, two dozen Saturn rockets, all lit up, pulled at the Earth's grip, eager to be gone. I started a countdown. What if there had been two of Munch's screamers and they held their faces as they walked toward each other? It was like that. Does anyone think that the most frightening power and greatest engineering genius isn't throbbing inside the flesh of every stranger? Doesn't everyone know that no matter how far we travel in space, the most alien creature we'll ever encounter is ourselves?

Within a few feet of passing, I quickly closed and opened my eyes. I could almost feel the hard impact as the other body collided with mine and sent me hurtling over the bridge. Instead, of course, the usual banality occurred, just as it had occurred to Christopher Knight when he'd suddenly turned a corner of a path and run into a hiker, forcing him to utter the only word he'd spoken for decades, the same word I managed to gasp out now.

"Hi."

The word came back, like an echo, an auditory reflection. But I didn't look into the man's face. I couldn't bring myself to do it. What did the hermit say? A face is too busy, has too many signals, creates a sensory overload. I kept walking, my own face like the *Twilight Zone* robot's, all the wires exposed and snapping.

When I'd gone far enough to be sure, I stopped and turned. Thankfully, the other person had kept going, his black coat returning, no doubt, to hang in the branches by the nylon tarp. For I had lost all normal sense of the world by now, unsure if I was even the same self. When I looked down at the shoe-tree, its dark gifts were pacing, pacing, walking out the lonely mania of all consciousness. The moonlight on my gloveless hands on the railing had never been so cold.

> 1:15 PM EST
> YOUR ITEM IS ALMOST THERE
> We are writing to inform you that your recent GSP item has cleared customs and is now out for delivery with the carrier.
> Lot of 3 Red, White, and Blue MPC Plastic Spacemen astronauts 2" in original package.
> Thank you for being an eBay customer.
> The Global Shipping Program Team.

Cleared customs? Surely they meant "left Earth's orbit." In truth, the black coat in the woods and the other man on the bridge seemed more real to me in the daylight than my own life did, though I tried hard to invest the trivial dailiness of Internet commerce, and all else, with significance. That is, I tried to maintain my sense of humour, the only kind of perspective that allows an atheist to cope with the absurdity of existing on a small and fragile world revolving in the midst of infinite darkness.

As I waited for my little astronauts to arrive, I remembered that I still hadn't booked myself a session at the Float House. It was about time that I did so, given the state of my nerves. Besides, where else was I going to experience at least some degree of weightlessness? The astronauts' steps on the moon had been light; mine were altogether too heavy. In any event, after the encounter on the bridge, running the gauntlet of a young hipster at a wellness place in the middle of the day shouldn't be too disturbing.

THE SEVENTEENTH-CENTURY FRENCH PHILOSOPHER BLAISE PASCAL famously wrote, "All of humanity's problems stem from man's inability to sit quietly in a room alone." So I decided to stop walking for a few nights, even though the moon was full and drawing me out like a murderer. I distracted myself by thinking. Firstly, I thought about Pascal's sentence in relation to Neil Armstrong's legendary comment after planting his footprint on the moon: "That's one small step for man, one giant leap for mankind." Apparently, Armstrong had said, "That's one small step for *a* man," etc., but the radio transmission either cut off the article or else the astronaut merely fluffed his lines. The debate has raged for decades, with most space fans now accepting that the article had been lost in lunar transmission.

But just as Robert Frost is famously paraphrased as saying about his own art form, "Poetry is what gets lost in translation," so too does the greatest meaning get lost in Armstrong's words. That is, are we mostly individuals or mostly some sort of team? If the former, then he took a small step for himself and thereby advanced our species' cause; if the latter, we all stepped with him, whether we wanted to or not, thereby leaping into the unknown. And if Pascal actually wrote, "All of humanity's problems stem from *a* man's inability to sit quietly in his room alone," then that would let most of us off the hook. Without power and influence, that is, it made no difference at all to humanity whether I went out for a walk under the moonlight or whether I stayed in my room and made an inward cerebral journey. Or did it?

But one fact was clear enough: I knew that walking alone in the woods at night to *forget* about the presence of other humans was a luxury that half the species couldn't take for granted, meaning that a small step for a man is using just one boot, and the other's very likely kicking someone without power right in the ass. Even after my encounter on the bridge – no, *because* of it – I longed to be outside again, if only to experience the mild electrical shock of plunging my own consciousness into conflict with the world. In a room alone, I didn't have to be all Zen and composed and domestic; I could scale the walls with self-probing. As Thoreau says, "A man thinking or working is always alone." But I had read too much Adrienne Rich to be sanguine about male thought. Here's the opening of her poem "Ghost of a Chance":

> You see a man
> trying to think.
>
> You want to say
> to everything:
> Keep off! Give him room!
> But you only watch
> terrified
> the old consolations
> will get him at last.

But a man can also watch himself in terror as he resists those consolations: the society he has structured and controlled, the power that sends some men to the moon and that drives others into the woods. I was equally afraid of my resistance and of the old consolations, if only because the resistance led to unchartered territory while the old consolations no longer struck me as consoling. Worldly success, the belief in the inevitable triumph of goodness and justice, the meaningfulness of work, my possible personal future as a grandfather: these consolations were rapidly losing their magnetic attraction. What, then, would be left? If there was an answer, I couldn't see it, and so had no choice but to let my consciousness carry my body through this carnival of odd time.

One final footnote about the moon men: Armstrong and Aldrin waited six hours in the *Eagle* before Armstrong took his famous first steps. Armstrong later joked that his wife suspected it took him that long to come up with his leaping mankind sentence (which, as it turns out, he basically stole from some forgotten writer of a NASA pamphlet). Given the couple's later divorce, it's obvious that her humour even in 1969 was as dark as the far side of the moon.

As I sat alone in my living room for two nights in a row, enduring my fifteen and more minutes of no-fame, talking myself out of putting on my boots and coat and following my familiar tracks (whether visible or not, whether Armstrong or Knight or not, I knew where they were), I thought a great deal about the difference between doing and not doing, particularly as it relates to human nature. Many philosophers, including Pascal, maintain that restlessness is our natural condition; in fact, without it, the argument goes, there's no human condition at all. Even the Buddhists acknowledge this innate human quality, referring to it as *tanha*, which literally means thirst. That thirst, however, can be directed, paradoxically, toward stillness, a journey that – judging by all the wellness therapies and, frankly, books about solitude, silence and disconnecting from the digital – has become more popular than ever.

One striking example among many: In his 2017 book, *Silence: In the Age of Noise*, Norwegian explorer, lawyer, art collector, publisher and author (no sitting around in rooms for him) Erling Kagge writes about his thirst for silence, a thirst that drives him, logically enough, to become the first person to reach the South Pole alone. How did he do it? He walked and skied for fifty days across Antarctica, the Earth's coldest continent. Often he froze until he wept. His nose, fingers and toes gradually turned white and the feeling in them disappeared. But why did he do it? Ah, there's the rub. In short, like Thoreau (yet also unlike Thoreau, who was cozy by comparison), Kagge wanted to live more intensely than his rat-race fellow humans. Here's Thoreau's explanation for why he took a two-year solitude at Walden Pond: "I went to the woods because I wished to live deliberately, to front only the essential facts of life, and see if I could not learn what it had to teach, and not, when I came to die, discover that I had not lived."

Kagge, father of three teenaged daughters, girls whose primary desire, or so he says, is to own a valuable Louis Vuitton bag (hey, thanks, Dad, for pointing out our shallowness to the world), refers to Pascal's famous sentence and admits that he mostly can't sit alone quietly in a room because he normally chooses "to do anything else rather than to fill the silence with myself." These little domestic trials led him to tell his restless soul, "Houston, we have a problem." Unwilling to endure the rat race like lesser mortals, unwilling to reach the end of his life without actually having *lived*, Kagge's solution is obvious: if he can't sit in a room with his thoughts for fifteen minutes, why then, he'll walk all by himself to the South Pole.

Somehow, the irony is lost on the man. Well into his fifties, he is exactly the kind of modern spiritual seeker for whom the Float House targets its marketing: you can't take time out from your busy life and just *think*; you have to give your thinking a *goal*. Who cares if a Norwegian lawyer and art collector travels inward unless he travels very extremely outward?

Interestingly, while on his epic walk ("The secret to walking to the South Pole is to put one foot in front of the other"), Kagge imagines the man in the moon looking down on the Earth and watching him in his blue anorak heading south, week after week, climbing out of his tent and repeating his same forward progress. The man in the moon, so Kagge writes, must think he's nuts. Yet that mysterious lunar observer also looks to the north and sees the millions upon millions of Kagge's fellows trudging into their cars week after week to go to their desk jobs and then driving back to their TV sets and computers, a pattern that repeats until they die. When our Norwegian explorer and art collector thinks up this contrast, which apparently can't be made unless you walk by yourself to the South Pole, he feels calmer and more at peace when he crawls into his little tent each night.

While I sat in my room, thinking about how much the quest for solitude, when put into writing and published, is predictably similar, a sop to those sentimental middle-class citizens who would happily pay to hear Mr. Kagge give a talk about his explorations so that they could simultaneously feel bad about themselves while adoring him, I began to be less quiet and much more angry, not so much at the world but at myself. Was my own plunge into whatever form of solitude I wanted merely a posture?

I concluded, at last, that it might have been, except for one thing: I had been on Alf Harley's island with my father and Dr. Kaney. I had tasted the wake of a solitude, like the brine on the estuary air, washing off a dying man who kept no record of his life and sought no acknowledgement for his isolation. Alf Harley was Christopher Knight if Christopher Knight had never been caught. Alf Harley lay in a capsule, a boat that no longer went on the water, and his steps amounted to exactly nothing. But Neil Armstrong was every bit as dead as Alf Harley, and Christopher Knight and I would join them soon enough. It seemed, more and more, that what mattered wasn't so much what one *did* or what one *knew*, but who one *was*. What does it profit a man (not just *man*) to gain the kingdom of the cosmos if he loses his own soul? Or, to come round to the orbit of Pascal again, "Knowledge of physical science will not console me for ignorance of morality in time of affliction, but knowledge of morality will always console me for ignorance of physical science."

Then only one question remained: Is it moral for an individual, seeing violence and speed and noise and distractedness everywhere, to make the whole world a room in which to sit quietly alone? The next night, I answered the question by putting on my boots and walking, one step at a time, back to the woods.

TECHNICALLY, THE MOON IS FULL ONLY FOR A MOMENT, BUT IT APPEARS full to the human eye for about four nights. So by the time I recovered from my mini-crisis involving the hanging coat and the stranger on the bridge, I returned in clear, almost palpable moonlight (like sperm whale oil) to the blue tarp. Immediately, I noticed that several more items of clothing had appeared in the trees, as if the warming air had brought splotches of its own blood to the surface. Even my own shadow lay on the ground before me as if I'd taken off my coat and tossed it there. Now the night seemed to breathe, and my solitude, as I had known it, slipped away. Great Birnam wood had begun its walk toward high Dunsinane hill. Suspended, like the half-dozen coats, shirts and pants of the massing army, I didn't move, except to tilt my head up at the moon, more visible now than it would be for another month. I felt I had come to the end of something, though I didn't know what that something was. My Buddhist thirst for solitude remained, as did my skepticism about all human aspiration, whether to land a man on Mars, to enter a monastery or to write another book. And yet, to do nothing brought to mind only the disturbing image of Anthony Perkins in his padded cell at the end of *Psycho*, vowing in his dead mother's voice that he wasn't going to move, not even to swat a fly. "They'll see," he says. "They'll see and they'll know and they'll say, 'Why, she wouldn't even harm a fly . . .'"

I was neither moving nor seeing, immobilized, if not by fear of strangers, by fear of myself. The craters on the moon stuck out vividly and yet were smaller than my footprints. I took off my glasses and rubbed my eyes, feeling much like the narrator of Robert Frost's "After Apple-Picking," who "cannot rub the strangeness from [his] sight." Caught between two worlds, night and day, the moon and the sun, solitude and society, not doing and doing, I too felt the ache in "my instep arch," I too had grown "overtired / of the great harvest I myself desired." The moon, hanging there like an unattainable apple drained of all its flavour, provided little succour as I balanced between a long hibernation and a brief human sleep, between states of consciousness, including life and death. The sensation was, to use a favourite Elizabeth Bishop word, uncanny.

I looked down, turning my head toward the large smudge of the blue tarp. With my glasses dangling from my hand, I thought of Christopher Knight again. His greatest physical challenge during the twenty-seven years of his hermitage involved his failing eyesight. Though he often tried out glasses when he broke into cabins, hoping to replace his ineffective, taped-together pair, he never found a better prescription and eventually had to settle for seeing the world, including the night sky, as a blur. The romance of solitude becomes decidedly less romantic as the body ages and the solitary is no longer capable of the same physical feats of strength and agility. Robinson Crusoe, after all, didn't arrive on his island as an old man.

As a result, putting my glasses back on and seeing the moon hove sharply into view as if through the window of an approaching Apollo module made me feel better – younger, stronger, more hopeful, almost like Ralph Waldo Emerson in his most famous paragraph:

> In the woods, too, a man casts off his years, as the snake his slough, and at what period soever of life is always a child. In the woods is perpetual youth. Within these plantations of God, a decorum and a sanctity reign, a perennial festival is dressed, and the guest sees not how he should tire of them in a thousand years. In the woods, we return to reason and faith. There I feel that nothing can befall me in life – no disgrace, no calamity (leaving me my eyes), which nature cannot repair. Standing on the bare ground – my head bathed by the blithe air, and uplifted into infinite space – all mean egotism vanishes. I become a transparent eye-ball; I am nothing; I see all; the currents of the Universal Being circulate through me; I am part or particle of God.

For Emerson in this passage, life *is* a liminal state, a crossroads between matter and spirit that becomes most palpable when one enters the natural world. While I wasn't buying the idea of a Universal Being, I nonetheless understood how my post-midnight walks were slowly eroding my "mean egotism." But the problem remained: To what purpose? If a man is an all-seeing nothing, what on earth (or on the moon) can he see except the end of sight?

The question took my transparent eyeball and, as in the iconic Luis Buñuel film that I saw in my university days, sliced across it with a razor blade. A chill shook me from top to toe. Unlike a Norwegian explorer and art collector, I was getting nowhere. So I decided to move, if not toward the South Pole, at least in another direction, back to the fateful bridge.

As I neared the Moravian Church, a rustling above caught my attention. Looking up, I saw, on the top of the steeple and bathed in the blithe air, a huge raven. It was like no bird I had ever seen before, as black as the other side of the moon and as large as an astronaut's helmet. I heard – or imagined I heard – its eyeballs turn to follow me. Almost flinching in expectation of a hoarse cry coming from its massive beak, I found that I couldn't face the bridge. In fact, I backed away for several yards, then turned and hurried away, all Emersonian reason and faith drained right out of me as if I'd been tattooed with leeches.

Back home, feeling at once as insignificant and monumental as the Underground Man, I turned on all the lights, including the desk lamps, searching for the electrical current of the Universal Being but finding only what Thomas Merton found at the end in his Bangkok hotel room with his dysfunctional electric fan. The whir of the imaginary blades sounded a lot like the wings of a raven as it flies overhead, deeper and deeper into infinite space, becoming, like the moon as it leaves fullness behind, the "Nothing that is not there, and the nothing that is," as Wallace Stevens once wrote.

IN *NOCTURNE: A JOURNEY IN SEARCH OF MOONLIGHT*, JAMES ATTLEE includes a chapter on the science of the eye, specifically drawing attention to how we do, in fact, see the world differently in lunar light. The eye, operating as a lens system, focuses light passing through the transparent ("window on the soul") cornea onto the retina through a crystalline lens. This "lens is made up of dead cells that cease to be connected to the body's blood supply when [we are] still in the womb, although it continues to grow and become thicker, rather in the manner of hair or fingernails." Between the lens and the retina lies a substance known as the aqueous humour "in which ghostly objects sometimes appear to float because of the shadows they cast." It occurred to me that floating in a tank of Epsom salts, then, ought to put me in an aqueous humour, if nothing else.

Attlee goes on to explain that the retina is filled with receptors that convert light into electrical signals that are sent along nerve fibres to the brain, where they are translated into vision. He also points out that the curve of the cornea bends the light it receives, displaying images on the retina upside down until the brain corrects the images, righting them. No wonder Bishop's Man-Moth travels backwards and slips a tear out of his aqueous humour; no wonder the astronauts leaving Earth face the wrong way; no wonder Buzz Aldrin's helmet automatically flipped the one image of Neil Armstrong the right way up; no wonder Chris Knight was like Melville's willful Laplander, blinded by his refusal to accept reality, doomed to see only a palsied universe.

The retina contains two different types of photosensitive cells: cones, which register colour and are used for daylight; and monochromatic rods, which we use for night vision. But when we go out under the light of the moon, we actually use a blend of signals from both receptors. That is, we experience a slippage, like Wakefield and Flitcraft, between two systems, two worlds. At night, though, we use more of the rods, and they can take as much as a full day, in a process known as dark adaption, to regenerate the photo pigments that daylight destroys (this is also why we can be, in a reverse way, blinded by the light). Contrary to popular belief, human night vision, once dark adapted, is remarkably powerful, enabling us to "detect light that is a billionth of the strength of daylight – the equivalent of the flame of a single candle seventeen miles away."

Once the rods are fully adapted, we see the black-and-white nocturnal world with remarkable clarity, all the shapes and shadows sharper somehow than in the full light of day. To prove his point, Attlee quotes passages of moon writing by Goethe, Italo Svevo, John Ruskin and Walter Benjamin, but it was his reference to my old friend Thoreau that stopped me in my tracks. I had little choice, of course, but to dive back into the writing of the *Walden* "hermit," looking for guidance along my own lunar path, using whatever rods and cones were necessary, turning the words around like little weightless astronauts.

THOREAU LIVED FOR THE AURORAL LIGHT, FOR DAYBREAK AND MORNING, equating that freshness with creation and possibility. But he also possessed a deep regard and feeling for the night, especially the moonlit night, seeing it as a necessary antidote to the "profane" day: "How insupportable would be the days, if the night with its dews and darkness did not come to restore the drooping world. As the shades begin to gather around us, our primeval instincts are aroused, and we steal forth from our lairs, like the inhabitants of the jungle, in search of those silent and brooding thoughts which are the natural prey of the intellect."

Thoreau's love of the night, in fact, relates directly to his independence and to his critique of the conformist mind. "Many men walk by day, few walk by night. It is a very different season." In it, the world appears like a fairyland: "In moonlight nights the bushes loom, the grain-fields are boundless, and the shadows of rocks and trees and shrubs and hills are more conspicuous than the objects themselves." Here, we enter the realm of mystery and drama, largely because senses other than sight take the lead. We become more aware of smell and sound, even as "new and old things are confounded. I know not whether I am sitting on the ruins of a wall, or on the material which is to compose a new one."

But for Thoreau, the night's special quality is emphasized by the solitary journey of the moon across the sky. In fact, the moon's passage is the very height of drama: "What an entertainment for the traveller, in such a night as this, the incessant motion apparently of the moon traversing the clouds. Whether you sit or stand, it is always preparing new developments for you. It is the drama of the moonlight nights, and event enough for a simple mind. . . . You all alone, the moon all alone . . ." At night, whether you have a simple mind or a brooding intellect, you have escaped the clutches of civilization. At night, plainly put, "there is less of man in the world"; you enter into "a different order of things." But when I read the following sentences, I knew just how intimately Thoreau understood my own attraction to walking after midnight: "I come out thus into the moonlit night where men are not, as if into a scenery anciently inhabited by men but now deserted by them. Their life is like a dream to me."

Not only that, but *my* waking life, too, had lost much of its reality, a fact that Thoreau also recognized: "That kind of life which sleeping we dream that we live awake, in our walks by night we waking live; while our daily life appears as a dream."

But I wasn't a brother to Thoreau. How could I be? He was a nineteenth-century man whose writings are peppered with references to the creator of the heavens. For him, the moon not only allows us to be more spiritual and less earthy in a receiving way, but it gives us an opportunity for growth: "What if one moon has come and gone with its world of poetry, its weird teachings, its oracular suggestions – so divine a creature freighted with hints for me, and I have not used her?"

If the moon – a barren rock and not a divine female – was teaching me something, I didn't understand the lessons. I certainly didn't know what use I was to make of my sojourns into its oracular presence. But I agreed wholeheartedly with Thoreau whenever he made a claim for the powerful contrast of the moon's world with the sun's: "The moon is a mediator. She is a light-giver that does not dazzle me. I can look her in the face. I am sobered by her light and bethink myself. It is like a cup of cold water to a thirsty man."

Sobered and bethought, thirsty like a Buddhist but not for enlightenment, I realized that my moonlit walks were important precisely because *something* was being mediated; that is, I walked with purpose even if I couldn't see the purpose. More paradox, but I was becoming used to accepting that "it is what it is" is really just another way of saying "it isn't what it is" or "it is what it isn't." The moon, much more than the sun, comfortably accommodated such thinking, as did that most solitary of walkers, Henry David Thoreau who, having begun life as David Henry Thoreau, even rearranged his feet on the path of his own name.

THE ASTRONAUTS OF APOLLO 18 DIDN'T SPLASH DOWN; THEY ARRIVED AT their destination with a loud clunk at about 4:00 p.m. Mountain Standard Time on a Monday (the same day of the week that Apollo 11 re-entered Earth's atmosphere). In fact, the clunk woke me up. More and more sleep-deprived, I was nodding off for five to twenty minutes at a time with increasing frequency. Once, making a snack for one of my teenagers, I burnt some nachos to a crisp and filled the kitchen with acrid smoke. My lunatic behaviour was becoming dangerous to more than my own nature. The moment firemen and insurance companies get involved, there can be no question of withdrawing from the world. I needed to move on somehow.

The capsule containing my little astronauts was a cardboard box about four inches wide by six inches high, and lighter than an eagle's feather. So light, in fact, as to be all but weightless. I wondered if perhaps a tiny portion of the moon's sky had served as a protective womb for my lunar team.

Upon opening the box, and pulling out the three plastic astronauts still sealed in their 1960s plastic, I couldn't help but feel that I'd stepped back in time, or at least that I'd walked through the wardrobe into a world of unchanging white. The moon loomed before me. The room filled with its light. How utterly strange it all still seemed – human beings travelling a quarter of a million miles to collect rocks and bring them back for scientific study. No wonder there were so many conspiracy theorists out there arguing that the moon landings had never happened, that they were all part of some devious Cold War scheme to distract everyone from the political and social turmoil of the era. Because the lunar landings *should be unbelievable*. We shouldn't be capable of splitting atoms and cloning cells and going to Mars. But we are. Even though we aren't capable of sitting alone quietly in a room for fifteen minutes; even though we don't know why we do anything at all.

Red, white and blue. Of course. And still quarantined behind their original plastic wrap after a half-century. Feeling foolishly sacrilegious, I removed the plastic and stared at the three little figures. After a while, I named the blue one Michael Collins and let him make the first step onto my desk (it seemed only fair). Spitefully, I put the choleric red Buzz Aldrin beside him (second for all time also seemed a just fate). But the white Neil Armstrong – white enough to blend into the moon and vanish, as he would have wanted – I couldn't decide where to put him. He just didn't belong with the other two, despite his life-sized predecessor's unwavering desire to be seen as one small cog in NASA's great leaping machine. No, the first man on the moon had to remain isolated, as he had been from the start, contained within himself, all systems go and shut down at the same time. Like me. Like you. In the end, I couldn't part with him. So I stuffed him in my pocket, thinking as I did so that perhaps I'd smuggle him into the Float House too, closed in the capsule of one hand, as alone as Crusoe on his island. Sure, it was a silly idea, but by this point, all I was learning, all I was reading, pointed more and more to the fact that every idea – from flying to the moon to living in a hermitage for nearly three decades to walking in the woods every night to stare at the moon – was, in some real sense, silly. If not, why would a lunar mission lead to an online marketplace where you can buy an astronaut's hair clippings? Why would twenty-seven years alone lead to fifteen minutes of unwanted fame? Why would a nightly moonlit walk lead to an increasing and impossible desire to be unselfconscious about unselfconsciousness? If, as Descartes posits, thinking proves our existence (I think, therefore I am), and if, as Bertrand Russell claims, "Most people would die sooner than think – in fact, they do so," why shouldn't a man withdraw into his own private genesis and awe?

At last, when the full moon had given way to the new moon, the phase when the moon is directly between the Earth and the sun and is therefore invisible to us, I made two long overdue decisions. The first stemmed from the fact that Christopher Knight and Robinson Crusoe shared almost the same number of years alone, well over three hundred years apart. And when I read that the North Pond Hermit confessed while in prison to an admiration for Daniel Defoe's classic work of solitude, and when I further read that the journalist Michael Finkel dismissed this admiration in a single sentence, remarking that *Robinson Crusoe* is fictitious (this coming from a writer whose career had been derailed because he had himself tried to pass off a piece of fiction as non-fiction), I knew exactly where I had to go. From the Apollo astronauts to Nathaniel Hawthorne and Henry David Thoreau, from Emily Dickinson and Wallace Stevens to Crazy Horse and the Stó:lō people of the Fraser River, from Montaigne and Rousseau to Thomas Merton and Alf Harley, all signs pointed to what the poet Paul Éluard is attributed as summarizing so beautifully: "There is another world, but it is in this world." The time had come for me, hovering so delicately between the Actual and the Imaginary, and hardly knowing the difference any longer, to reread *Crusoe*.

When I did so, all in one sitting, with a toenail clipping of moon watching through the branches and the windowpane, I felt the pull of what I'd been feeling from the start, but it was greater now, as if I'd been grabbed by another orbit after drifting aimlessly for months. Almost frightened by what I found in the book – certainly unnerved – I finally acted on my other long overdue decision. I walked my tired body and embattled imagination, one foot and one thought in front of the other, up the melting urban snowscape to the Float House. All the way there, with the little astronaut in my pocket, I thought about the book I had just read for the first time since I was nine or ten years old, the book that had fired the imaginations of so many human beings in so many countries for three centuries. It didn't read like fiction to me; it read like fact. But then, what was the line between if it wasn't as thin and dissolving as the Earth's protective atmosphere?

Propelled forward as a strange gravity pushed me back, I knew that the cozy, silky blackness redolent of salt that I would soon immerse myself in was going to mark the end of deep winter and herald the middle of summer. One world would give way to another. Time and space blurred at their coronas.

Alone, more unsure than ever of the journey, I walked up the tarmac, my footprints of fire visible to no one as they immediately flamed out and turned to ashen craters behind me.

THE FLOAT HOUSE

"Monk."

Silence.

"Monk."

Just one word, coming from a long distance away. A word smelling like ripe blackberries and salt. Something else too.

"Monk."

Yes. Cigarette smoke. But faintly. One word as freighted with the world as a honeybee staggering back to the hive from a field of clover. I tried to see where the word was coming from, but though my eyes were open, I could see only thick night. I could hear water, though. A light liquid slapping. Strangely, my back was warm but my face and hands were cold. Though I did not move, I was in motion, a kind of gliding.

The one word came again. Spoken gently. I took a deep breath of the rich musk wafting off the calm voice and opened my eyes wider. At the very end of my sight, a small, fuzzy white light – like the little dot that used to appear on the TV screens of the 1960s when you first turned the sets on. How I used to love watching for that split second when the little dot would burst into a full screen.

Now it wasn't a loving anticipation I felt, but a kind of mild fear bordering on a desire so long thwarted that it had almost lost its pull. A soft splash off to my right, a sound as familiar and yet unknown as the voice, ushered me into a fuller attention. The light trembled as it widened.

Suddenly, the darkness turned the colour of a lustreless pearl. I saw the black-fringed tops of trees, off under the pale colour. Much closer, directly to my left, I could make out the trunks and branches, the shadows playing amongst them. Though I was still gliding, the trees remained. I could almost reach out and touch their rough wood.

Before the voice spoke the word again, I saw it – a face, moth-sized, frozen between a trunk and a shadow. A man's face, as terrible in its stillness and remoteness as the full winter moon. Though it hung beside me, and I was pulling away, I seemed to be on a collision course with that unchanging expression. I tried to cry out, but my voice died in my throat.

"Tim. Are you awake? It's time to pick up."

The still face dissolved as the world burst into mercurial motion and light. Blinking, I saw only the thick cluster of trees and ground shrubs, now bathed in the same dull pearl colour spreading rapidly around me as the black river moved under our boat. To my right, the multicoloured corks of our net, set out in large loops, flowed on the same blackness.

My father, standing in the stern, a cigarette dangling from his mouth as if he'd been hooked by it, said, "You almost made it this time. I tried to keep you up."

I LIFTED A MAN'S HAND HEAVY WITH EPSOM SALTS AND, IN A WEAK benediction, touched it to my forehead. But there was nothing human to bless that hadn't already been turned to ashes. Unless I blessed the cold water on my face. My back, as warm as my boyhood back pressed against the heat of the exhaust pipe on the main deck of my father's gillnetter, floated along with the rest of me, as if the bones had been taken from my body. By the time I realized I was contained within a sensory deprivation tank in the middle of a city of a million people nowhere near the Pacific Ocean, my father, the word he spoke and the terrible face in the island trees all blended again into memory. Though I could still see the images, it wasn't the same kind of seeing – too many years had thickened the lenses; most of the world stayed in the shadows, and already I understood that the drifting on the river would take me as much to the bare rock of half-remembered fact as to the rich waterscapes of lived experience.

Numbed by my own body's warmth, the same warmth as the tank water, I tried to shake off the unnerving dissolution of my current life into its distant past. But when I shifted, a little of the salty water got into my mouth, and the taste of it decided me, as the taste of a madeleine in a cup of tea had once decided Marcel Proust.

Had I once seen Alf Harley looking out from the trees of his island as we drifted past, about to pick up our net and remove the dying salmon? Seen him before I'd ever seen his smoke or thought to ask about it? Or had my fifty-five-year-old self simply wanted his face there, as a spur to exploration, or perhaps as the light to a harbour of black and motionless vessels? Twenty minutes in the tank, and I'd already dozed off, staying awake not even as long as I had done as a boy, when, night after night on the river, I desperately tried to stay up to see the daybreak, something I wouldn't manage until I was old enough to go with my father and Dr. Kaney on a mysterious mission to one of the silt islands we passed so closely without ever setting foot upon.

But there'd be no more sleeping in the tank. That one word, dredged up from the silts of lost time, seemed to have been spoken by the face in the trees and not by my father, though I knew the idea was absurd. Even so, it was true that my father's nickname for me had been Monk. Even in the tank, forty-five years later, I could hear him saying it. Perhaps he'd been saying it ever since his death and I hadn't been able to hear. If so, what was the reason for my hearing it now? A summons to some action, as if I was Hamlet going out into the shifting mists to meet his ghostly father's challenge? Or a warning, a way to make clear to me that I wasn't a boy and that he was twenty years dead, if, in fact, anything lodged in the consciousness can die?

Fully awake now, but long past seeing the sun rise to touch my hairless and unwrinkled face, I waited, like the Apollo astronauts, to climb out of the capsule and get on with the job. But I wasn't an engineer and military man trained to detach himself from the natural blend of thought and feeling. I wasn't Neil Armstrong saying that he hadn't gone to the moon to meditate, I wasn't Tenzin Palmo who said she had gone to a Himalayan cave exactly for that reason. No, I was like all of the rest of the species, who must travel back to travel forward. All of us, hurtling toward death as we carry the recorded messages of our own origins. What is the home planet except what we make of the time we have left? My father called me Monk because I was a quiet boy who often played alone, probably with one of the little astronauts that now floated with me, Friday to my Crusoe, in this great bath of unavoidable tears, the crying of a normal life.

Time must be bided, despite the self's imperatives. I couldn't float all the way to summer, nor could I shrink the hours, but when I climbed out of the sensory deprivation tank, I already felt that my small steps were the giant leap that we all experience when we try to make sense of our solitary condition. The present is liminal without the fuel of the past. This time, I would stay awake for the rise of the moon and the sun, on the river that would tell me whose eyes really stared out of the face of the hermit as he died.

III

ALL OF MY CHILDHOOD'S UNINHABITED ISLANDS ARE DENIED PUBLIC access. Alf Harley's island, for example, has been leased by the British Columbia Ministry of the Environment & Climate Change Strategy to a local hunting society in exchange for the growing of crops for migratory birds. This is exactly the sort of logical arrangement that defines the world of affairs with which I have become so disenchanted. If you agree to grow crops to feed the birds, we will grant you the exclusive right to shoot those same birds, and because you will be hunting, we must deny access to the island out of a concern for public safety.

So I invoked the spirit of Thoreau and his famous civil disobedience (he spent some time in prison for withholding taxes in protest against a war with Mexico) and decided to break the law. I anticipated my presence on the island to be very quiet, but should my trespassing be noticed, I would simply plead ignorance. In all likelihood, I'd manage a week or two without the interference of wardens and hunters.

Time was, a man in the little salmon-fishing town of Ladner could slip down to the harbour of tiny, interlocked floats and moss-sided, tin-roofed net sheds after dark and borrow (okay, take) any loosely roped skiff or rowboat and slide into the current and be lost for hours or days to the world of the au-tomobile and real estate. Time was, Ladner *was* a little salmon-fishing town, but when I arrived on a sunny, early July morning in the original section of the 1858 settlement, in which my elderly mother still lived in my childhood home, Ladner was under siege. The cost of housing had doubled in the past few years, and my mother's mailbox was daily littered with real estate flyers. The rather decrepit old house beside hers had recently sold for close to a million dollars, and the new buyers were doing renovations in preparation to flip the property and capitalize on the Wild West nature of the market. My parents had built their 1200 square foot bungalow in 1965 (with the help of the Department of Veterans Affairs) for fifty thousand dollars, but the place is tiny by contemporary standards, so will likely be torn down upon my mother's death. I arrived in Ladner, as always, feeling that I had stepped into a beautiful past on the verge of being obliterated and forgotten forever.

This time, to intensify the feeling, the old main street was undergoing a major facelift. All the trees on both sides had been cut down to create new sidewalks, and the whole street had been dug up. Workers in bright yellow hard hats climbed down from and up into various kinds of large, noisy machinery, and bright yellow caution tape steered pedestrians away from the busiest areas. Jackhammers hammered at the remaining concrete, dust filled the air and I worried that the town's Depression-era granite clock tower might accidentally be felled in the chaos.

Except, of course, that this wasn't chaos at all, nor was the proliferation of expensive condominiums and floathouses all along the dike west from the town centre for several miles to where the Fraser meets the Pacific; this was just the world, busy about its business. Negotiating my way past the Porsches and Mercedes along the narrow gravel dike my father had helped to fortify after the last major flood – in 1948 – I noticed a bumper sticker that neatly summarized the town's zeitgeist: *People are nice. Business is booming. Life is great.*

The Extrovert Ideal had covered over my hometown just as the pum-ice and ash of Vesuvius had buried Pompeii. Except to the west, to the silt islands and, beyond them, the Gulf of Georgia. Out there, of course, species had become endangered or extinct due to the toxic runoff of all this extroversion, and more sewage-spewing cruise ships and expensive pleasure craft plied the waters than wild salmon, but still, if I closed my eyes, the ever-expanding coal port just south of Ladner, on the ocean shore by the Tsawwassen ferry terminal, and the megamall on the local First Nations reserve on the approach to that same ferry terminal might just disappear. And if I shut my ears, perhaps the hum of the power grid rising up off the industrial greenhouse operations that had cemented over some of the most arable farmland in the world (and neatly circumvented the spirit, if not the law, of the Agricultural Land Reserve) would fade away, leaving only the prehistoric squawk of the great blue heron and the trilling of the red-winged blackbird.

The American poet Philip Levine says that, in North America, we can't go home again because home isn't even there (Thoreau's Walden has been utterly changed, whereas the view from Montaigne's tower today is virtually the same as it was in the sixteenth century). That was almost true for me of Ladner, except for its natural geographic bounty of location, location, location. That is, if I trespassed on the private condo property, and stood at the end of someone's gangway to get an unobstructed view of the little silt islands that begin a mere stone's throw away, I might see the lively ghosts of 1975 again. With my back to the wheeling and dealing, the getting and spending, the Wi-Fi Starbucks and Walmart plastic, I could face the continuance of myself and my place; maybe I could hang, like the silent film comedian Harold Lloyd, high above the urban maelstrom, off the hands of Time, slowing them down a little. Thoreau famously raises a rallying cry of "Simplify! Simplify! Simplify!" and I wanted to raise a slightly different one: "Slow down! Slow down! Slow down!" But I was shouting at the years as much as at the world, and neither was going to pay me any heed.

But, of course, just as in the deep Edmonton winter on my moonlight walks, I had my own society for comfort. "There is no nothing either good or bad, but thinking makes it so," Hamlet says. And Montaigne quotes

Horace, "It is reason and wisdom which take away cares, not places affording wide views over the sea." But perhaps reason and wisdom can spring from a conception of what is heavenly rather than hellish. Perhaps a wide view over the sea, or, more specifically, a river, in a place that I was born into as a child who would become a worker and not a speculative investor, might channel my cares a little more toward reason and wisdom.

OF COURSE, BECAUSE MY FATHER AND DR. KANEY WERE OVER TWO decades dead, I had no way to answer unequivocally the questions about what really happened that chilly October morning in my twelfth year. Even now, even after its legalization, doctor-assisted suicide troubles our society, for religious, philosophical and ethical reasons. Nevertheless, I knew that 350 pounds of dying hermit-fisherman flesh had not needed to linger in an antiseptic hospital room, and my father had known it, and Dr. Kaney had known it too. Perhaps he had to hold out for a few hours for the sake of appearances, or perhaps – and the possibility, albeit small, exists – Alf Harley actually drew his last breath without help. No matter how sharp, memory can't penetrate the unknown.

But as it turned out, memory relates to the past as wet relates to the river; that is, it's only a partial truth. Alf Harley lived and died a hermit on a silt island in the south arm of the mouth of the Fraser River, but I couldn't be sure I'd find any remnants of his beached gillnetter, nor could I even be certain of what grove of cottonwoods he'd taken shelter in. In the end, I decided to honour the spirit of his enterprise if I couldn't exactly replicate the physical reality.

My ninety-year-old mother suggested that Alf Harley had previously lived in a shack in the woods opposite the government wharf on land intersected by sloughs but not technically an island. She also said that for many years he'd been a cook on a seine boat plying the treacherous waters off the north coast. My older brothers said that Alf had definitely been a cook on a seine boat, but that he'd retreated from the world in order to drink as much as he wanted without any interference from church ladies or anyone else.

"I guess he had to get to one of the islands for that to work," my brother Rick explained. "Anyway, Howard Benson used to row booze over to him. On slack tides. At least until Howard was murdered."

"What!"

"Well, that's what everybody figured, except the cops. This was in the summer when all the outboards were being stolen off the wharf. Don't you remember? I used to carry my Merc home after every opening."

Memory did provide me with a sudden vivid image of my Jesus look-alike brother carrying an outboard engine in his arms like a frozen mermaid down off the dike, but I had forgotten about the thefts.

"Sure, they said he was drunk and fell and banged his head on the wharf. But I figure he came upon somebody messing about where they didn't belong, and he probably recognized them, and so . . . bop on the head and into the drink. The cops would just think the old rummy got careless."

My brother stared off into space as if the town he'd spent his whole life in had been moved to another planet. "But Howard made that trip hundreds of times," he added. "Piss-drunk every time on the return too."

I interrupted the long silence almost guiltily. "What about Alf? Where did he get his booze after that?"

"I don't know." My brother blinked as if the idea had never occurred to him before. "He sure as hell didn't row into town himself. I guess he just stopped drinking."

"He can't have been an alcoholic then."

"I didn't say he was. He just didn't want to be bothered when he drank. Anyway, he died not long after Howard, if I remember correctly."

"About that . . ." I shifted in my chair, suddenly feeling as if I was sitting beside a large, alert skeleton who had turned its heavy skull toward me. "Did Dad ever say anything about Alf's death?"

My brother's eyebrows lifted. If Jesus had lived to seventy, and his hair had thinned, his eyes would have been no less vivid.

"What was there to say? Alf was a big man, and no spring chicken.

His heart just gave out. Dr. Kaney was there with Dad when it happened."

"I know. I was there too."

"Oh? I never knew that."

After I briefly summarized my memory, including the possible euthanasia theory, my brother smiled indulgently.

"Dad probably just didn't like the idea of trying to get Alf off the island. Better just to leave him there. Or else say a few words and dump him into the slough."

"Is that possible? Do you think they would have done that?"

My brother shrugged. "Well, definitely not Dr. Kaney. He might have turned a blind eye, though. He was decent that way."

The horror must have registered on my face, because my brother chuckled and said, "Don't worry, I doubt it happened like that. They probably buried him on the island somewhere. One thing's for sure: there wouldn't have been any service."

So, I'd be searching for a gravesite as well as the remnants of a hermitage. After all, most people went to the trouble of marking a dog's or a cat's grave. Then again, fishermen – my father included – were decidedly unsentimental about certain things.

"I never did hear," my brother added, "about anyone taking his body off the island. They might have done, though. It wouldn't have been something to talk about, unless they'd dropped him on somebody's foot."

Listening to my brother, I suddenly realized that I had to keep my hermitage plans a secret, from him and the rest of my family (except for my wife back in Edmonton, who'd just have to say that I was out of town doing research on a book, if asked). I also realized – or at least confirmed my inchoate plan – that I'd get to Alf Harley's island the old-fashioned way, the way that would honour my family's own rich life in the salmon fishery.

When Rick was in his late twenties, he fished a wooden skiff without a drum and pedal for his net, without a cabin or mast, and with only an outboard engine for power. Aptly enough, this bare-bones vessel – only about sixteen feet long and a half-dozen feet wide – was named the *Driftwood*.

In truth, it wasn't much larger or more fishable than a slab of waste lumber. For the channels of the lower Fraser, though, it was sufficient for the job, even if my brother got drenched and chilled in the rain or sunburned in the heat and had to pull two hundred fathoms of silty lead line and nylon mesh by hand all day and night until his back and shoulders and arms, by summer's end, were sculpted rock.

I wouldn't be working nearly so hard, or even travelling so far, which meant that my barely navigable vessel – a round rubber dinghy with plastic oars that I found stored on top of a mouldering pile of fishnet in my father's dilapidated backyard shed – would suffice for the twenty-minute row west out of Ladner harbour and slightly north to Alf Harley's island.

Of course, I already knew I couldn't leave via the old government wharf where so many of my childhood memories still drifted on the changing tides. A padlocked door curiously fixed into place in a solid hedge of head-high blackberry bushes brandished the following discouraging signs: *Members Only. Keep Out. No Trespassing. Private Property.* Beyond these signs (I had walked the half-hour around to the other side of the harbour channel to see), a half-dozen sleek pleasure craft were moored – presumably the municipality had leased the old wharf-site to a yacht club.

Feeling like Nick in *The Great Gatsby* – an insider and an outsider, within and without at the same time – I decided one calm midnight on a slack tide to launch my little hermitage enterprise from the dike at the foot of my childhood street. Yes, it felt ghostly to make the dark walk from our little bungalow past the corner street lamp and up onto the fifteen-foot gravel dike with a backpack of provisions and a small dinghy at my side.

The town still became 1970s' quiet after working hours, and the river still flowed in the same place, still headed out to the same ocean, so it was easy, and somewhat unsettling, to hear Dr. Kaney's laboured breathing in the stillness, even if, in truth, the breathing and the middle-aged weight and consciousness were definitely my own.

Clumsily, and, I must admit, apprehensively, I managed to push off, briefly seeing myself as a passenger in one of the lifeboats drifting away from the *Titanic* at the end of *A Night to Remember*. Terror and loss, after all, had always been a part of my maritime heritage. I had absolutely no romance about the natural world; in fact, I had too much respect for it *not* to be frightened of its power. Where the Fraser River was concerned, I knew of at least six people who had drowned within a hundred rowing strokes of my launch point: one was a boy of five who had pedalled his tricycle off the wharf; another was a teenager I'd played soccer with who'd tried to swim home from an island bonfire party and misjudged the strength of the current; and another was, possibly, the unfortunate crime witness Howard Benson. More intimately, I recalled a night toward the end of my working life as a fisherman, when I scrambled up into the bow of my brother's much-larger gillnetter to hoist the anchor so that we could make a set. Almost falling overboard, I happened to note the tide; it was raging toward the sea with such ferocity that I'd have been fifty feet below our position before resurfacing, that is if I'd even been able to fight to the surface. Now, returning to the fishing grounds where almost no commercial fishing ever happens, I'd be more apt to write poems that focused on questions, uncertainties, even simmering anxiety rather than straightforward terror.

But consistent in my writing and attitude over nearly three decades has been my recognition that the estuary of the Fraser River is no mere playground for the leisured or work yard for industry; it is a complex sphere of shifting energies utterly indifferent to human existence but not immune to human presence, which might just be an accurate definition of a middle-aged man in his pursuit of meaning. Montaigne entering his tower retreat in 1571 quickly discovered that he knew no subject better than he knew himself, and that even that knowledge was suspect because of the complexity and malleability of human nature. His famous motto of skepticism – Que sais-je? – which he had struck on a medal as a kind of reminder and challenge, somehow continues to be ignored by most of us, who much prefer to believe that we know a great deal about many subjects.

I knew only one thing as I rowed west out of the harbour in the summer stillness: I was afraid. It wasn't that I expected to capsize the dinghy and drown, or that I thought a fisheries officer would nab me for poaching; rather, my fear was almost the same as my hope – that I would take to this island solitude as a smolt to water, or at least as I had taken to my winter hermitage in Edmonton. If that happened, how on earth was I going to bear my life? I was, after all, in the thick of it – a son, a husband, a father, a worker (albeit an unemployed one). If I discovered that my lust for solitude truly was authentic and not just a passing phase of lunar-inspired mini-resistance to a connected, controlled world I didn't trust or wish to participate in, then I was destined to be a hermit in the marketplace.

In a way, I suppose I was testing my humanity, or humanity itself, just as ardent readers of *Moby-Dick*, in the late nineteenth century, often gave the novel to others to read as a means of evaluating their potential as friends. My Moby-Dick was a tiny, unpopulated silt island in the mouth of one of North America's wildest and most under-celebrated rivers, and here I was, either Ahab or Ishmael, setting out to slay the tenor of my times. Put the island and the man together, and what would result?

For Christopher Knight, the factors in the equation were slightly different (Maine woods, young man), but the result was crystal clear: nearly three decades without touching another person. And for Alf Harley (silt island, middle-aged man), the result was a lonely, cold October death, even if, before that, the result was often drunkenness punctuated by a kind of sobriety I couldn't begin to fathom. Regardless of my own place in the equation, at least my withdrawal was an active one.

I rowed a few strokes and paused, letting the dinghy drift. The surface of the channel was sleekly black and flat, like a vinyl LP that has stopped spinning on the turntable. To my immediate left, a light shone from a floathouse and made a yellow square on the water. To my immediate right, a dark line of bulrushes and a higher dark line of poplars offered a preview of my destination.

Within minutes, I would start to row north up the fishing drift where my father had spent most of his working life. But first, as if to give me a final taste of what I was about to leave behind (or so I thought), the channel picked up and amplified the voices of a man and woman calmly conversing. The sound emanated from the floathouse, and was punctuated by the light clatter of cutlery, so obviously the couple was sharing a meal. I didn't pay much attention to the content of the conversation, for I was immediately stricken by both the intimacy and antiquity of this scene that I could not see but only hear. Could anything have better symbolized the simple, straightforward argument against solitude? Only the presence of a campfire would have strengthened the bond between our twenty-first-century sociability and that of our ancestors. Food, shelter, language, the ease and comfort of being in another's company: I would retain the first three graces of life, but what would they mean without that final grace? What, indeed, would language mean after a thirty-year period of isolation like Christopher Knight's? Finkel, in his subsequent book on the North Pond Hermit, mentions that many people doubted Knight's story because of how articulate he was immediately upon capture. Surely such a prolonged isolation with such a pressing need to be quiet would affect his speech? After all, the most famous marooned sailor of the seventeenth century, Alexander Selkirk, spoke an incomprehensible Scots brogue after only four years of solitude. If Christopher Knight had not spoken aloud for nearly three decades, how could he sound as if he'd just stepped out of the world for fifteen minutes to catch his breath?

Even though I wasn't going to be gone more than a week, the question wasn't entirely moot. One ninety-minute session in the float tank listening to my central nervous system and the circulating of my blood had already taught me a great deal about the mysterious memory-arousing power of silence. Plus, as a poet and an apprentice solitary, I understood just how much language – written or spoken – formed a bridge of sociability; without speaking or writing, even for just a week, would thought itself begin to change? Put another way, how many people even laugh out loud when they're alone? Some, perhaps, but doesn't that begin to veer toward loss of sanity?

I was headed for deeper waters in a physical sense as well, as I rowed north up the broader channel toward Alf Harley's island. Suddenly, the waters around me brightened, causing me to stop rowing and hold myself perfectly still. I felt like a prison escapee when the spotlight strikes him. But after a few seconds, I looked over my shoulder at the moon, which was already vanishing, a broad band of black cloud placed like a gag across its expression. Within seconds, the heavy dark dropped around me again, and I could feel, rather than see, the little silt Tortugas breathing through their bulrush gills. Ten more minutes, and I had slipped across the timeline of memory to the world of the past, which, deceitfully but without human guile, continues to exist in the present.

THE EIGHT SMALL ISLANDS OF THE LADNER MARSH AREN'T FAMOUS. Far from it. Even the people who live within shouting distance on the nearest mainland dike don't know the official names; if anyone needs to refer to the islands at all, they don't even use unofficial names, but rather locations – "The island across from the float homes just before the bridge" – or vague descriptions – "The island where we saw those eagles roosting." With few exceptions, they are indistinguishable one from the other – flat, sparsely treed, surrounded by sedge and bulrush, and possible to circumnavigate on foot in no more than a couple of hours. The islands are also very young. In a curious sense, they're rather human in their makeup, being at once products of nature and of civilization. Made of the accretion of silts and muds washed down from the province's interior to the estuary, the islands took shape when European and American settlers began altering the river's flow in the mid-nineteenth century. Dikes, dams, dredges and other forms of human interference, increasing throughout the twentieth century and now at a rabid peak, have essentially clogged the Fraser's arteries right as they connect to the Gulf of Georgia's great beating heart. Because these black blood clots in the river mouth have no particular physical appeal, especially in relation to their more spectacular surroundings (the ocean can be smelled on the wind; the ski mountains beyond Vancouver are still visible through the smog haze), no one's ever developed them. And because they're undeveloped and inaccessible except by boat, the government of British Columbia manages – in effect, mostly ignores – them. Public access is not allowed, but the public, almost universally, doesn't bother with these islands anyway. All sorts of pleasure craft go by them, as do a few leftover fishing vessels. Kayakers, canoeists, jet skiers and water skiers pass down the sloughs, and the occasional nature study group is allowed a supervised field trip. But as far as I know, no random writer-hermits ever set foot on these muddy, tide-surrounded acres.

Of course, as even Robinson Crusoe discovered, no island is ever truly a desert, and my island is a far cry from the remoteness of an eighteenth-century island off the wild coast of South America. In the south arm of the Fraser River, between the heavily used George Massey Tunnel and the Gulf of Georgia a few miles away to the west, a clutch of silt islands bear the following official names: Gunn, Barber, Rose and Duck. The much larger, and most well-known (because of its popular waterfowl refuge), Westham Island has been farmed and populated for over a century, and the small wooden suspension bridge that connects it to the mainland has done so for sixty years. But my island (officially called Rose) is known to me as Wilkie's, because that's what my father always called it (Wilkie having been a warden there at some long-ago time – not a permanent resident, but permanent enough to have left a small dock along the bank, overhung with weeping willows).

Operating purely on body memory, I pulled for the spot, which was significant not so much because of any human presence, but rather, like so many other places on the river, because it marked the presence of a snag, a submarine hazard that could cost the unwary fisherman several fathoms of net if he didn't know enough to move off the bank. Ah, but if you could get as close as possible to the bank near Wilkie's dock, you'd be much more likely to catch the large spring salmon who, the old-timers always said, liked to scratch their bellies on the silt. It was a delicate, risky negotiation, one that I was keenly attentive to thousands of times between 1970 and 1995, but one which no longer happens, because there are no old-timers and almost no commercial fishery. Already, I began to hear voices and to see phantom shapes; already, the hair was rising on my forearms as I slipped the oars and slid over the calm moments of my father's solitude. Here, when the net was finally set (laid across the water), and the tide carried our boat toward Wilkie's dock, my father would put his bare hand on the lead line and "feel" for the big springs or even bigger sturgeon to bump into the hanging meshes. The creatures of the river were canny; that was why you had to set your net across the channel in big loops. If you set in a straight line, the meshes would hang tight as guitar strings and the salmon would nudge them and back right up and try another path. For the same reason, fishermen always made a special effort to make the "dark" set, when twilight shivered into blackness, because the fish had a harder time seeing the web.

But my thoughts weren't with those fast-moving desperate schools out in the middle of the channel. Appropriately, my thoughts were with the human and the non-human old-timers — all the fishermen of my youth who were dead now, and the white sturgeon of the same generation who very likely were.

I SAT RESTING FOR A FEW MOMENTS, SLIDING GENTLY FORWARD ON THE slack tide, my whole body as sensitive as my father's fingers as he felt for the slightest touch along the lead line. Most often, he would sense the presence of a spring salmon — the largest of the five Pacific salmon species, and the most valuable if its flesh was red not white. But every now and then — in memory, it always happened in the dead of night, in a stillness deeper than any I've ever known — my father would pull the net in slowly by hand, to keep the meshes slack (using the powered drum would make the web tense and might almost fling a fish to freedom), and a ghostly shimmer would begin to rise in the dark fathoms as I leaned over the stern to watch.

Then the head — prehistoric, frightening, long and flat and covered in scutes not scales — would burst from the water, the whole thick body following, perhaps ten or fifteen feet in length. It was as if the arm of a dead giant had thrust out of the afterlife to reach for our throats. So pallid the creature, so strange and forgotten to the surface world, it seemed to have been forced underwater against its will a million years before. Always, I jerked back, even though I'd been tensed for the surfacing. The head would sink again, and the powerful underwater flexing of a great muscle would begin to test my father's strength. With his left arm pulling the web, he'd hold his gaff hook in his right, waiting for that ghastly zombielike return from a mystery we couldn't possibly understand until we made the journey ourselves.

I closed my eyes. Sixteen years before, my father had made the journey, and I had sat by his deathbed the moment his heart stopped, feeling as if I'd gone partway with him, just as being on the river always felt like an incomprehensible marriage of realms, a subtle yet irrevocable shift from sound to silence, twilight to darkness, loneliness to solitude to whatever lies beyond solitude.

I looked over the gunwale, willing that old terror to emerge, because in it also lay the delicacy of my father's touch and the depth of my own capacity for wonder. The sturgeon remained down there, though the likelihood that many venerable giants had escaped the habitat destruction and general toxicity of the age was almost nil. Once, the great mysterious creatures could reach the size of small whales and live well over a hundred years; they were like the adzed trunks of massive cedars, slipped into the river before they could be carved into totem poles.

I caught my privileged summer breath and tried to think my way back to pre-settlement times, before any commercial fishery existed, before my island had formed enough to walk on, to a darkness and a silence that belonged so much to the Earth that they also belonged to the cosmos. Can a man with his thought slowly pull a constellation in, hold back the terror to do the work he's born to do? Never mind Ted Hughes and his legendary stilled depth of England. I had to think beyond the limitations of nationhood.

But the truth is, I do not know exactly what lies at the bottom of the river now, in the summer of 2018, what might be gliding under my small craft and (to all animals) dangerous human reflections. I suspect, though, that the great sturgeon, like the old-growth cedars, are mostly gone. One of the last years I worked as a salmon fisherman, in fact, was hauntingly noteworthy for the mysterious deaths of giant sturgeon – dozens washed up on shore from the mouth of the river to beyond Mission. Several theories were put forward (including shock from underwater explosions set off by the Department of Fisheries and Oceans to control the salmon returns, massive increases in water temperature and some sort of psychological trauma), but a toxic incident of some kind seemed most likely. What I remember most about that summer is the irony. In 1994, the salmon harvest on the Fraser reached record levels, with twenty-four-hour openings netting individual catches of several thousand sockeye – and with each fish selling for approximately ten dollars, the money made that season was considerable. Routinely, nets would be "sunk" – that is, so much weight of fish in the net pulled the corks below the surface of the river. My brother Rick and I benefited from the largesse, though 40 percent of our earnings went to the cannery from which we rented our boat, but the next year would be as poor as 1994 was good (and would, in fact, mark our last season fishing together, the end of our family's – and almost every other non-Indigenous coastal family's – many decades in the industry).

I remember the high, blood-sun-drenched slack tides of late August evenings as we carefully picked the dead and dying fish out of the nylon meshes. I remember the pungent odour of brine, mud and salmon, an odour that seemed to rise up out of the earth and sink down from the sky and, in fact, become the only element that mattered. I remember the scales and slime and blood specks on my glasses. I remember, too, an undeniable sadness at my participation in the slaughter, along with that unmistakable proud fatigue that comes from hard manual labour performed outdoors. But more than all that, I remember an evening several weeks after the height of the salmon run, when the fish were still plentiful but beginning to diminish, and the summer itself had almost reached its end. September was always poignant in the fishery, either a calm time of looking back with satisfaction at the rich harvest or a sad time of recognizing that the harvest had been disappointing and that the fall dog salmon fishing would be more of a necessity than a bonus.

Nearly two hundred fathoms from our boat, right next to our bright red Scotchman buoy that marked the end of our net, drifted what appeared to be a log. Certainly, the black shape was too large to be a salmon or even two salmon tangled on the cork line. And it couldn't be a seal poaching a meal from our net either, because the blackness didn't move once it caught on our net. By the time we had picked up to within thirty fathoms, we suspected that the shape was a sturgeon, though we couldn't quite believe it until we brought the creature below the stern.

At first, we thought it was dead. It lay oddly against the cork line, one strand of web hooked on one sharp scute, its white, sandpapery belly to the sky, its vacuum-mouth open and unmoving. But the stillness of a sturgeon is deceptive, and we knew enough to be cautious. My brother began to pull in the net by hand as I bent over the stern, gaff hook at the ready. Twice the length of my extended arm, twice as wide as my thigh, the sturgeon looked as they always looked – ghastly in their otherworldliness, like the skeleton of a sturgeon. But this one lacked the familiar visceral sense of a paused explosiveness; it was, if not dead, more lethargic than any sturgeon I'd ever encountered. When its mouth opened wider and then closed, and the fluked tail made the fan pass of a dying geisha, I didn't pull back in anticipation of a more violent stirring. Something was wrong. The river felt it. The sky felt it. The whole day contracted to the air still engaging with the animal's dying gasp. My brother and I looked at each other.

I couldn't bring myself to gaff it. My brother understood my hesitation without asking. He stopped pulling the net, held its dripping bunches in his hands like grapes killed by a frost. We both stared at the sturgeon, waiting – indeed, hoping – that it would deliver on its familiar traditional promise, waiting, perhaps, for the promise of our own past. We didn't admit as much, because we didn't have to. For at least a decade, we had been returning the smaller, younger sturgeon back to the river, but any sturgeon over three feet long was a legal catch and brought as much per pound as a salmon – no small amount. And this fish – at a glance we could see it surpassed a hundred pounds, which translated into over two hundred dollars (the value of twenty sockeye). Even so, something was seriously wrong. If the earth suddenly stopped all tectonic activity –

Even when I touched it with the gaff, the listless sturgeon didn't react. It was exactly as if the corpse of a man still took in air through the mouth. I could feel the whole dead weight before I slipped the hook up through the gill and tried to lift. The tension across my shoulders turned solid, like a steel beam. And I was afraid too, for if the sturgeon suddenly thrashed and twisted, I'd either feel the pain of its motion or else I'd drop the gaff and lose both it and the two-hundred-dollar fish.

But the sturgeon didn't move. I pulled it right underneath the rollers in the stern so that my brother could stick his own gaff in and help pull the creature aboard. Carefully, just as I had done, Rick didn't pierce the sturgeon's head or body; he just slipped the steel hook up through the gill, the way we'd put our index fingers into the gill of a large salmon when we carried it home from the wharf; the way our father had taught us, twenty years apart, in the 1950s and 1970s. Already we both knew that we were thinking of our father, seventy-one and on kidney dialysis, without having to think of him. He had killed fish for a living, but with as much respect for their otherness as possible under the dictates of economic survival. Besides, irresponsible stewardship was simply a form of suicide. To tell our father, as we would have to tell him today, that the orca whale is the most toxic marine creature on the planet and that its carcass must be treated as "hazardous waste" would be to run a blade across all our throats. By the same token, to gaff a listless hundred-pound sturgeon and not recognize all the decades it had survived to that point, to gaff it and not consider the greater advantage to the whole life of the biosphere its survival meant, would have been to be another man's children. But if the fish was going to die regardless?

We waited, carrying the whole burden of our culture in our nerves, muscles and brains, uncertain how to proceed.

After a half-minute, we heaved the creature aboard and let it slowly die. Later, we heaved it like a decapitated body in Spanish armour onto the deck of the packer. Later still, the cannery, owned by the billionaire

Jim Pattison, paid us our two hundred dollars. We spent it as quickly as most working men spend any income. Not long afterwards, our time – and almost everyone's time – fishing on the Fraser River was done. In about 130 years, the tradition as we knew it was over, marked by that summer's ominous appearance of giant dead sturgeon, floating and drifting like un-exploded WW II mines under the city's ever-expanding grid.

Except the sturgeon, even in its most motionless state – of healthy feeding, comatose recovery or even death – always contains the opposite. So what didn't explode in 1994 was still ticking slowly away in 2018.

I sat still, with the small paddle across my lap, and listened. I couldn't hear the ticking, but I could hear, distantly, the hum of traffic, the occa-sional car horn and siren. Closer, I could hear the trickle of current, the wind, the voice of my own thoughts. There I was, in the midst of one of the Earth's two great processes (erosion), waiting for a metaphorical/spiritual eruption of the other (tectonic). According to science, if all tectonic activity on the Earth ceased, erosion would completely flatten the Earth's surface within fifteen to 110 million years. But what of the relationship between the erosive quality of consciousness and the wellsprings of life from which our material selves emerge? Was the aging man flattening the dynamic surface of the child's imagination?

It was why I had come – to see if the final thirty years could be more like the first ten. If they couldn't be, surely they could be more than what my culture was selling. At least some of the places of my childhood still remained, and in a condition much as they had been for fifty years, at least on the surface. Below the surface, where the white sturgeon once grew like red cedars, the erosive changes were constant and often deadly. In fact, all over the estuary, above and below, change was visible. But here, on this one island, arrived at by my own free will, I could exist, if not in a different time, at least in time differently.

I pulled the dinghy in tight under the overhanging willow and strained in the darkness to find the shape of Wilkie's old dock. For the moment, I couldn't see it, and assumed that my memory had steered me wrong, as memory so often does. Instead, I scrambled up onto the bank, tied the rope to the tree and let the feeling of earthly solidity take hold of my body. The strangeness of the sturgeon's kingdom – past and present – had threatened to unseat my senses, a condition I hadn't yet prepared myself to accept. All I knew, at this point, was the memory of experience and my readings into solitude, silence and isolation (the hermit life). Combined, these two forms of knowledge overwhelmed my ability to focus fully on the immediate present, which was, in short, the motivation for my hermitage project in the first place. Clearly, the river's erosive action had much work to do.

But at least now I stood on Alf Harley's island again, for the first time in over forty years. Illegally, but I stood there. And the sky and the water and the darkness did not reject me, even though I did not, in truth, feel at home. What I felt wasn't even relief, and certainly not contentment. My separation from this place was akin to my physical body's separation from the digital world – the former had once been much less; the latter was increasing to the point where I had come to see myself and my whole generation as centaurs, with an analog body and past and a digital consciousness and present. Which creature would finally enter the grave? What role would this pilgrimage to isolation have in working out an answer?

In his 1933 book, *A Philosophy of Solitude*, the English author John Cowper Powys presented his theory of elementalism, its chief tenet being that we must have the courage to develop our tragic vision of life. And this courage necessitates solitude: "When our loneliness is invaded and the magical silence in which every spirit has a right to live is impinged upon by the crowd there is a wonderful comfort to be derived by stripping ourselves, not only of our clothes but of our flesh and blood, until there is nothing for them to torment but a forked, straddling skeleton and a skull that may be held in human hands a thousand years hence!"

For Powys, the way to enlightenment and peace isn't for dilettantes, the sort of resort hermit that Christopher Knight saw Thoreau to be. Indeed, Powys is bracing precisely because he doesn't mince words: "It is a vast solace to think of the huge rondure of the terraqueous earth beneath our skeleton feet, how it is forever carrying us forward with its luminous and its darkened atmosphere, like a great, dim, soft projectile, through inter-stellar space."

Standing in the gentle summer darkness, I realized that I was a great distance removed from "vast solace" at the condition of my mortality. Rather, I felt like an alien who had returned to his home planet and found that his own changes, more than the planet's, had cut him off from his origins. Where Powys found liberty in the idea of his skeleton, I found, if not horror, then an almost numbing melancholy. Time, as it diminished, became a material foe, which was exactly why I could not see the sturgeon out there in their fluid reality as anything but chains on the floor of a dark, cold cell; I could not carry my own intestines as anything but the same chains coiled and growing heavier with each ticking hour.

I wanted, of course, to feel an immediate peace. But either the world was still too much with me, or I was too much with the world. Only a few months before, I had left a place of noise, trivial distraction and banal interactions to arrive, in Thomas Merton's words, "at the doorstep of [my] own being." The change was too swift, as if I had tried to fall asleep immediately after playing video games for five straight hours. I still couldn't settle. I could hardly even catch my breath or slow my heartbeat. I was the hunter in the canoe, and I was the semi-conscious sturgeon, at the instant of tipping. Whatever balance I needed to find hadn't happened, and perhaps it never would. The latter fact had to be faced; I took the sharp barb of it in my skull and terror chased me across galaxies, though I did not move from my little silt island at the mouth of my father's river.

Is extended solitude a prison? Had I already entered it mentally and emotionally? If so, I had not chosen it, at least not consciously, and, as the old maps used to read, that way monsters lie. As Ian O'Donnell explains in his book *Prisoners, Solitude, and Time*, "It is probably fair to say that solitude is often damaging if it is involuntary, sometimes damaging if it is an unavoidable corollary of a chosen course of action, but seldom so if it is sought out." He goes on to qualify the above statement: "What is less clear is whether the mark [solitude] leaves is indelible, or deleted when normal living circumstances are restored. This depends on the duration of confinement, the reasons for it, the individual's prior mental health status, how well it is administered . . . At a fundamental level, the isolated prisoner fears that he will lose the authorship of his life."

But how could I lose the authorship of my life, returning as I was willingly to the first chapters where all the magic and mystery of my intrinsic capacity for solitude began? I couldn't. Even as I stood in the terror of the indifferent universe, more aware of it than I had been in decades, something was steadying me, righting the canoe of my unpredictable passage through time. And I knew exactly what that something was. Powys also knew, as if he stood right beside me to repeat his words: "Flung up against pain and mockery and brutality, [the lonely self] allows its aura of memories to melt away. They will re-form again, quickly enough, this cloud of disembodied images and ideas, when once the immediate tension is removed. They will return like reflections coming back to a pool of water that has been rudely disturbed."

I had rudely disturbed the surface, and Alf Harley had come back. I had rudely disturbed the surface, and my brother and my younger self had also come back. If I was patient enough, and trusting enough, the foundation of my life would return, and on it I could build a more tenable future. Powys concurred:

It is as though these memory-pictures that come floating by were "intimations of mortality," witnesses to some curious and beautiful fatality amid the casual happenings of our life, not recognized in the least by ourselves at the time, but deepening now in its meaning and significance to something ineffable . . .

. . . there is more in these memories than just what happened to us as individuals. They seem to have a life of their own, over there in that strange country, from which they floated in upon us, or slid down to us, along the slippery corridors of Time.

I stood still and let that strange country float around me. Once, I had been more natural in it, less plagued by consciousness – perhaps I could be so again. Motionless, I heard the current's trickle and the wind's trickle in the black cottonwoods – nothing else. The night remained heavy, and I could just discern the darkness below the ragged top of the tree line. It made no difference now how I felt about the greater world and our species' role in it – I had reached the island of my youth, and I was alone. If the past, present and future – linear time itself – had somehow conspired to form "slippery corridors" where reality might not appear so simple, where fact and fiction might even collide, I had certainly arrived with the appropriate book in my cargo.

DANIEL DEFOE'S *THE LIFE AND STRANGE SURPRIZING ADVENTURES OF Robinson Crusoe, of York, Mariner*, published in 1719, was immediately and immensely popular and has remained so, despite, or perhaps because of, its uniquely English mix of pragmatic fact and neurotic fancy. For Samuel Johnson, it was one of only three books he would have wished longer (*Pilgrim's Progress* and *Don Quixote* being the other two). For Jean-Jacques Rousseau, most of the story was garbage (*fatras*), but he thought a young man's ideal education should emulate Robinson Crusoe's life on the island, particularly with regards to handling the practical challenges of such isolation. Walter de la Mare sees Crusoe as representative of "that poor forked radish, a Man – with a thickish vigorous active headpiece, legs, hands, a Bible, a hatchet and a gun – face to face with grisly circumstance." The sheer ordinariness of Crusoe's intellect – Samuel Taylor Coleridge claims he represents the middle degree of mankind – is in de la Mare's eyes the whole power of the story: "Crusoe's industry is at the same time absurd and entrancing. It saved his life and sanity, it is the sovran charm of his book." James Joyce darkens this theme, seeing Crusoe as the "true symbol of the British conquest," and the "true prototype of the British colonist." Indeed, "the whole Anglo-Saxon spirit is in Crusoe; the manly independence; the unconscious cruelty; the persistence; the slow yet efficient intelligence; the sexual apathy; the practical, well-balanced religiousness; the calculating taciturnity." Virginia Woolf, too, zeroes in on (almost begrudgingly) the admirable practicality of Defoe's hero, "his shrewdness, his caution, his love of order and comfort and respectability." Everything about Crusoe's experience, she writes, is seen through his "middle-class, unimaginative eyes"; his "naturally cautious, apprehensive, conventional, and solidly matter-of-fact intelligence."

But what does Crusoe experience exactly? Decades of solitude on a tropical island. And therein lies the book's true power. Crusoe's character, in fact, is almost beside the point. A less famous early critic of the story, James Sutherland, succinctly explains its abiding appeal, an appeal that transcends race and culture: "To read *Robinson Crusoe* is to be compelled to face up to all sorts of physical problems that civilized man has long since forgotten. It is in some sense to retrace the history of the human race; it is certainly to look again with the unspoilt eyes of childhood on many things that one had long since ceased to notice at all."

For the child I was, who grew up in a watery world that included boats and islands and deaths by drowning, and whose distant Anglo-Saxon heritage included such sayings as "God helps those who help themselves," *The Life and Strange Surprizing Adventures of Robinson Crusoe, of York, Mariner* was not an extreme exaggeration of reality. I seemed to have spent every day of every summer between 1970 and 1975 building Crusoe fortresses out of driftwood and chopping Crusoe caves out of blackberry bushes; moreover, other people, especially the dangerous adults, might well have been pirates and cannibals as I made my solitary way over my island of early consciousness. The critic O. Mannoni not only explains my natural inclination toward Crusoe's story, but also, more intriguingly, my current attraction to the whole idea of hermitage: "There is in the child some trait which is partly misanthropic, or at any rate anti-social, a trait which, for lack of a better term, I would call 'the lure of a world without men.' It may be repressed to a greater or less extent, but it will remain, nonetheless, in the unconscious."

If that trait had once lain dormant in my unconscious, that was clearly no longer the case. Like Crusoe, I had come face to face with "grisly circumstance," except mine wasn't so much about how to survive alone on an island as how to survive alone amongst the crowd. The shipwrecked Crusoe didn't choose his solitude; of my own volition, I was on the verge of making mine a way of life.

In any case, as a fiction passed off as fact, *Robinson Crusoe* is the progenitor of the modern novel as we know it, but the lines between fiction and fact in all human endeavours have always been blurred, and they certainly haven't found any sharp clarity in 2018. Regardless, the themes of Daniel Defoe's eighteenth-century narrative, if not exactly the content, are timeless and fitting to my purpose: The relationship between the material and the spiritual. The will to endure. The role of solitude in human existence. The unbearable presence of time. While most children of my generation, and perhaps even of today's generation, experience *Robinson Crusoe* as an adventure tale filled with exciting exploits involving cannibals and mutineers (just as it was experienced from the beginning), the book itself mostly dramatizes one man's long wrestling with himself, which, inevitably for a book written by an eighteenth-century Englishman, is a wrestling with God. For a secular man of the twenty-first century – indeed, for an atheist who finds his Eurocentric culture alien and unappealing – Defoe's most famous work is a hard slog redeemed by periodic passages of compelling narrative action. But *Robinson Crusoe*, much like Bram Stoker's *Dracula* and Mary Shelley's *Frankenstein*, remains a powerful presence in contemporary culture, a kind of myth that enters our reality as if by osmosis and provides a blank page on which we can write our own fears and aspirations.

Who hasn't been asked about their desert island books? Their desert island discs? That's the lighthearted, comical side of the Crusoe myth, a companion – at least for those old enough to remember it – of the goofy '60s TV sitcom *Gilligan's Island*. But there's also the bluntly practical side, the one that appeals to the DIYer in any of us. Crusoe's ingenuity and sheer work ethic to construct a bearable existence, his building of fortress shelters and his sowing of crops, speaks to our admiration for resourcefulness and makes us speculate on our own practical abilities.

More than the comical and practical, however, the haunting side of the book spoke most dramatically to me as I settled into my island retreat.

Ironically, I didn't even need to face the prospect of an indeterminate solitude caused by the mercurial circumstances of a mariner's fate: what haunted me was the prison of my own consciousness, this island we're born to and must always survive on. Robinson Crusoe's anguished confrontations with isolation and time, with fate and purpose, don't require a desert island for resonance, and therein lies the explanation for why many critics, and Defoe himself, regard Crusoe's adventure as allegorical as much as historical.

As for me, I had reached a point when I could not see reality as anything other than a forced confinement. My childhood and youth in this very landscape, in fact, were almost exactly akin to Crusoe's life in England and Brazil before his shipwreck: irretrievable. In that sense, all our lives are more confined than Defoe's character's, for he eventually escapes his solitude even before leaving the island, when Friday, the ultimate TGIF, shows up as a prisoner of cannibals (to be rescued from the menu by the shotgun-wielding Crusoe).

I looked around at the darkness again. This was no tropical island with a tropical shore of sand exposed at low tides. I knew that much without having to see the actual physical reality. A silt island at the mouth of the Fraser River is more like a decapitated head held in the invisible grip of an executioner: the edges drop off abruptly and violently and the access is no easier because of tidal changes. To see a footprint would mean pushing back a thick cover of sedges and rushes and locating the print before its outline dissolved in the mud. More commonly, the new arrival must simply hoist himself up onto the bank, as I did in my boyhood on my only other visit to Wilkie's island. Even now, looking just behind me, I knew that whatever trace my passage left on the ground would be vanishing rapidly and certainly not taking any firm shape to be pondered over later. Perhaps, in this sense, the contemporary situation for an intelligent human being can never be equivalent to Robinson Crusoe's fate, for Crusoe, in the middle of his strange narrative, has a bizarre and troubling encounter that Defoe readers and literary scholars continue to puzzle over nearly three hundred years later.

Fifteen years into his enforced solitude, after he has wrestled with God over his lonely condition and reached a certain level of acceptance and ease, Crusoe is suddenly plunged into even greater fear and doubt:

> It happened one day about noon. Going towards my boat, I was exceedingly surprised with the print of a man's naked foot on the shore, which was very plain to be seen in the sand. I stood like one thunderstruck, or as if I had seen an apparition; I listened, I looked round me. I could hear nothing, nor see anything; I went up to a rising ground to look farther; I went up the shore and down the shore, but it was all one, I could see no other impression but that one; I went to it again to see if there were any more, and to observe if it might not be my fancy; but there was no room for that, for there was exactly the very print of a foot, toes, heel, and every part of a foot; how it came thither I knew not, nor could I in the least imagine. But after innumerable fluttering thoughts, like a man perfectly confused and out of myself, I came home to my fortification, not feeling, as we say, the ground I went on, but terrified to the last degree, looking behind me at every two or three steps, mistaking every bush and tree, and fancying every stump at a distance to be a man; nor is it possible to describe how many various shapes affrighted imagination represented things to me in; how many wild ideas were found every moment in my fancy, and what strange, unaccountable whimsies came into my thoughts by the way.
>
> When I came to my castle, for so I think I called it ever after this, I fled into it like one pursued; whether I went over by the ladder, as first contrived, or went in at the hole in the rock, which I called a door, I cannot remember; no, nor could I remember the next morning; for never frighted hare fled to cover, or fox to earth, with more terror of mind than I to this retreat.

Over the next several pages, Crusoe records his experience of coming to terms with this solitary footprint. He speculates that it must have been placed there by the Devil, but then, in his very rational way, concludes that the Devil would surely have found an abundance of other ways to terrify him. Then Crusoe considers the presence of savages who had arrived in canoes from the mainland. This seems more credible, and in fact convinces Crusoe that he is in great danger, for the cannibals might eventually return to destroy his fortifications and crops and to devour him. After facing this horrible prospect, he then strikes upon another idea:

In the middle of these cogitations, apprehensions, and reflections, it came into my thought one day that all this might be a mere chimera of my own; and that this foot might be the print of my own foot, when I came on shore from my boat. This cheered me up a little too, and I began to persuade myself it was all a delusion; that it was nothing else but my own foot; and why might not I come that way from the boat, as well as I was going that way to the boat? Again, I considered also that I could by no means tell for certain where I had trod, and where I had not; and that if at last this was only the print of my own foot, I had played the part of those fools who strive to make stories of spectres and apparitions, and then are frightened at them more than anybody.

But when he goes to investigate a couple of days later (yes, the print is still there!), he finds that his own foot is not nearly as large as the footprint, a fact which "filled [his] head with new imaginations, and gave [him] the vapours to the highest degree; so that [he] shook with cold, like one in an ague."

Even more terrified than before, Crusoe is nonetheless able to philosophize conclusively: "Thus fear of danger is ten thousand times more terrifying than danger itself, when apparent to the eyes; and we find the burden of anxiety greater, by much, than the evil which we are anxious about."

But in the moment, Crusoe cannot console himself, and in fact spends the next two years in a state of feverish anxiety, improving his fortifications, building a new and more secluded one, and generally fretting that he is going to be attacked by savages. Ultimately, looking back, he is confounded by this paradoxical quality of man, in which "Today we love what tomorrow we hate; today we seek what tomorrow we shun; today we desire what tomorrow we fear." For fifteen years, Crusoe's only affliction was his loneliness, his banishment from all human society, his sense of himself as having been condemned to a silent life. And yet, when a footprint appears, the very sign of another human presence, Crusoe does not regard this as a deliverance or as a "supreme blessing of salvation"; instead, he trembles "at the very apprehension of seeing a man."

When I stopped and considered my own situation, I realized that I shared this much of Crusoe's attitude: like him, I felt cut off from human society at the same time that I regarded a reconnection to be a matter of some apprehension, even of horror. Before coming to my actual silt island, I had started to construct a fortress (using mostly books, long moonlit walks, a general avoidance of social engagements and mass media); and now that I was here, I already dreaded the prospect both of staying and of leaving. Worse, I couldn't believe that the paradox even mattered, perhaps not even to myself.

In his book *Perpetual Euphoria: On the Duty to be Happy*, Pascal Bruckner presents the modern dilemma of self-fulfillment quite neatly:

> There is nothing more vague than the idea of happiness, that old prostituted, adulterated word so full of poison that we would like to exclude it from the language . . .
> . . . The very abstraction of happiness explains its seductive power and the anguish it produces. Not only are we wary of prefabricated paradises, but we are never sure that we are truly happy. When we wonder whether we are happy, we are already no longer happy.

Interestingly, Bruckner identifies Defoe's time, the eighteenth century, as the time when notions of the self, individuality and personal responsibility for happiness originated. Certainly Defoe's depiction of Crusoe suggests, by his character's very isolation, that freedom of thought and action without a belief in God would lead to the kind of modern anguish where, as Bruckner writes, "the promised land in the future recedes before us . . . It evaporates every time we try to seize it, disappoints us as soon as we approach it."

In this receding sense, we are more Jay Gatsby than Robinson Crusoe. Both characters are heroic isolates, but Fitzgerald's hero is so trapped in his own conception of the self's happiness that he can't live unless the past is also the present and future. Crusoe, the more practical Englishman, never really loses sight of the rightness of linear time or of his actual place within it. Yet individual consciousness is clearly the island that both Gatsby and Crusoe must learn to survive on. I had reached the same point, and literature, much to my dismay, seemed unable to provide the support it had always provided. My island, then, was familiar and also completely new territory at the same time. I was almost afraid to make the first print on the surface.

In the same way, many readers and critics of *Robinson Crusoe* are afraid to face the haunting nature of that one footprint on the sand and somehow let themselves believe that it was made by Friday. But as the critic Robert Folkenflik points out, "Despite Crusoe's penchant for probability, he never computes or asserts the odds of the footprint's being Friday's, nor with his interest in probability would he have been likely to have considered it probable, for it is not." Reality is most horrible to consider when it can't be explained, as Roland Barthes realized when he proposed that "the irrelevant detail is the very sign of the real, an excess like life itself, its purposelessness the reality effect the novel desires." In other words, Defoe's footprint – haunting, inexplicable, but absolutely real – is a symbol of life, and, intriguingly, perhaps most powerfully of twenty-first-century digital life. Is the real even real? Did I see what I thought I saw, and can I go back and find it again? The shifting sands of the earth, the shifting screens of the Internet: Where do we place our bodies and our spirits in the shift? Can anything stay, or take hold, even if it's never erased, even if there's no end to the amount of stored memory?

Defoe, living three centuries before the Digital Age, would have appreciated and recognized our precarious state. His own life – which has been shrouded in secrecy and muddied by his own fictive negotiations with fact – never attained lasting security.

Exactly like his most famous fictional counterpart, Defoe rose and fell often in the world, losing a fortune in failed commercial ventures, moving in and out of favour with various patrons and royals, and constantly feeling that life's basic foundation was instability. In short, he never really belonged. Born into the new mercantile class (at Cripplegate, very close to Henry Welby's Grub Street), he was routinely sneered at by the established classes for being vulgar; his success as a highly productive pamphleteer, essayist, poet and political operative never granting him full access to privilege and power (in this sense, he represents an eighteenth-century version of Jay Gatsby). Just as Crusoe spent time as a slave before his famous period of seclusion, Defoe spent time among common criminals when imprisoned in Newgate Prison and even suffered the indignity of being pilloried when his writings ran afoul of the authorities. (In fact, he spent three days in the public stockade, the same amount of time it took for Apollo 11 to reach the moon.) His great success as the first novelist didn't occur until he was almost sixty, and even then, even after the massive popularity of *Crusoe*, Defoe faced considerable criticism from the literati who doubted the veracity of his narrative and who, for centuries afterward, questioned the degree of craftsmanship that went into his novels. By this reckoning, he was, in essence, an artless hack, an upstart from the class of tradesmen who just happened to catch the public's fancy for adventure in exotic locales. Besides that, Defoe was accused – and this idea still persists – of pirating *Robinson Crusoe* from the real-life experiences of Alexander Selkirk, a Scottish sailor famously marooned for four years on a tropical island who had become something of a celebrity in the years just prior to Crusoe's appearance.

Finally, despite the immense popular appeal of the first Crusoe book (there were two others, not even remotely as popular then and certainly not read now except by the odd curious trespasser like me), Defoe's life ended with creditors so hotly in pursuit of him that he couldn't even dare to come out of hiding to stay with his beloved daughter for a visit. A letter he wrote to her at this time poignantly captures his situation: "It is not possible for me to come to Enfield, unless you could find a retired Lodging for me, where I might not be known, and might have the Comfort of seeing you both now and then; upon such a circumstance, I could gladly give the days to Solitude, to have the comfort of half an Hour now and then, with you both, for two or three Weeks. But just to come and look at you, and retire immediately, 'tis a Burden too heavy. The Parting will be a Price beyond the Enjoyment."

So not only did the Age of Enlightenment discover the modern self, it also discovered, or at least intensified, modern notions of solitude and isolation. Defoe's restlessness – especially as exemplified in Robinson Crusoe – is our modern Western restlessness; and Defoe's capitalist society/desert island is our rapid-paced/Digital Age/Buddhist yoga self-help flotation theory twenty-four-hour screen entertainment reality. But a real version of Crusoe's island, as Defoe himself made clear, and as Montaigne made clear before him and Thoreau afterwards, involves an exploration of the self that doesn't require an island at all. Defoe's largely unread third Crusoe book, which is moralistic without providing much in the way of dramatic scenes, in fact opens with a lengthy treatise on Solitude (important nouns always being capitalized by eighteenth-century authors) that undermines the whole attraction of Crusoe's experience from the reader's point of view. Gone are the cannibals and the fortress-building, replaced by the idea that, no matter where he is, on a desert island or in the middle of London, "Life in general is . . . one universal Act of Solitude." We are, that is, isolated by our own senses: "The World, I say, is nothing to us, but as it is more or less to our Relish: All Reflection is carry'd Home, and our Dear-Self is, in one Respect, the End of Living. Hence Man may be properly said to be *alone* in the Midst of the Crowds. . . . All the Reflections which he makes, are to himself; all that is pleasant, he embraces for himself; all that is irksome and grievous, is tasted but by his own Palat."

He continues, "What are the sorrows of other men to us?" Crusoe writes. "And what their Joy?" While we might feel sympathy and affection for others, ultimately, "we love, we hate, we covet, we enjoy, all in Privacy and Solitude: All that we communicate of those Things to any other, is but for their Assistance in the Pursuit of our Desires." There's simply no getting around it: "'tis for our selves we enjoy, and for our selves we suffer."

If that isn't sobering enough, Crusoe goes on to say that he never experienced real solitude on his island because he wasn't often in the proper contemplative frame of mind. Unlike Tenzin Palmo in her Himalayan cave, Crusoe, a kindred spirit of Christopher Knight, expended more thought on practical matters than on "sublime Things." Moreover, if a person has to seek a hermit-like solitude in order to escape the corrupt world, then that person is simply acknowledging his own weakness and failure. In short, desert islands aren't necessary for a person to live a good Christian life; what's needed is strength of character.

Not surprisingly, this third volume of the Robinson Crusoe story, completely unromantic, left readers stone cold. In fact, I might have been one of its few avid readers, intrigued as I was by Crusoe's belief that "every solitary person must be an Angel or a Devil." But how was one to know? Perhaps I could have discovered the truth without even leaving the city, without even walking alone at night, if I had more strength of character. Perhaps I just needed fifteen daily minutes sitting quietly in a room.

Yet here I was, on an island similar to Robinson Crusoe's in at least two senses: it was a body of land entirely surrounded by water, and it was unpopulated. But unlike Defoe's hero, I had come here of my own volition, and I had been here before. My version of a shipwreck wasn't of the romantic, page-turning variety to be found in the first volume of the myth, nor was I in danger of being eaten by cannibals or wild animals. I could also leave at any time. In fact, within two or three hours, I could be sitting in a café in downtown Vancouver, watching the whole panorama of the fractious hurry of the world go by

So why did that mysterious footprint in the middle of Crusoe's adventure seem so relevant?

Beyond the obvious reason that I had just spent a winter speculating on footprints – my own and others', including the most famous human ones of all – I saw the solitary footprint in Crusoe as the palpable yet ephemeral sign of the true nature of our brief time between the two great silences. A trace, destined to vanish, as the west coast commercial-fishing culture had vanished, as my father and his whole generation of workers had vanished, as perhaps all human civilization was destined to vanish, leaving no trace, no written history, no three-century-old stories of shipwrecks and solitary communions with the self or God.

I had reread *Crusoe* for the first time not long after my visit to the sensory deprivation tank, as a kind of encouragement and possible guidebook, a spur to the boyish exuberance I once possessed in this very place, building rafts out of driftwood and spare lumber to float along the sloughs, carving fortresses out of chest-high blue-joint grass and blackberry bushes, surveying my whole riverbank neighbourhood from a bower high up in a Douglas fir, returning and returning again to every abandoned Edwardian house with the hope of finding some surprise salvage I had overlooked before. What struck me wasn't so much Crusoe's enforced solitude, but rather the duration of it – for twenty-eight years he lived on his island (the last four of those with Friday), which is the exact amount of time that Christopher Knight had haunted the Maine woods before his capture. By nature and vocation prone to look for uncanny signs, I couldn't dismiss the coincidence – it seemed to pull me toward my own island destiny, just as the haunting appearance of the singular footprint began to resonate in numerous unbidden ways.

It was a lovely summer night, and I chose to wait until the morning to pitch my pup tent. One night fully exposed to the elements seemed only a small homage to Crusoe's trembling fear and Christopher Knight's alienation. Besides, I had nothing to worry about except perhaps a sudden shower of rain if the weather shifted, but that would undoubtedly wake me in time to seek cover. The tide was up, the smell of brackish mud heavy on the air. I could hear vague remote noises from the mainland, like hearing a battle from across many farm fields, but nothing close, no owl calls or flit of bat wings, not even a mosquito drone. The silence, which wasn't quite silence, seemed friendly. Even so, I decided to risk a fire. It seemed appropriate somehow, another longing gesture for a boyhood of random flame, whirled up out of Eddy matches and driftwood and bark and grass. Who was going to notice? I wasn't isolated like Crusoe, but I *was* isolated. Only the ghosts of my own past and the almost-as-palpable characters of my literary adventures kept me company. In any case, gazing into a fire has a kind of stirred cauldron power for a reflective human, and it was precisely to immerse myself in magic that I had come.

Gathering bark, twigs and then cumulatively larger pieces of wood was easy, even in the dark. Without exaggeration, my island could have been the floor of a sawmill after a long season of work; the river washed up all sorts of burnable detritus, and the wind in the cottonwoods contributed enough fall to start ten thousand fires. The summer heat and dryness also helped. I had a fire going within minutes, and soon stretched out beside it, no longer quite as anxious but not yet relaxed either. Strange images and sensations began to disorient me. Under the plankton squall of stars, I couldn't separate myself from the great sturgeon I had recently envisaged, down there in the murk at the bottom of the river, patiently, patiently waiting for sustenance to drift its way. How patiently? Science tells us that the white sturgeon can enter a stillness so deep that it's equivalent to a coma in humans, a kind of half-life, or perhaps a more-than-full life. Given that we have so little respect for any state other than frenzied production – even the Float House markets its sensory deprivation business as a way to increase productivity – the sturgeon's natural stillness, not to mention its antiquity, is easy to dismiss.

But I couldn't dismiss it. In fact, despite the fire's warmth, I began to shiver with the idea that some kind of sustenance, or perhaps accusation, was about to descend through the vast black fathoms above me. Robinson Crusoe's strange vision came suddenly to mind. Early in his stay on the island, his anxiety for the state of his soul threatens to shipwreck his consciousness, leading to the following passage:

> I thought that I was sitting on the ground, on the outside of my wall, where I sat when the storm blew after the earthquake, and that I saw a man descend from a great black cloud, in a bright flame of fire, and light upon the ground. He was all over as bright as a flame, so that I could just bear to look towards him. His countenance was most inexpressibly dreadful, impossible for words to describe. When he stepped upon the ground with his feet I thought the earth trembled, just as it had done before in the earthquake, and all the air looked, to my apprehension, as if it had been filled with flashes of fire.
>
> He was no sooner landed upon the earth but he moved toward me, with a long spear or weapon in his hand, to kill me; and when he came to a rising ground at some distance, he spoke to me, or I heard a voice so terrible that it is impossible to express the terror of it. All that I can say I understood was this: "Seeing all these things have not brought thee to repentance, now thou shalt die"; at which words I thought he lifted up the spear that was in his hand to kill me.

Though I lacked Crusoe's Puritan sensibility, or any religious faith at all, I couldn't shrug off the essential chasmic mysteries of life that could, in one fleeting instant, take me from a creature's stillness at the bottom of a river to the stillness howling from the light side of the moon to the dark side and back again. How many months, how many years, before such rapid imagining unloosed itself from reality and led to madness? Neither Christopher Knight nor Robinson Crusoe had any difficulty speaking normally after several decades alone, and yet Alexander Selkirk was unintelligible after just four years of desert island solitude.

According to *Prisoners, Solitude, and Time*, a common result of solitary confinement is self-abuse (biting off fingers and toes, for example), often leading to suicide. In a recent case in New Brunswick, a prisoner ended 118 days in solitary confinement by hanging himself in his cell. Who among us can honestly predict our capacity for isolation, whether voluntary or forced? My late-night walks and my ninety minutes in a sensory deprivation tank had taught me a little about my capacity, but only a little. And even that teaching left me skeptical of the advantages in a solitary life. Certainly, the books I'd read hadn't done much to convince me that those who were most capable of long periods of isolation were healthy, contented individuals. Christopher Knight, Tenzin Palmo, Thomas Merton, et al. are enviable only to the extent that a person feels the same aching void, a void that, on most of the evidence, doesn't appear to be fillable. Solitaries, in fact, are just like the moon: broken from a lost wholeness, and shining on the one side that others see; the private side, like the dark side of the moon, is inaccessible, as Dostoevsky understood. Already I knew from the deep winter that my relationship to solitude and society was much more complex than I had assumed, and that, if I wrote about it, I would have to work very hard not to present a half-truth for the sake of rhetoric.

The minutes drifted by. I tried to clear my mind of all images by gazing into the flames, but the sturgeon, true to its nature, would not swim away. It remained out there in the night like an open casket waiting for my life to fall, as it had no doubt waited for Alf Harley's life to fall, a Salish hunter's life, any life over these tame-seeming but wild currents. The sturgeon's patience, its capacity for stillness, could outwait any human state of consciousness, including whatever category mine fell into.

In the hermit world, or at least the spiritually motivated version of it, the main threat to peace is acedia, a condition described by an early desert Christian, Evagrius Ponticus, as the noonday demon that attacks the believer when the sun is at its highest and the heat unbearably oppressive. It is an outside force more than a flaw of character, an alien agent that drains a person of energy and life, ultimately leading to spiritual death and possibly even suicide, tearing the soul to pieces "as a hunting dog does a fawn." In the grips of the noonday demon, a person hates precisely what is available, says Evagrius, and desires what is not available. Also known as sloth and despondency, acedia is considered by most religions to be the most dangerous sin, for its presence overwhelms all other thoughts and feelings. To be unconcerned with one's position or condition in the world, for most people, is indeed considered a form of living death, a comatose state, a sturgeon's inhuman stillness.

Solitude taken in great doses is therefore seen to be a threat. Certainly Robinson Crusoe, who discovered the terrifying footprint "one day, about noon," fell into a state of acedia when he couldn't enjoy the pleasures of the island available to him and desired only the lost English island that was so unavailable. Certainly, many people in the privileged Western world, battling anxiety and depression to the point of not being able to get out of bed, or of not wanting to live in material rather than digital reality, understand the demonic nature of acedia. Binge-watching whole seasons of TV shows on Netflix without getting out of your pajamas for days might not lead to suicide, but the experience can become dangerously addictive, a barrier to living a rich and fulfilled existence.

But the salient point is that the hunting dog can tear the fawn to pieces whether the fawn is blinking into a screen or gazing into a fire. The urban technophile and the rural hermit, in other words, run the same risks.

Where had I landed on this first island day of my withdrawal from the great sins of busyness and efficiency? Well, not being a Christian and therefore having no real belief in sins, I nevertheless recognized that I had indeed lost interest in the world and its affairs, as well as in my own worldly position. Thomas Merton says that the hermit is one who, accepting in his very essence the inevitability of death, gives over his cares to God. Thomas Merton doesn't say, however, to whom a non-believer relinquishes his cares.

I poked at the fire and watched a demonic face twist in the flames. But that face couldn't hold my attention. I still saw – no, I felt – the sturgeon on the bottom of the river, the inevitability of its appetite, its indifference to the world above that sometimes dropped surprising meals through the murky fathoms. As a small boy, I had been witness to the gutting of a seven-hundred-pound thirty-foot-long sturgeon, had seen the contents of that capacious stomach laid out on a moonlit wharf – many bones of different species, tin cans, more recent undigested fish. But most disturbing of all, when I look back, was the small greyish woman's shoe with buttons and a high heel, possibly hoovered up during the Victorian era. I remember how one of the fishermen made a joke: "Too bad there's not another one. Make a nice gift for the wife." I remember how the laughter of the gathered men sounded hollow, fearful, even to my innocent ears. I remember, above all, my father's strange solemnity as we returned to our boat, almost more solemn than his demeanour as we left Alf Harley's island.

This island. My long-dead father. That I could put my hand out and touch the very ground over which my father, Dr. Kaney and Alf Harley had once drawn breath struck me again as the most debilitating and haunting fact, a palpable strangeness, the source of my own noonday demon. But the memory of that gutted sturgeon, along with acedia's ever-present companion of suicide, quickly reminded me of other horrors, as if, in a desperate poet's game of association, I had to leap to keep ahead of my own images.

THE SINGLE FOOTPRINT ON CRUSOE'S ISLAND. THE SINGLE VICTORIAN shoe in the gut of a giant sturgeon. The astronauts' footprints. The shoe-tree. Being where I was and what fancies played upon my imagination, how could I avoid thinking of one of the most bizarre, haunting and ongoing episodes of gruesome news to trouble the west coast in years?

For the past decade, disarticulated human feet, always one at a time and always in a running shoe, have been washing up on British Columbia's shores. To date, thirteen feet have been found, including one just a few hundred yards away, on a neighbouring silt island.

A longer, deeper tremor ran through me, as if the fire had suddenly snapped out. I heard the river now as deep space flowing without any solid mass to touch. Pulling my jacket tight at the collar, I tried to shift my mind to other subjects, but, of course, I had been in the grip of strange forces since arriving on the coast and I wasn't going to escape so easily. For two years, Crusoe ruminated on the meaning of that single footprint. As a twenty-first-century man, self-marooned, soft, impractical, a little neurotic, I had no choice but to continue sacrificing the calm reflection I had come here for in order to face whatever the solitude dredged up.

Thirteen feet. Each one in a running shoe. Each one thereby protected from scavengers. The authorities say that thousands of bodies fall into the world's oceans every year, that it's not unusual for feet to disarticulate from those bodies, given the thinness of the ankle joint and that running shoes basically act as tiny flotation devices that inevitably find their way to shore. The public says, as the public will, a grisly serial killer must be out there. Or the feet must be from the victims of a downed Asian aircraft that was never found (all the sneakers appear to be models manufactured around the same time). The authorities, trying to calm public fears and fancies, explain that the feet likely come from suicides and accidents – in fact, eight of the feet have been identified as belonging to six victims. The thirteenth foot, discovered in early December 2017, remains a mystery, but an even more grisly one, given that part of the lower leg, including a tibia and fibula, is attached to the foot. One thing is for certain, the authorities insist, no foul play is suspected, nor is there any connection between these haunting dismemberments. The public, unconvinced, responds, how do they know? What aren't they telling us?

But surely suicide itself is a major connection. Cold by the fire, I could hear in the river-silence the million footsteps of those lost people no longer walking on the earth. I could hear my own faltering footsteps approaching my inevitable end, and the footsteps of Christopher Knight as he walked out of his car at the edge of nearly thirty years of invisibility, and the fog-shrouded footsteps of Weldon Kees walking along the Golden Gate Bridge, on his way to end his own and Robinson's life. Instinctively, I looked skyward, but couldn't find the smeared lunar surface containing the footprints Neil Armstrong tried so hard to walk away from for the rest of his life, as if he sought to kill the man he had been.

When is a person ever more solitary than at the instant of suicide? No foul play? No connection? The words of authority, which are the words of the busy world, so rarely console.

I stood up from the fire and tried to walk without self-consciousness toward the river. But each step was leaden. I had a terrifying sensation of my own feet being dismembered, then joining the flow of the lost. Out there, the river seemed clogged with bodies, their eyes open like salmon's, gazing ferociously at a future that was only death. The bodies of strangers, and the body of Alf Harley, dumped out of his seclusion like a sailor, like Neil Armstrong's ashes buried at sea.

This wasn't any good. This wasn't Thoreau stretching his legs as he went outside to check on the pond, or even Christopher Knight on a midnight raid for radio batteries and junk food. This was more like Captain Lawrence Oates, famously saying to the three surviving members of Scott's doomed Arctic expedition huddled in a tent, "I'm just going outside and may be some time," and then vanishing forever in a swirl of snow and ice.

That "time," obviously, happened under extreme conditions that led to the deaths of the whole party, but that "time" was purely a matter of the individual in his own mind, like the suicides washed up on British Columbia shores. That "time" is the only time that matters, once you've reached a certain stage of your own explorations. I thought again of Thoreau's sentence in "Civil Disobedience": "A man thinking or working is always alone."

But Thoreau didn't live in the Digital Age. He didn't know about online communities, cellphones, laptops or the ubiquitous nature of virtual reality that has completely altered the whole concept of "alone." Thoreau sensed the coming invasion, though, in his loathing of mass media, telegraphs and railroads; he recognized, even in the middle of the nineteenth century, that the human capacity for individual reflection was being eroded.

Still, he remains a creature from another planet, even if we seek to make a kindred spirit of him. How could it be otherwise? Over a century of capitalist progress and technology has intervened. What would Thoreau make of all these Starbucks franchises filled with people plugged into laptops and sitting by themselves? Would he understand that, even though they might be thinking and working, they are not alone in the same way as he was when strolling along the streets of Concord? More to the point, would he understand how much more a person retreating from 2018 civilization into what remains of wilderness has to shuck off to recover some sort of natural state of being?

By the time I reached the river's edge, Thoreau's promenading footsteps and his two years of convivial solitude had faded away, replaced again by Christopher Knight's vanishing footsteps and his nearly thirty years of touching no one. In Finkel's first interview with the North Pond Hermit, one remarkable fact about invisibility stands out: the diligent and masterful way Knight left no trace of his passage through the woods. Not only was he obsessive about never leaving a print, but Knight also came to know the exact number of steps required to reach certain cabins. It was as if he existed without existing, as if he had committed suicide but had somehow kept on living. But then, after his capture, Knight spoke those haunting words that I was just now beginning to taste as a kind of horror: "When I applied my increased perception to myself, I lost my identity."

As disturbed as Crusoe, I looked back, half expecting to see a whole sequence of enigmatic solitary footprints walking toward me, a sequence I would have to follow in order to reveal myself to myself, just as Claude Rains as the Invisible Man is revealed only by the trace of his passage over the ground.

The stars were faint; the moon, my less-than-comforting companion of a colder season, obscured by cloud. The black was deep over my hands and on the water as I stood listening to the current gnaw quietly at the muddy banks. A dozen fathoms down, the single shoes rested in the guts of the few remaining sturgeon, and out in the gulf currents the dismembered feet of the dead floated on their strange journeys to sad discovery.

What a mystery and power is our consciousness, and how true Dostoevsky's statement that we can hardly know others because we can't even know ourselves. Invisibility. Isolation. Identity. An appropriate trio of words to sum up the modern age, which is everywhere, and especially in matters of popularized wellness – I, I, I. For Christopher Knight, the loss of identity resulted in a sense of great freedom. Without anyone to observe him, without anyone to communicate with, he was "just there," a being in a world free of human interaction.

But clearly that wasn't so. In fact, in his long seclusion, Knight was ironically more attentive to human presence than he might have been plugged into a laptop in a Starbucks in the middle of New York City. His desire for solitude, in other words, demanded a sensitivity to the presence of his own kind that was primitive and even more stressful than a rush-hour commute. Was this, then, freedom, or merely a special kind of cage? Can there ever be freedom in a mind saturated with memory and experience? And is freedom without memory and experience, that plane of being Tenzin Palmo tried to attain in her cave, really worth the foot-candle?

A siren sounded very faintly in the distance. I could see the white sturgeon phosphorous shimmer of the Ladner town clock on the southeast horizon. But it was the black water flowing a mere foot from my stance that my eyes kept returning to, water that, in mid-July, wasn't ice cold, but somehow the murkiness and the grimness of the contents made that water as chilled as any current in deep space, as chilled as thought itself. The current took me back, almost against my will, to another night on the same stretch of river.

PAT BRODY'S SMALL, NEAT GILLNETTER BELIED HIS IRISH ECCENTRICITY. Everything about his vessel reflected the order and control of his previous life as a policeman; everything about his face and manner reflected the wildness of his Celtic blood. His boat with the puttering Easthope engine suddenly quieted as he slid alongside my father's gillnetter.

Out of his long face corded with muscle shone eyes black as wet slate. Unlike the other fishermen of my father's generation, he rarely wore a skullcap, so his greyish white hair, jowl-length, appeared to whip around his expression like so many small seething snakes. Normally, when he spoke, his voice, unaccented, boomed. But not on this night.

"Hector," he said softly from the deck of his main hatch, "I wonder if you'd have a drink with me?"

I was maybe eight or nine then, and always a quiet child. It was easy enough to take little notice of me under any circumstance, but I sensed, even at that age, that Mr. Brody had a good reason for overlooking my presence.

My father must have understood as well, for he didn't drink on the river, and in fact drank only rarely on land. After only a few seconds of hesitation, he said, "Okay, Pat. I'll just get the top off my Thermos."

Our net was out, the corks stretching away like a constellation strand in the dim moonlight. I stayed on the main deck, against the exhaust pipe, to pick up the lingering heat from the switched-off engine, but a whisper over still water can sound like normal conversation, and I was only ten or twelve feet away from the two men.

With the boats roped together securely at the stern, and after a clink of glass, Mr. Brody put one arm of his dull orange Floater jacket onto the high bar of his rollers, and said, "Something terrible, Hector. I've done something. I'm not sure . . ." Even as his voice trailed off, I could hear the fear in it falling on the darkness out beyond the faint glow of the mast lights. I was even sure that I could hear the long swallow in his throat as he tilted his uncovered head back slightly, the snake heads quivering at his cheeks.

"I thought it was a stump, you see. Or a big spring. I wasn't thinking." He brought the orange sleeve across his brow, momentarily vanishing. My father hadn't raised his Thermos lid.

"It was a body," Mr. Brody said, the last word stopping his breath. His hand seemed to make a benediction with his glass as he raised it. "The smell was the first thing. Then . . ." He spat abruptly over the stern, as though the smell had reached him again. The tide, which was running out, moved even faster in the pause.

"It wasn't a woman. Thank the good Lord for that." His arm had dropped to his side.

My father nodded, and when he took a sip from his Thermos lid, Mr. Brody seemed to gain strength from the act. At least he spoke more clearly and fluidly. "I didn't see the face at all, Hector. But the shoulders, the width of them. I could tell it wasn't a woman. You see the tide? I was right at the bottom of the drift, picking full speed, and it wasn't really in my net. Sort of hanging on the cork line. Then it twisted away. Like it was still alive."

So slightly that I barely noticed, my father turned his head to me. Then he put himself between me and the speaker. But his effort made no difference, for Mr. Brody suddenly gave one shocking sob and said, "I had my gaff in my hand, and I made a swipe at it. I wasn't thinking, Hector. The sound. Not the sound. The feel. You know. Up your arm. I felt that. But Hector . . . it must have been in the river a long while. It wasn't hard. It just . . . well, most of it . . . pulled off. The current took it under. But not before it rolled on me. You know, the way a stump does. Sweet Jesus."

He poured from the bottle so hastily that I could hear the slosh of liquid in the glass. Then he took a long drink, which seemed to enter his mouth like lead, for the upper half of his body slumped forward.

"Heaven help me, but I'll be damned if the arm didn't come right off. I had it gaffed. Properly gaffed. That's not the worst of it, Hector."

His face appeared and disappeared, as if he too was roiling in the black current, his orange arm reaching up for help.

"I wasn't thinking clearly. It happened so fast. Probably instinct, or maybe the smell, I don't know, but I shook it off, you see. I didn't think about it. Once the rest of it had pulled away, I just . . . I couldn't stand it, you see. That arm on the end of my gaff. But I shouldn't have done it, Hector. I shouldn't. The poor bastard's family. I should have kept the arm. Jesus, what was I a policeman for if I didn't know that much?"

"It was a shock. Who would have done anything different?" My father's voice was admirably calm, but I knew him well enough to know that he was just as upset.

"I've been to crime scenes. Accidents. It's not my first corpse. Not even close."

"But the surprise of it. You can't have been prepared for something like that."

"No. You're telling the truth there, for certain. A man can't be prepared, can't ever be. Not even when I was a cop. I threw up for years before I got used to it."

Our twinned boats had almost reached the slough at the south end of Wilkie's island. We would have to pick up our own net now. But how could we? The speed of the current meant that the body would be moving faster than us, but that was no comfort to a child's — or probably even an adult's — imagination.

My father lit a cigarette for himself and for Mr. Brody. The scritch of the match and the little flare of light seemed to occur in an even deeper darkness, as if we were drifting in a cave.

"The family won't know, Hector," Mr. Brody said, all the fear in his voice suddenly replaced with sorrow. "It's the most terrible thing, not knowing."

Then he untied his stern-rope and our boats pulled apart. My father stood still for a moment, one hand on the taut cork line between the drum and rollers. I wondered if, like me, he felt anxious about picking up his net, if he felt the same cold along his spine. If so, he kept the anxiety to himself, as he always did.

But after he told me to start the engine, I noticed that he took a quick swig out of his Thermos lid before he flung the rest of the contents into the river. A minute later, when I joined him in the stern, the smell of whisky hung above the gasoline fumes and the brine until the drum's turning brought the first salmon over the rollers, its silver jaw working and working without sound, as if the desperate creature was afraid to utter a verdict on its own fate.

MY LOGICAL NEXT STEP WAS TO SLEEP. BUT IF CHARLES DICKENS couldn't sleep in 1857, and Tenzin Palmo in her cave refused to sleep because it was a waste of meditation time, and Christopher Knight couldn't afford to sleep because the cold would kill him, who was I to differ? Besides, I had that memory of my young childhood inability to see the daybreak on the river, so I decided to stay awake. Perhaps some special insight would come to me now that I was on the island, or perhaps sleep would take me suddenly, as it had sometimes done on my couch under the moon in Edmonton, as it must have done to the astronauts of Apollo 11, running on adrenaline but exhausted as they waited between stages of their iconic journey. One thing was obvious: I could no more go traipsing about the island in the dark looking for Alf Harley's grave or the remains of his hermitage than the astronauts could let themselves out into space to drift around. Here, sunlight, not moonlight, needed to be my walking companion.

Mosquitoes whined at my ears, so I moved even closer to the smoke of the fire, almost hanging into the flames. Bats flitted overhead, their erratic flight like a series of tossed handfuls of oily dirt. The wind tickled the cottonwood leaves, making each tree shudder briefly before going still again. After a few minutes, my eyes started to sting from the smoke, so I pulled back and looked upward. There, just creeping out from the black scud, was the full moon of midsummer, what the Indigenous people of the area call a Sturgeon moon.

Was it the moonlight or my own sleep-deprived imagination that turned the trunks of all the trees to dead and hanging giant sturgeon? If I stood and walked toward them, would I find inside each trunk the missing shoes on the missing disarticulated feet? Once, thousands of these huge prehistoric fish were yearly hauled out of the murky depths and left to hang, like otherworldly bell-tower ropes that no one dared to pull for fear of the revelation that would come, consigning us all to doom for our unthinking disrespect. I could smell the brine of that flesh and feel the sharpness of those scutes. Now I even heard the whine of the mosquitoes as a far-off infant cry arising from the gut of what we had killed and continue to kill with impunity.

As the night wore on, growing darker and darker, as I began to slip in and out of consciousness, fighting, like the little boy I'd been, to use whatever warmth I could find to keep myself awake even as most of my body turned cold, the trees became more alive, blood-filled, fighting and gasping on their invisible hooks. When the wind picked up and the leaves trembled, the sound was half weary sigh and half despondent moan. Like Crusoe, I plagued myself with my own imagination, convinced that in the first light I would find a remnant of Alf Harley's presence, and that remnant would be a pair of boots containing decayed stumps. Even the current's barely audible eroding of the muddy bank sounded macabre, as if a baby was suckling blood from a breast.

At some point, I knew I had lost my battle with the darkness. The pre-dawn cold penetrated all my defenses, and I felt myself inviting sleep, eager to escape my waking fancies.

"Sorry, Dad," I said softly as I lay beside the fire. "Still can't make it."

His voice, even more softly, replied, "That's okay, Monk. You can try again next time."

A split second before the smoke of sleep buried me in its folds, my mind registered the hard fact that all the next times had gone forever.

I WOKE TO THE BURNT SMELL OF SIZZLING ASHES, THE PATTER OF RAIN and a pre-dawn as cold as I remembered it from my last summer of fishing in 1995. A daybreak as thin as egg white streaked with pale blood rose moon-like over the North Shore mountains. The actual moon had disappeared behind the overcast again, so the moment was darker than the moment I had fallen asleep. My whole body was chilled with the kind of cold that makes it hard to stir. I knew it wasn't the deep winter cold of Alberta, and that therefore it wouldn't kill me, but somehow it felt much more penetrating, as if ice had formed on my skeleton. The rain, not heavy enough to soak me, also wasn't enough motivation to get me on my feet. I just lay there, damp, beside a scorched crater of my own making, trying to orient myself, trying to determine what world and time I existed in.

At some point, I must have dozed off again, for I was back on the deck of my father's boat, slumped on the main hatch near the exhaust, with a thick blanket over me. Two men's voices spoke out of the same kind of thin pre-dawn light I had just wakened to.

"We'll have to cut him down. These knots aren't budging."

"Is he conscious?"

"Passed out, from the smell of it."

"You'll have to tie us to the piling."

By the time the voices paused, I recognized them as my father's and my brother's. Their tone dropped, but they might as well have been whispering in my ear.

"What about Tim?"

"Sound asleep. He'll stay that way until we go in."

"Good. He doesn't need to see this. The little bastards . . ."

The rest of my brother's sentence died under a sudden brief thump. Because I felt it, I knew that our boat had bumped into my brother's boat or vice versa.

IN THE WORDS OF EMILY DICKINSON, THE RECLUSE-POET WHO WAS really just an intelligent woman desperate for freedom from social constraints, "I could not see to see." The bump shifted my consciousness again. What I looked out on wasn't my father and brother, but the still-oncoming daybreak. This time, stiffly, I pushed myself up into a sitting position, determined to use my familiar waking logic to brush away the insistent palpable dreams.

The light and colour seeped over the mountains. Already, the faint random squawks of Vancouver traffic mingled with the first bird pipings from the rushes, telling me exactly where I was. The cottonwood trees fifty feet away no longer hung like dead fish. The scent of ripe blackberry mixed with the burnt ashes of my fire and the heavy musk of the current to work like smelling salts.

I stood and, like Crusoe, took stock of my property. One silt island, a few miles in circumference, out of eight silt islands in the Ladner Marsh;

one of twenty-eight original islands in the mouth of the Fraser River that now numbered only nineteen, as several channels had been infilled with the ever-accumulating silt, turning two islands into one. Twenty miles to the north, under the pale-blue mountains, the global metropolis of Vancouver; to the east, a thousand miles away, Edmonton's smaller metropolis; a half-mile to the south, the original townsite of Ladner, where I had spent an idyllic childhood of Thoreauvian freedom; and a few miles to the west, the Gulf of Georgia, where the last endangered resident orca splashed down like returning Apollo capsules.

The image stopped the pretense. I stood in a world of science and industry that, allied with religion, waged constant battle against nature. Neil Armstrong detached from his emotions flipping 477 switches on a console a quarter-million miles from Earth and his mother on the ground praying to Jesus non-stop. Both armies terrified me; I was a refugee from hundreds of years of civilization. There was no place to stand except in my consciousness, no place except the past where I felt at home.

But even that home was a mythology. While I played with my tiny plastic astronauts in the alluvial dirt, Michael Collins looked down from his orbiting and saw "some green along the west coast of Canada," and then paused to eat a plastic pouch of salmon that might have been caught in a net on this very stretch of river. Before I was even born, our species had decided that, as Armstrong put it, "man's destiny lies in the stars." Not only that, I was an invasive species, just like the Himalayan blackberry bushes and the ring-necked pheasants and the old English and Greek women who formed such a rich part of my memories. Another form of fellowship with the barren and reclusive moon, itself an invader, spun off and now stuck in a middle zone between a dying planet and a blazing star.

I stood and walked to the bank. The tide was running out, and a great deal of drift cluttered the dark-grey surface. Several large candelabra-like stumps and scorched and jagged tree trunks progressed southward like a herd of bucks, doubtless the products of raging forest fires in the interior. After a hundred plus years of industrial abuse, the Fraser still contained considerable power to shift material. When I was a boy, fishing with my father at freshet time, we could even hear the silt scraping the bottom of the boat; at night, our watery world flowed as black and matter-filled as the cosmos that stretched impossibly above us.

I looked to the north, to the main river, where larger and larger freighters crept inland to the shipping docks. The towering black masses of their hulls, the warning blasts of their horns, had caused particular anxiety for fishermen who had just set their nets in a freighter's path. With the current running fast, and the great ships spinning their massive propellers and moving with surprising speed against the outflow, the nights were fraught with anxiety.

All at once, I looked to the hard-packed ground at my feet. It was as if the island itself had bumped into my memory, jolting it. I already knew that Alf Harley wasn't the only hermit on the Fraser River. Far upriver, near Williams Lake, a hermit nicknamed the Mad Russian had lived alone on a rocky island between 1958 and 1970, until he vanished without a trace, leaving the table in his little shack set. His overturned boat was eventually found, so it was assumed that the man, rumoured to be a western spy hiding out from the KGB, had drowned. Much closer to where I was, in the peat bog near Surrey twenty miles to the east, a nameless hermit had constructed a hermitage on the riverbank more in keeping with Christopher Knight's sort of set-up. However, by 1998, the bush-shrouded ramshackle cabin had burnt down, the little garden had gone back to the wild and only a few relics remained, including thousands of plastic bags (akin to all the plastic pouches that the astronauts strewed across the moon) and, mysteriously, a rusted globe of the Earth on which only the word *Timbuktu* was legible.

STANDING NOW ON THE UNCOMFORTABLE AND SHIFTING GROUND OF LATE middle age, I looked upriver, trying to imagine that nameless hermit as a kind of Robinson Crusoe who had built a fortress and garden in the bog and had managed to survive otherwise on salmonberries, blackberries, perhaps even a stone-struck mallard or a salmon caught bare-handed in the shallows of a slough. The idea was ridiculous. These silt islands possessed no caves or wild goats, and the amount of passing marine traffic, not to mention the proximity of civilization, made it obvious that hermitage was much more than just a matter of physical endurance.

The question was always the same and it always returned: For whom do we live? For whom *can* we live? Even filled with the selflessness of a saint, we simply cannot create peace of mind in another person. Material support, yes, and sometimes even emotional support, but not mental health *at the deepest level*. As Defoe, Crusoe's creator, understood so well nearly three hundred years ago, every person is, in fact, an island, at least when it comes to ultimate matters. So the question isn't whether we shall be rescued and taken off one day, but rather how can we keep the isolated self from being eroded. With Twitter? With endless scrolling? With the work, work, work of personal destiny, Armstrong on the moon and Christopher Knight breaking into cabins? "Beware the barrenness of a busy life," Socrates said, the philosopher who walked everywhere barefoot, unafraid to leave a trace.

The deep winter had resolved nothing except the hunger for resolution. I still possessed it. That is, I couldn't agree with Tenzin Palmo's words long after she had left her cave: "The more you realize, the more you realize there is nothing to realize. The idea that there's somewhere we have got to get to, and something we have to attain, is our basic delusion. Who is there to attain it anyway?"

Yet she had devoted her whole life to attaining yogi status, as I had devoted mine to writing books. If there is indeed nothing to realize, how does one proceed? I wasn't any further along that path of self-wisdom than I'd been at the end of March. Between leaving the Float House and arriving on the island, I had maintained my withdrawal from the main currents of the world, though I had been unable to sustain the pace of my sleep-deprived nights. Slowly, over the weeks, as the deep winter had turned, unconvincingly, into the not-quite-as-deep Edmonton spring, I even lost track of tracking the moon. Occasionally, I'd catch sight of it, almost guiltily, and try to re-enter my obsession, but the intensity of my self-awareness had diminished with the severe cold. I had crossed a frontier but wasn't yet sure whether I'd landed in a new country or, like Thoreau, just retraced my steps. The flapping blue nylon tarp and the lonely shoe-tree remained in place, but I saw them only by daylight – as a result, some of the magic had drained out of them. In fact, with the arrival of a warmer season, even more clothes and blankets began to emerge with the foliage. One morning, walking the dog, I even saw a couple of figures through the trees, and knew that the homeless had resumed their summer camps. Increasingly, my footprints blurred with other footprints on the path; I no longer felt like I was leaving eternal traces in the lunar light.

Even so, I was a different man. For one thing, I no longer had a job; for another, I refused to reconnect. The desire just wasn't there. I had no clear idea of what was going on in the greater world outside of my own physical limits, nor in the lives of the people I knew. Even my three children mostly existed to me as shadows, like the flickering images of illusion on the walls of Plato's cave. I did what I needed to do – shopping, cooking, engaging in ordinary conversation – but I felt the lure of Alf Harley's island almost every minute, awake or asleep. It loomed in my imagination not as a place but rather as a decisive event beyond which I might never return to my former self.

NOW I STOOD IN THE GREY DAWN LIGHT, SO COLD THAT I FINALLY DECIDED I had to move. So I walked a hundred yards to the edge of the broad, deadhead-filled slough running between my island and its neighbour to the north, whose name I couldn't remember. The world of official names on human maps just couldn't compete with memory, but then, memory has a hard time competing with itself. Where was I, really? On an island I knew mostly only by drifting past it in the company of a man who'd been dead for almost twenty years, a man – I recalled now – who rarely socialized and who, on many occasions in my childhood, disappeared into his backyard greenhouse whenever anyone came to visit. Was I just the apple not falling far from the tree? Perhaps. Studies have shown that there can be a genetic predisposition to solitude. I had my father's blue eyes, why not his longing to be alone by a fire long after midnight staring into the flames or watching the sky for shooting stars? Perhaps I had to stop resisting my own inheritance and let myself withdraw into whatever hermitage I was born to.

The tide had almost stopped running out. The coffee-brown surface crept along, thick and sludgy, covered with drift, almost like a lava flow. Now the muddy banks were exposed, creating opportunities for the day's first hunters. A great blue heron, that masterly creature of stillness, the visible companion to the sturgeon's invisible patience, stood in the shallows on one thin leg, gazing with its unblinking yellow eyes at the almost-still water.

It had been over forty years since I'd played the game of trying to outwait a blue heron. As a boy, I used to stand completely still, daring the bird to make the first move. I wouldn't even blink my eyes. Sometimes the waiting would last a minute, and sometimes much longer; sometimes I would win, and sometimes the day of sensory pleasure would call me away to pick blackberries or cherries or to just lie in the chest-high blue-joint grass before the heron lunged for its prey.

Now I played the game again, admiring the bird's colours, so much like the colours of the mountains and the islands to the west on a clear summer day – a pale blue body, with dark blue at the wing tips, and that curious head to body/neck ratio, giving the heron its prehistoric brontosaurus quality. With the neck thin and curved as a garter snake, and with the small head like the yarmulke on a Hasidic scholar, the heron was an intimidating rival, seeming at once to predate our species by eons but also to contain a penetrating human intelligence. However, this striking bird, unlike the sturgeon, doesn't live for centuries; in fact, it lives, on average, only about the length of a childhood.

The daylight brightened around us, moving faster than the river flow. Tired as I was, I fought the desire to blink and tried to clear my mind of all thought. But I wasn't Thich Nhat Hanh about to wash a delicate blue plate; I was nothing but a vessel so filled with memory that I was sinking from the present and the future. The river might well have risen over the banks to bury me in its Vesuvian ash. My form of mindfulness was always going to be fully conscious of the past.

Staring at the heron, I recalled the only person I knew who'd ever killed one. Just as that specific face and body returned to me, the bird lowered its head and, with a snake's quickness, struck the dark water at its feet, jolting me back to the present. Seconds later, as the heron shook its catch down its long bill and longer throat, I was back on the deck of my father's boat, surreptitiously watching my brother and father at their unusual task.

THE LIGHT HAD JUST BEGUN TO BREAK, AND THE PRE-DAWN CONTAINED the usual penetrating chill. When my father and brother moved closer to the body, I shifted my own as quietly as possible until, lying on my side, I had a clear view through the fingerlings of mist.

Our engine idled against the current, which was low and running out, but my brother's outboard was lifted in the *Driftwood*'s stern. Apparently, we were keeping him in place beside the tall black piling, one of the remnants of a late-nineteenth-century cannery that had shut down in one of the periodic slumps that has always defined the salmon fishery. My brother, with black hair almost to his shoulders, a stained red-and-black mackinaw jacket zipped up tight to his full beard, stood in the bow of his skiff, a long knife in his right hand.

Above him, roped so tightly at the waist that the rope appeared to divide him in half, hung a thinly clothed teenaged boy. His uncovered close-cropped head slumped like a broken flower onto his bony chest, which was covered by a thin dingy white T-shirt, and a pair of frayed cut-off jeans that reached to just above his prominent kneecaps. His feet were bare and pointed downwards.

My brother reached up and around the boy in a kind of embrace, feeling for the knot at the wood of the piling. I could hear him gasp as his arm slid back and forth, almost as if he was sawing wood. My father, meanwhile, reversed our boat against my brother's boat, pinning him in place. He said something but I couldn't make out the words.

"I'm not going to let him drop," my brother said. "If the tide was just a little higher . . ."

I took a small risk and lifted myself on my elbow to look closer at the bank. The river was a vicious trickle about five feet below the hanging boy's feet. He must have been roped to the top of the piling to keep him from drowning, though he likely wouldn't have known that. I could just see the dull green line of the high-water mark on the wood of the piling, at about the boy's shoulder height.

"Watch it!" my father said, not quite in a shout but his voice rolled across the channel and over the nearby silt island.

The hanging figure had slumped as the knife sliced through the knot, and my brother had been forced into a kind of sideways leap, his left arm tightening around the body and piling.

"Give me a hand, Dad. I don't want to lose the knife."

When my father stepped up onto the side of the stern, his back fully to me, I sat up to get a fuller view. Beyond the boy's profile, in a cluster just upriver, a dozen or so untenanted pilings shone blackly in the daybreak light. Hundreds of bulrushes, their heavy brown heads partially torn to white tufts by red-winged blackbirds, stretched hundreds of yards beyond the pilings to where the first rust-coloured net sheds simmered like embers on the dike. We were at the very bottom of the drift, with no other boats in sight. I could just see the top corks of my brother's heaped net glistening in his stern, as if he'd dragged in some sort of rare marine creature. Over the sound of the idling engine, I could hear the sucking of the current at the hulls and the erratic pipings of birds in the reeds across the channel. Looking skyward, high above the hanging figure, I noticed a sprinkling of stars, faint as salmon scales on ice. Then, suddenly, my brother grunted, and the boy's face emerged over his right shoulder, just for a few seconds, as if a ventriloquist had shifted his dummy in preparation for the act.

But I knew the act was over, though I wouldn't know exactly what it had been for another few years. By that time, I understood my place and its people well enough to accommodate, if not to understand, these almost ritualistic forms of violence, the playing of a seagull on a fishing line and the shooting of a great blue heron in flight.

This boy, hanging in the dawn light so that the tide would rise perilously close to covering him, was one of several who skirted the fringes of our small-town life and who suffered the consequences of being vulnerable and available, especially at times of much drinking. I knew him then, and still know him, by the ugly nickname he'd been given: Bullhead. Not given because his head was large, or even because his bulging eyes resembled the bullhead fish's, but because he would, for money, bite the eyes out of those fish and swallow them.

All of this knowledge would come later. But when I saw his sun-bronzed, narrow face with the rubbery lower lip and crooked nose, the exposed throat covered in a rash of mosquito bites, over my brother's shoulder, I knew I was seeing solitude. It didn't matter that my brother held his body and that my father waited like a father to bring the boy back into the world; it didn't matter that we would warm him up, feed him and take him safely into harbour. He was alone, and he was going to be alone. If my brother had tossed him under the drum where each caught salmon was tossed, the isolation wouldn't have been any more individual or any less universal. What belonged to any dying creature belonged to him. But what didn't belong . . . I couldn't access it at eight years old and I can't access it at fifty-five. The consciousness, the will, the particular rotting cask of vital memory – it was his; just as Alf Harley's was his, face turned to the briny wall of the bunk on a boat that never moved; just as mine belongs to me, standing here at the mouth of a dying river under a limitless reality of stars and worlds as foreign and unreachable as the billions of humans who carry out their life's limit of steps without counting them.

Before my father turned back and dropped into the stern, I lay down and closed my eyes, assuming again the image of sleep, a sleep I had only recently entered and from which I have never fully awakened. Tell me what world we do our living in. Our keenest living. And are we destined always to be alone there?

I WATCHED THE HERON TAKE A FEW STEPS INTO THE MURK AT ITS FEET, moving, as always, as if miming the moves of a heron. Then it expanded its wings and lifted off, flying in that low angular fashion that seems to pull all the world's shadows behind it. I closed my eyes, seeing body after body on the blackened pilings along the riverbank – children, men and women. All the heads were slumped, the faces hidden. But what did they matter? If Neil Armstrong had almost drowned at high water, or Christopher Knight, Montaigne, Thoreau, Rousseau, Tenzin Palmo, Charles Lindbergh, Weldon Kees, Nathaniel Hawthorne or even Daniel Defoe; what did the faces matter, in childhood or old age? Someone hung them up, and someone either brought them down or let them die. Or they chose to grow the tightened rope like an outer rib and take the higher water to the filling of the throat.

The morning came on without pause: the branches of the cottonwoods gaining clarity, the mountains rising above the city, the auroral light once more scouring the night's inefficient mysteries. I watched the heron diminish until he was a small dark speck on the western horizon, and then, almost undone by the haunting image of all those bodies roped to pilings (I had not known that memory had undone so many), I began to walk away from the cluster of trees. I wasn't in the mood to look for the grave of a hermit who had faced the high water alone; suddenly, the solitude only seemed tragic, the result of a longing that could never be fulfilled. Either you had a wounded childhood and continually seek wholeness the rest of your life or you had an idyllic childhood and want the feeling of it back. Either way, the journey's impossible; it's easier to fly to the moon.

I kept to the bank but found the going difficult. The sedges and rushes were thick and the ground uneven. After ten minutes, I had progressed only far enough to realize that another, much narrower slough intersected the island. Could this be the slough that my father, Dr. Kaney and I had drifted into all those years ago? It was barely wide enough for a kayak now. But I couldn't jump it, so I had to cut across the interior of the island, thinking again, with some envy, of Crusoe's tropical home. How neatly, and allegorically, it contained two completely different parts, almost like the light and dark sides of the moon. In one, he could cultivate his isolate civilization; in the other, he could only descend, like Conrad's Marlow, into fancies and terror. My distinctions were much less clear. The past and the present? One bleeds constantly into the other. Solitude and society? I was still buffeted between. Waking and sleeping? The same.

Careful of my steps, for the ground beneath the rushes and sedges was uneven and there might even have been narrower sloughs branching off the nearest one, I progressed slowly inland. Meanwhile, the daylight lifted the island out of the night's dark water and held it like a gem discovered in a puddle. I could hear the trilling of red-winged blackbirds and the pipings of widgeon, but the day's industrial noises hadn't begun: planes weren't flying out of the Vancouver airport just to the north, nor had the blarings and hummings of rush hour started in the distance. I realized I was as close to the summer silence of childhood as I could ever be. Within a few hours, the clamour of the age, like a battle fought in a neighbouring field, would be pervasively audible, and the closer artillery of jet boats pulling water skiers would encircle the island's stillness. But I had some time, maybe time that would never return.

Suddenly, I came to the edge of surprise, the edge of what I had forgotten because it wasn't a part of my memory of this place. Pushing back a few tall rushes, waving away the droning mosquitoes, I emerged at the edge of a field of chest-high barley.

At first, the brilliance of the frilled golden seed heads seemed unreal to me, as if the grass of my childhood daydreaming had been touched by Midas. The light almost pained my eyes, so I made a small visor of my right hand as I stepped into the stalks. The seed heads were heavy and tilted the stalks at different angles. I stopped and touched a seed head, its thickness and dryness strangely alive to my fingertips. An unnerving stillness hung in the air. I wondered if I had stumbled upon some bizarre gilding of grasshoppers as they had descended onto the crop. In a minute, perhaps, the whole swarm would shake off the rich summer dust and darken the waking sky. But for now – stillness, and that untranslatable hum of the earth indistinguishable from the central nervous system and just as infrequently heard in the ceaseless bruit of our accumulations.

I stood with gold at my chest but the usual bulrush-green the rest of the way down to my feet. And all around me the tidal musk of the Fraser River estuary wafted its familiar drugging scent, one-third childhood, one-third salt, one-third death. Somewhere on this shifting ground Alf Harley's bones rested, remembered perhaps by no one other than myself. Or else, long ago, his bones had dissolved far out in the gulf. I suddenly felt dizzy and overwhelmingly tired, like a child in the birth canal who cannot force his birth. With nothing else to do, I did exactly what I did as a boy in the fields of chest-high blue-joint grass: I lay down.

How many minutes passed before I fell asleep I do not know. But I remember lying on my back, as close to the sizzling generative hum of our planet as I had been in over forty years, and watching a fringe of cumulus cloud overhead change depth with the growing light. "Bella Bella," I murmured, "Ucluelet," the words like a nursery rhyme. "Bella Coola, Bamfield, Rivers Inlet, Nass, Skeena." I partially closed my eyes and looked through the blur of my own dark eyelashes and the grain's golden lashes at a sky I hadn't noticed in a long while, a sky, in its way, as deep and enigmatic as its nocturnal sibling. After a while, either awake or asleep, I recalled the torn untriumphant face of a teenaged boy after he'd blasted a sacred bird into the kind of stillness that doesn't fascinate but only terrifies and wounds. Then I saw that boy's body roped to a piling, blue wings cracking through the shoulder blades and a long hoarse cry rolling across the almost unlived decades. It's even possible that tears frayed my lashes and the grain's either just before or just after I finally lost consciousness.

WHEN I WOKE, THE SKY WAS LIGHTER AND THE DEEPER DRONE OF AN airplane now worked its way across the stillness. I lay motionless, letting the world return to my senses, my senses return to the world. No one knew where I was. If my heart gave out, how long would it be before I was found? When the hunter-farmers came to check on the barley, perhaps. In any case, I was as vanished from the world as I'd ever been.

The sound of the plane increased but couldn't bring me back. When it grew to a certain pitch, I couldn't take the sensation of sliding underneath waves of grain and island earth any longer and stood up, more perplexed than offended by the interruption of my reverie. I watched the machine emerge overhead, its cross-like shadow racing over the grain, just as the English schoolboys in *Lord of the Flies* had watched it, waiting for their island captivity to end and for normal life to resume.

But they were characters in a story, just as Robinson Crusoe was a character, just as the dead, perhaps, become actors in our memory-play, so many locusts in honey weakly failing to resume a living flight. I was alive, gold-bounded, as if touched down on the surface of the sun, protected only by my desire not to die, the desire that defines us and moves us in consort with the energies – vital, dangerous and impenetrable – of our kind. And if I was alive on the Island of the Solitaries – Christopher Knight sheltered somewhere in the cottonwoods, Thoreau kneeling by the bank, Neil Armstrong in a cloud shadow waiting for night and the return of his second and inescapable self – I was nonetheless alive. It struck me then, with greater force than I'd known since my last visit to this uncelebrated little island in an abused and unappreciated river, that a gravity was working on my body and my mind that had worked on billions before, that was working on everything with the same indifferent tenderness, the green-fringed branches of the cottonwoods on the horizon, the golden seed heads of the barley torsioned around my chest, the sobbing man or woman on the bridge railing upriver who, if things had gone differently, might have been me.

It took Apollo 11 three days to reach the moon and what did the astronauts learn there? Nothing that would help them in their ordinary human lives. It had taken me a winter and a single summer day to discover that the choice is always banal and monumental and always the same. Live or die. But within that choice? I knew the moment I began to count my steps out of the ripe barley that irresolution was, in fact, its own resolution; that I could spend Christopher Knight's twenty-seven years in the Maine woods or Tenzin Palmo's twelve years in a Himalayan cave and still know nothing worth knowing. Why else should Thomas Merton regret the life he'd spent on a spiritualist path? "It's too late now," he said ruefully not long before he died, wondering if all the seeking had been a waste of time – some people even believe that he killed himself in despair over the ending of his affair with a woman. And Neil Armstrong's ultra-devout mother, as she lay dying, said to her daughter that there probably wasn't any God but that she was happy she'd lived all her life as a believer.

The grain parted before me, its gold sliding away like yolk. Within minutes, the barley stalks turned to bulrush stems and then to open ground bordered on the bankside by black-and-red-dotted blackberry bushes, trumpets of morning glory, purple thistle and loosestrife. The trilling of red-winged blackbirds – the whistle my mother always used when she stood on the porch to call me in from play – called me in for the remainder of my solitary time on this blue planet, whose blue so few humans have ever seen, so few that it might not even be a real colour. But what is real? Even Crusoe, that pragmatic Englishman, couldn't say with certainty. Still, he left his island, as Armstrong and Aldrin left the moon, as Christopher Knight left the woods, needing to live again among men, and needing, just like those who never leave in any dramatic way, the always newly discovered and long-tended inner fire as both comfort and beacon.

I stood beside the rubber dinghy a long while, staring out at the murky channel where I had fished with my father. Life itself just isn't believable – the rapid passing if it, how it enfolds so many lives into one life, so many altered stages in the single journey. I had never really accepted that I wasn't still a boy, though I lived with the body and responsibilities of a man. That capacity for wonder, so hated by the world, couldn't slip from me. Without it, what did I have for sustenance? My only remaining task was to protect that instinct, and if a greater solitude was necessary, a greater solitude I would have to accept.

So I spent the day on the island, walking the banks, scanning the ground beneath the cottonwoods, looking for what I already suspected I wouldn't find: some trace of the man who had gone into isolation before me and died there. But nothing of Alf Harley remained. Perhaps the hunter-farmers had burned his boat, perhaps he had never been buried on the island or else the grave had been given no marker. Regardless, his secrecy, like yours and mine, remained inviolate.

At last, in the early evening, with the heat of the day subsiding and the river once again bathtub-full and calm, I decided to leave the island. There simply wasn't a compelling enough reason to stay. What I had found under the winter moon was no different than what I had found here: the necessity of crossing the threshold of myself. What Apollo mission can rival it? What can an astronaut bring back to Earth comparable to what a man can find in the recesses of feeling and memory? As Montaigne knew, as, hopefully, Alf Harley knew and Christopher Knight would survive long enough to discover, the inward journey is the most perilous and rewarding, perilous for what it threatens to travel away from, rewarding for the peace of the island that the voyager might discover.

But I had found no prescription for anyone's illness but my own, if illness it was. Nor did I even know what I was curing. For a few terrible moments, the surface of the river was tender as skin as I broke it with the oars. Then the water, as our consciousness must do, repaired itself and prepared again to flow out to the sea.

AFTERWORD

I RETURNED TO EDMONTON IN MID-JULY, TO AS CLAMOROUS A CONTRAST with my little silt island as possible. Because of the unwelcoming climate, Alberta's construction season is short and so a great deal of work must get done over the summer. I woke every day to the construction of new homes (our neighbourhood is being infilled) and to the repairing of infrastructure. Hammering, sawing and jackhammering combined with the revving of motorcycles, the long pealing of sirens and the droning of leaf blowers and lawn mowers to create a soundscape of unrelenting if impersonal violence. Nights were more peaceful, though the warmth of the long days kept revellers and drivers out well past midnight, and any 2:00 a.m. excursions were bound to include more people than had the walks I'd known in the deep winter.

But I needed to repeat my winter walks just once, in order to enact a small ritual to mark my unusual sojourn into solitude. Atheists, I had come to realize, are as misunderstood as hermits. Somehow, people associate atheism with darkness, negativity, even violence, and believe that atheists are coldly pragmatic, anti-wonder and anti-ceremony. Nothing could be further from the truth. In fact, once you have accepted that you will not see this earth or its people ever again, the desire to make your brief existence meaningful, even in small personal ways, grows in significance as you age.

My winter and one summer day of inwardness needed to be marked with more than words. After all, I wasn't the person I'd been only a few months before: I was closer to the sources again, and I knew I would stay that way until my last breath, humbled by an awareness of human vanity and fragility that belied all the mythmaking of our commercial culture. In a year, when the fiftieth anniversary of the moon landing rolled around, I knew that the Apollo 11 astronauts would be gods again, that much talk would focus on space exploration, on China's plans to land on the moon by the end of the 2020s, on the idea of a moon colony as a base for a Mars landing and even on PayPal billionaire Elon Musk's more ambitious hopes of colonizing Mars for the sake of preserving the human species in the event of a nuclear war (or for the sake of his personal profit margin). In a year, I knew that the moon would briefly make another public appearance, just as Neil Armstrong had reluctantly made them, and then the moon and the astronauts would vanish again.

But my relationship to the moon was now older and more powerful than anything our media and marketing powers could generate. I stood firmly with Thoreau, who asked, "What if one moon has come and gone with its world of poetry, its weird teachings, its oracular suggestions? So divine a creature, freighted with hints for me, and I have not used her!"

I didn't count my steps or leave any footprints as I made my way to the bridge over the creek; this walk just didn't have the weight of the winter variety, nor was it as isolated. More traffic passed, even a few pedestrians and cyclists. And no one else probably took much notice of the moon, since it was only in its first-quarter phase, its light not strong enough to rival our grid's usual violation of the darkness.

Thirty feet below me, the branches and dangled objects of the shoe-tree were just visible. Human dreaming had brought me this far, as far as it had brought the astronauts of Apollo 11, but just like on the moon when Armstrong needed to manually land the *Eagle*, human physical skill would have to finish the task. I counted to three and tossed my laced winter boots over the railing.

Did they catch? I thought I saw their dark shape swinging in the air. I certainly didn't hear anything land on the ground. Well, it's necessary, even for an atheist, to have faith in something, so I accepted that they had snagged on a branch. It was strangely moving to imagine them there, as if I'd been that nomadic boy on the Internet who always threw a pair of running shoes over the telephone line to tell the neighbourhood that he'd existed.

Today, if you stop halfway over the bridge between Mill Creek and Bonnie Doon, in south central Edmonton, you'll likely see my boots, numbers fourteen and fifteen on the shoe-tree. But only if you're reading this will you know that taped securely inside one boot are two plastic astronauts, and inside the other boot, one plastic astronaut. Still travelling, between one world and another, between the past and the future, visible and invisible to everyone else, just like all of us, solitaries of the teeming islands.

ACKNOWLEDGEMENTS

EARLIER VERSIONS OF SOME OF THESE ESSAYS APPEARED IN THE FOLLOWING publications: *Eighteen Bridges* ("On the Rails"); *Alberta Views* ("Initiation"); *Queen's Quarterly* ("The Common Currency of Life," "Should I Really Read *The Remains of the Day* in What Remains of My Days?," "The Proof of Love" and "The Floating Library").

"On the Rails" was a finalist for the 2012 National Magazine Award, "Initiation" received the 2021 Alberta Magazine Awards' Gold Medal for the Essay and "The Floating Library" received the 2021 Writers' Guild of Alberta James H. Gray Award for Short Nonfiction.

I wish to thank the following organizations and juries for their support of this manuscript: the Access Copyright Foundation, the Alberta Foundation for the Arts, the Canada Council for the Arts, the Edmonton Arts Council and the Edmonton Artists' Trust Fund.

My gratitude to Noelle Allen and Ashley Hisson for their editorial expertise in helping these essays achieve their final form, and to everyone at Wolsak and Wynn for their support.

Tim Bowling is the author of twenty-one works of poetry, fiction and non-fiction. He is the recipient of numerous honours, including two Edmonton Artists' Trust Fund awards, five Alberta Literary Awards, two Writers' Trust of Canada nominations, two Governor General's Award nominations and a Guggenheim Fellowship.